D1730567

台灣

Bicycle Touring

Taiwan

Roads above the Clouds

Mark Tovell

addoil Publishing

Bicycle Touring Taiwan: Roads above the Clouds

Author Mark Tovell
Edited by Eldes Tran and Sheri Quirt
Indexing by Eldes Tran

Cover by Mark Tovell
Illustrations, photography and maps from
original copyright © reserved by Mark Tovell

ISBN: 978-1-7384798-0-1
First edition
Printed in U.K, US and Taiwan
Published by addoil Publishing
addoilgo.com / ig: addoil_go

Nothing is made alone. Thank you to everyone who has
supported me along this ride, but especially

Annie,
without your friendship, kindness, support and late-night coffees
I would never have gotten through my early drafts, countless rewrites and
endless hours of drawing.

林建良,
the No. 1 mechanic in all Taiwan, whose skills always kept Jimmy on the road.
If you need some bike support on your journey, hit up the lovely
Cycle Element bike store in Tainan, *p117.*

Jewel,
your inspiration and collaboration will never be forgotten.

To all those riding companions, hosts, friends, strangers and encouragers who
handed us a beer, a bottle of water or a smile, thank you.
To everyone who has shared a thumbs-up, a waving hand, or shouted a
cheerful "加油,"
all I can offer is a humble
謝謝你.

The moment ...[a person] traverses a mountain range on a bicycle, ...[they are] like the first Mongolian who ever leapt onto a wild horse on the steppe—

German bicycle designer, Karl Nicolai, in Wu Ming-Yi's, *The Stolen Bicycle*

Read a novel that has no relation to the place you're in.

Paul Theroux, *The Tao of Travel*

Describing something is like using it—it destroys; the colors wear off, the corners lose their definition, and in the end what's been described begins to fade, to disappear.

Olga Tokarczuk, *Flights*

Contents

Index
Key & GPX maps

Taiwan

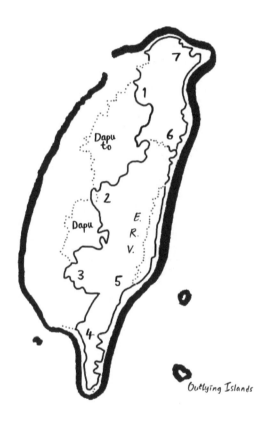

Dapu
to

Dapu

E.
R.
V.

Outlying Islands

1	2	3	4	5	6	7
Taiwan Spine	Nantou	South West	Taiwan Tail	South East	Hualien & Taroko	North East

Preface

Cycle touring is, for me, the subtle art of looking, searching, for those special places, the hinterland of life, the edges of our world. Obsessed with quiet back-country roads, the spaces between city streets, the nooks and crannies, where our built world blurs with the force of nature. Out across the big plains, in the wilds of it all, that's where the tourer goes.

One day, sitting in a friend's flat in London, I was nose deep in another book. There, baked into the pages was a sense of one of these hinterlands, a new place to explore. Seeping out of the story was a land that felt so real.

Wu Ming-Yi's *The Stolen Bicycle* instantly grabbed my imagination, pulled me in close to this land called Taiwan, and convinced me that this emerald island in the Pacific was to be my next riding adventure. Little did I realize at the time just what effect that book was going to have on the direction of my life and the burning passion that would come from a journey along roads above the clouds.

When I first arrived in Taiwan, years ago, I stayed with a Warmshowers host—fellow cycle tourers who host riders on tour. My companion and I were looking for an interesting route around this island, how to escape the maze of concrete and metropolises. Our hosts kindly offered up some advice for those seeking the unknown and beauty that was eluding us. Had we listened to them that day I would have experienced the adventure, and challenge, I was so dearly craving.

They spoke about quieter highways that twist and weave through the hills and high mountains. These jungle-lined roads pass up across cloud and rain, gliding through rural villages, up into high mountain vistas and panoramic, clear, clean skies. Soaked in fresh, crisp air, these places, they assured us, would feel a million miles away from the heavily populated cities of the west. This was the adventure we were looking for, we were excited.

Two routes south were offered up that day. The first, a simpler ride down to the western flats heading directly for the southern cities, a pleasant journey to be sure but sticking to the fringes between the hills and the flat roads of the industrial heartlands.

It was the second route our hosts were really animated about. Instead of heading south directly, why not first ride into the heart of the island, up and over the central mountain ranges, and across the rural valleys that lie hidden between soaring peaks?

The route traverses the highest roads and passes and sped down through the heart of the lush mountain national parks. They spoke about the experience of rolling through the wild and unique areas that these awesome landscapes offer. It sounded glorious, challenging and unique...

Safe to say we took the simple way out. We rode fast to the western flats, riding the lower hills and passing through the western cities. I had taken myself away from the very thing I had come to Taiwan to see. It wasn't until later that I went back to those high mountain roads, to the routes that display the island in all its glory. That initial conversation stuck in my head. I never forgot what I had missed out on. I knew that one day I would fully explore Taiwan's landscapes and find it again.

After that first trip around Taiwan, we fell in love with this wondrous island, its nature, beauty, and of course, its arrestingly cute peoples and their unique ways of life. So, we decided to stay and carry on exploring. We were fortunate enough to make friends, fellow riders who would come on adventures with me. We would go for multiday rides along the east coast, long weekends through the tea fields, trips across the southern beach roads. We would ride across coffee hills and through the western hills that split up the cities. Explorations into the narrow warrens of Taiwan's badlands. Island hopping to swim with sea turtles and camp under the stars. Hiking trips to the island's tallest peaks and rides through the giant city of Taipei and its lush hillsides.

My first few months I took solo trips up narrow farm roads that twist and turn their way up through bamboo forests, pine trees and into hidden farming regions. All the while I thought about that original route, through the heart of the island, over the mountain passes and across into the national parks.

My second Huándǎo, in the heat of the summer, finally took me across those passes and through the central roads. My third, fourth, fifth and sixth tours would see me traverse every inch of the island, all of its routes, every direction covered and still the joy and fun were found. Every new turn, every fresh village, town, island, meal, night under the stars and descent through the clouds felt like a reimagining of this great and unique land.

This book is the culmination of years of exploration and adventure that Taiwan has gifted me and I would like to pass that on so that others can have the chance to see this island, its challenges and its pleasures in all its full glory.

Cycling is a journey, the route, the ride, the people you meet and adventures you have along the way are more important than the destination, and as such it is a truly personal, emotional choice selecting your way, your path through. Are you a planner, needing to lay out every single meter of path before you arrive at the start? Or perhaps you throw the maps away, ride blind into the day willing to turn the handlebars on a whim, a feeling? Well, for all of you, this book is an invaluable resource for pointing you in the direction you want to go. There will never be one perfect route around a country like Taiwan, with so many options and landscapes thankfully there are routes that will appeal to every rider.

With this in mind, *Roads above the Clouds* provides a set of options and guides to the different paths around Taiwan that highlight what we think are the best vantage points to take in this illuminating island. We visit its challenging environments and landscapes, experience its cultures and cities, bask in the mountains, weave along its ocean roads. We smell the jungle canopy, listen to its wildlife in play and watch its seasons transform.

This book is a personal voyage, pulling together some of the country's more famous regions, routes and highlights, with its least known paths, back road challenges and natural regions building a unique adventure that covers all of the island's beauty and intrigue. Using local knowledge and the experiences of riders of all types we consider daily distances, side trips, locations for camping and highlights that cannot be found on route planners, apps or government websites. Be careful out there, even with Taiwan's safe roads and calm communities we cannot guarantee our routes and the state of the roads as you travel down them.

Every journey is personal and should be full of the unexpected. I just hope this resource can bring more people to experience this incredible land, its roads above the clouds. To see it from a similar lens as I have seen it, to feel free and alive riding along the misty highways and sun-soaked coastlines. To enjoy life and to love the feelings so often hidden from view.

Introduction

How to Huándǎo—clockwise or counter?
The term *Huándǎo* (環島) directly translates as "around the island," but broadly means a complete journey taken around the island by bike or even on foot! For Taiwanese cyclists, this pilgrimage is often a must, a dream and a challenge to take on, at least once, if not every year. Made famous by several riders and walkers of old inspiring future generations of riders, hikers and young students who, upon graduation, attempt this bucket list challenge.

Taiwan is a stunning, complex and often misunderstood island. Wedged between the coast of China and the great, never-ending blue of the Pacific Ocean, Taiwan is often seen as simply an overpopulated industrial part of Asia. Nothing could be further from the truth. The natural beauty in Taiwan is dense, literally. Despite its small size, the island of Taiwan has one of the highest densities of high mountains anywhere in the world, perhaps even the highest. There are more than one hundred peaks over 3000m in height. Add in Taiwan's position along the Tropic of Cancer in the Pacific Ocean and you have the perfect mix of sea and summit. Crystal blue waters, unbelievable mountains covered in jungle shoot straight up out of the ocean.

There really is no island on the planet with such a rich mix of landscapes, and all on such a small landmass. Combine that with a thriving, progressive and determined democratic society steeped in a unique set of histories, traditions, cultures and values and you have the makings of very special place indeed.

On the surface, riding around Taiwan seems like a simple affair. A teardrop island that lends itself to a near-complete coastal ride, a circular tour that travels just under 1000km in length. The Taiwanese government's own marked route Cycle Route 1 (CR1) is advertised as a ten-day journey. This highly unobtainable aim would require you to stick stubbornly to a daily constant grind in the saddle, maximizing the flatter, smoother sections of the country's road networks. It is often attempted in as short a time as possible. Sadly, to those on their first trip to Taiwan this information gives a false sense of what is achievable in a short time, and more critically, it ignores the simple truth: Taiwan is not a fast, flat ride around a small island, far, far from it.

A quick note on the CR1: for several reasons this, the country's first official cycle route, skips, avoids and straight up ignores some of Taiwan's highlights and best areas. It provides followers with days of dull, flat riding through the industrial heartlands, highways and built-up towns, keeping riders on some of the busier, heavily traffic-laden roads crossing traffic lights at an almost constant frequency on the western half of the road network. It is a beautiful route in places and of course even portions of our route travel along the same path, but only in parts where the road is nonnegotiable. Within our book we highlight when we cross alongside this useful, if limited, piece of infrastructure. Maps and information on this route can be found here; *eng.taiwan.net.tw.*

Your first choice, upon planning any tour of Taiwan by bicycle, is between traveling along a clockwise or counterclockwise direction. Due to Taiwan's geography, most of the mountains are situated in the center of the island, clumped together across several connected ranges that reach like a spine from the top, all the way down to the southern tip, splitting the land in two. Taiwan is one of the most densely populated places on the planet. But the vast majority of the large population is concentrated in the greater Taipei region and its western cities. The mountain ranges are sparsely populated and the eastern shores' lack of land make population growth there almost impossible. As a result, avoiding some of the western region means you can complete a near-monthlong trip around the island and feel a million miles away from it all.

These towering, remote landscapes lift high up into the clouds. On the east coast the mountains rise sharply from the edges of the Pacific and across a major fault line; in the north and west, mountains fall over themselves as they all bunch up together. As such, any road that navigates their valleys and peaks is prone to destruction from landslides, earthquakes and typhoons, making road construction and upkeep a stark challenge. Cross-island roads are limited, and the ones that exist are always exposed and prone to closure. Having said that, Taiwan keeps its road conditions in impeccable order. Expect smooth asphalt at every turn.

Crisscrossing the island in any direction you wish is near impossible and therefore, which way you turn at the beginning will have a large effect on your journey, experiences and enjoyment. Below we set out some considerations to keep in mind when you make that first choice.

The way

This book at its heart follows one main, counterclockwise route that travels around the island, enjoying every type of experience to be had. This is no forced "take it or leave it" journey, but simply a strand that binds your individual adventure. There are alternative routes and add-on side trips, hiking highlights and outer island getaways. We have covered almost all of the island's main route options. We discuss entry and exit points of major cities and ports so you can pick up our tour no matter where you're starting from or if you take a break and rejoin farther down the road.

Our west coast alternative route, Dapu to Dapu, avoids the high mountain route, while keeping you well away from dull, polluted highways and industrial heartlands. This alternative is perhaps a better overall route for those on their first tour, riders who don't want the slog of daily climbing or if the weather simply doesn't allow for the high mountain passes.

On the east coast, we have included a guide to both the coastal road and an inland East Rift Valley route. While our main route follows the coast, this inland journey is just as enjoyable, it's all about the flow and feel at the time.

The main, eighteen-day journey is our personal favorite route around Taiwan, with what we think has just the right mix of fun and adventure, trial and tribulation, relaxation and exploration. It starts, ends and crosses the Taiwan that best serves your body, mind and soul. It places hot springs, beaches, jungle, mountain passes, towns, cities, cultural highlights, remote regions and re-sources in just the right moment. Relaxing days follow tough ones, views are over your correct shoulders while climbs are at their best and the descents, well, they can't be described, can they?

People often ask us how far they should travel in a day. It, of course, differs person to person, group to group, and as such take our day's start and finish points as a broad sense of what's possible. Some riders can combine days while others will need to take it easier and add in additional stops. As a rule of thumb, including days off the saddle, a twenty-one-day itinerary is minimum for an entire Huándǎo. If you have less time than that, consider adding in train journeys to break up the route or just pick one side of the island to explore. Chill out, not all roads can be explored.

If you spend your time worrying about your limitations, then, instead of missing out on what you can't see, you will miss out on what you can. As they say in Taiwan, *màn màn lái,* take it easy.

Navigating the book

The start of our journey in the sleepy village of Sanxia (三峽) is a perfect jumping-off point from both Taipei and Taoyuan (桃園), allowing you to escape the traffic and noise of Taiwan's major cities quickly. See our *To the Start* pages for bike trail routes from Taipei and Taoyuan to the starting point.

While our journey follows a counterclockwise route, there are many reasons you might just choose to ride clockwise. At the end of every chapter we have included notes on that section's journey for those traveling clockwise around the island. You can use our maps in reverse using the km markers as a countdown, just bear in mind any directional turns are reversed.

We have tried to cater to every type of rider along our trip. And we have ridden our route with inexperienced riders and experienced riders alike. Whether you're a solo cyclist ready for the wild, in a small group looking to have some laid-back fun or a group with a support system, our book will provide lots of useful information both before you embark on your adventure and while on the road. We hope you will build your own bespoke journey using us as the trusted friend who can provide those missing pieces of vital information...as well as anticipation for what will surely be a trip of your life. But at points just let the wheels do the talking, exploration that includes jeopardy can be called adventure.

We have split Taiwan up into seven sections, each covering an area that our main route passes through. Starting at the edge of Taiwan's mountains we travel down through the island's spine before heading through the wild heart of Nantou. Leaving the mountains behind we roll down through the fruit-filled southwest before arriving at Taiwan's Tail, the sunny, unmissable southern peninsula.

We then turn up the southeast coast, following the surf highway before arriving at Hualien and visiting the stunning Taroko Gorge. Finally, we hit up the northeast as we ride though the northern region and circle the north coast around to a sunset finish on the riverbanks in Taipei.

Each section is composed of two or three days from our route, with every day coming with its own map and direction notes as well as km markers. All of our routes match our .gpx files that you can access free using the QR codes throughout the book or by downloading from our website.

Specific turning instructions and junctions are marked in bold while other markers might just reference stores, highlights or interesting aspects of the ride. Alternative routes and roads that lead to other useful locations are also marked on our journey. Each day starts at the exact end point of the previous day's journey to ensure continuity. I would still recommend using individual day's maps as a way of accessing the information quicker and not losing track of your bearings.

Our hand-drawn daily maps offer a sense of direction and a degree of accuracy as to the route's junctions and facilities along the way. They offer a good companion to anyone who rides without GPS maps or who just wants a quick visual reference when reading through a day's set of markers.

Our alternative routes have their own chapters with separate day guides. Their start points and end points both link directly to the main route.

Throughout the book are notes on side trips and a short chapter on Taiwan's outer island adventures.

This book is not a full travel guide to Taiwan. Apart from specific choices that aid our journey or fit in with our cycling ideals and sense of exploration, we don't recommend specific hotels or hostels, we don't rate or grade restaurants or attractions. There is no wrong choice in Taiwan and all its cities deserve exploration; even if we avoid most we are simply thinking about the journey, we highlight roads and highways that lead off our trail, connecting to other cities and sights along the way.

Cycle Touring Tips & Wild Camping Taiwan

If this is your first time touring by bicycle there are plenty of resources out there. Social media, videos, blogs and books offer insight into what to buy, what to take, how to ride, how to sleep, how to plan, how to train, etc., etc. There are many terms out there to describe essentially the same activity: riding a bicycle for more than one day with bags attached to the bike that are full of the materials needed to support yourself along the way.

Any bicycle can be a touring bike, any bag will hold your coat and what you wear doesn't really matter. Of course, we have our preferences and after touring on different bikes, replacing gear, our setups and bikes have become bespoke to us.

After years of cycle touring, hosting and meeting many riders from all backgrounds around the world, there is one simple truth. No two touring setups are the same. We have never seen two groups live the same life. Everyone rides different distances, sleeps in different places and lives on different time scales.

We once met a five-year tourer with a trailer of incalculable weight who was adding to it by picking up rocks they found blocking their path. Equally, we once met a couple speeding across North America with one change of clothes each, just one saddlebag, no helmet and no hidden support vehicle. All of these people were as happy as anyone we have met. There really are no bad choices.

That being said, besides a bicycle, here is our essentials list. These are the things every cycle tourer, bike packer, adventure rider, road traveler needs to carry, no argument. The purpose of this list is to show not how much you have to take, but that essentially whatever else you take is really up to you.

-Multitool set, puncture repair kit with tire levers.
-Bike pump with gauge; trust us when we say you need a gauge.
-Two, TWO, spare inner tubes; that includes you, tubeless riders.
-Water bottles/bladder capacity to at least 6 liters.
-A decent, lightweight, waterproof jacket.
-Padded cycle shorts, preferably a bib. We get asked this question a lot and the answer is always yes, yes and yes.
-At least one 100 percent waterproof pannier/bike bag/bucket. (The joy of a dry sleeping bag is priceless, the pain of a wet one is incalculable.)

That's it! Whatever else you take depends on your ride, the environments you will travel through, your adventure.

Note: We did consider adding helmet to the list as, from personal experience, it's essential, but, it's your life, live free.

Taiwan is an island of a nearly never-ending chain of convenience stores. These 24hr beams of light take away any stress of being stuck without supplies. That is not to say you have to use these places, it's just a truth. But our route does travel through Taiwan's most remote regions, and even on the east coast highway, you can always get stuck between resources. Our daily maps highlight locations to get food and water.

There are only a couple of locations on our tour where planning ahead and carrying some supplies are essential. The first stage travels through Taiwan's Spine; these remote roads offer only occasional villages with stores. Day 6, riding up and camping on Tatajia Pass (塔塔加) requires water and food for the climb. And our multiday side trip to the mountain lakes of Qi Cai Hu (七彩湖), this remote adventure is as wild as it gets.

There are few safer places to travel on this planet then Taiwan. The kind and helpful people care about visitors as well as each other. Personal theft is near non-existent, your bicycle and cargo will be left alone. Outside of major cities we rarely use our locks. At night nobody will disturb your sleep, safe in the knowledge that your privacy and personal space are upheld at all times.

In our experience Taiwan has a very welcoming approach to those wild camping and traveling by bicycle. Sleeping in a tent is a safe, enjoyable and hassle-free experience. Police stations, especially on the east coast routes, will offer up possible locations. There is an endless number of rest stops, beach pull-ins, mountainsides and hilltops to pitch up for the night, just be respectful and take everything with you. Riders have found that temples, churches and schools will lend their lawns for the night if you ask. One note of warning, Taiwan has many wide, dry riverbeds that look great for camping, but during rain seasons flash floods fill these areas quickly. Wild camping in the national parks is not allowed and be respectful of any areas with no-camping signs.

Paid campgrounds are, with a few exceptions such as Shady Tree in Kenting, expensive affairs. There are a few fantastic free campgrounds and camping spots around the island, and where possible we note those on our route.

Jimmy

Jade

Route Considerations

Where is your starting point?
Most travelers enter and exit from Taoyuan International Airport, in the northwest of the country. This makes a complete circle easy, but there is also an international airport in Kaohsiung in the south and a ferry port in the west that links to China.

Our main route spans eighteen days, nineteen if you take one of our alternative routes. We see this as a bare minimum; as a general rule, if this is your first time riding around Taiwan, give yourself at least twenty-one days, a month even. Relax, take it easy and immerse yourself. No point in rushing around in this life.

Some riders might need to consider visa constraints, or perhaps you only have a two-week break from work. Whatever your reason for a set timeframe, choosing certain sections that appeal to you will determine your direction. Trying to fit a Huándǎo in fewer than ten days is not feasible, not if you want to spend any time off the saddle or away from dull highways.

For shorter trips, consider combining an east coast ride with the northeast loop. Or perhaps you want some ocean swims and dives, then you can combine the southern tail with trips to the outer islands by ferry from Kenting or Taitung.

For the most adventurous with a time limit consider combining the Taiwan Spine and Nantou chapters, taking in all those high peaks, perhaps even a ride down the best descent of the country, from the high pass at Wuling down through to Taroko Gorge, ending up by the ocean in Hualien.

Whatever route you take there are no bad choices. It is a blast out there and Taiwan is stunning at every turn, with every stop and every highlight all worth your time.

What time of year is it and how is the weather?

Everyone who rides in Taiwan will need to approach this question differently. Certain times of year there are incredibly strong southerly winds that make riding north on the east coast a daunting task. But to be honest, this is often interchangeable and you can find good tailwinds in both directions any time of year. During the spring, winds in the southwest riding up from Kenting toward Pingtung are equally horrid, for example. I would simply consider the potential road closures in the mountains during the late winter season and the east coast road closures if a heavy typhoon is on its way.

The summer months bring the clearest skies in the west but with sometimes unbearable heat. Typhoon season runs through the summer months and you need to be ready for a one- or two-day shutdown should a big storm pass by.

The shoulder seasons of late Autumn and early spring offer the greatest chance of dry days and warmer weather. But be warned it can rain at any time of year on this tropical island.

How adventurous do you feel and how much city riding?

Should you head straight for the mountains, the hills, east coast or western cities, your first desires will determine tour direction. Starting from the north, if you want the coast life then you really should head around in a clockwise direction. If you want remote mountain rides then head down the spine before choosing a direction a little later. Equally, if you want to stay flat to begin with, then heading southwest along Cycle Route 1 will take you through all the northern masses, but be warned these large industrial cities are sprawling and often dull.

Taking public transport

Taiwan's trains operate around the island and are a vital resource. The High Speed Rail line connects cities on the west coast whilst a myriad of regular trains connect all over the flatter parts of the island. There is more than one type of bicycle car and with multiple reservation policies, dependent upon the train type, it can get confusing. You can pack a bicycle into a soft bag and take onto any train, without reservation, including the High Speed Rail. Giant sells them in most of their stores. On the railway website you can find trains that allocate space for bicycles and reserve tickets for some. tip.railway.gov.tw/

Intercity busses operate across the island. You can take a bicycle on any of these privately run coaches as long as you pack it into a soft bag covering the wheels, pedals and chain. Make reservations at bus stations in advance.
There are provincial busses that head up the mountain roads. These much smaller busses have limited storage space but are excellent for reaching trailheads and the national parks.

Notes on Culture, Food, Language & Bicycles

Without going too in depth, it's fair to say Taiwan has had a complicated history, a present that feels at a crossroads yet full of confidence, and a future of uncertainty and possibility.

From settlement, colonialism, subjugation, defiance, revolution, to autonomy and the white terror, to democracy, hypercapitalism and the looming threat of a strong China, that leads us to its current, unique political situation. But this ever-changing set of identities has created a contemporary nation as proud of its diverse makeup as it's possible to be.

Perhaps the most progressive nation in East Asia, Taiwan can boast of being the first in the region to introduce gay marriage and to guarantee equal rights for women and the LGBTQ+ community as well as having one of the world's most respected democracies for its representation, empowerment, openness and legitimacy.

Despite a desperately aging population, the youth of Taiwan are engaged in their communities, politically active and staunchly opinionated. Don't be afraid to approach any subject with the Taiwanese, they will happily chat; just don't expect the answer to be predictable.

Taiwan is a patchwork of peoples made up of the original indigenous groups who have lived here for centuries. Then groups of Han settlers from China came around the same time as Dutch colonialists started their building of Tainan in southern Taiwan. The Hakka communities, a subgroup of Han people historically persecuted, migrated to hill towns in Taiwan's west, and are still a recognized group, with its language as one of Taiwan's official ones.

Sadly, the plight of the indigenous peoples follows a similar pattern seen all over the world. For centuries, they had to fight invaders and pillagers, including the Dutch, Portuguese, Chinese Han and Japanese. At the sharp end of the white terror the indigenous populations in Taiwan's mountain regions and outer islands had to endure heavy subjugation, persecution and a lack of recognition. But many of their cultures, languages and communities survived and they are finally getting their recognition in Taiwan's modern land.

As you travel around Taiwan you will pass through communities of Bunun in the central ranges, Amis, the largest group, all along the east coast as well as Hakka communities in the northwest. You will be happily greeted by strong, independent indigenous communities all over the island. The Taiwanese are friendly and talkative, but often their demeanor needs disarming. Just crack a smile in their direction and more often than not you will get a smile back.

Language is another fascinating part of everyday life in Taiwan. Mandarin is the first official language spoken. Taiwan still uses traditional Chinese characters as opposed to China, which uses a simplified Chinese system of characters brought in during the Cultural Revolution. The Taiwanese language, Tái-yǔ, is spoken by about 70 percent of the population, with its everyday use more public in the south of the island.

English is being pushed as Taiwan's second language and as such all road signs use different forms of Romanization alongside traditional Chinese characters, so finding your way around the island is simple enough. See pxxxii.

Taiwan's food has roots in Chinese cuisine but the flavors of Japan and other neighboring nations play a heavy role. As does the unique array of cooking styles from the different indigenous populations that lived on this small volcanic rock long before anyone else arrived. A place of contradictions, due to a large Daoist population, the country has a long vegetarian history as well as an addiction to stinky tofu and all things soy, and yet, meat is almost a religion here too—beef noodle soup being one of the country's signature dishes and street BBQ restaurants being the staple of community life.

I would be remiss to not mention another staple of the Taiwanese food culture: its ubiquitous night markets. These centers of street food with stalls of cheap products and eccentric carnival-style games are a unique experience and a must do on anyone's trip around the island. Every large town and city has at least one if not dozens of night markets, some open every day, some open certain days a week. Each city takes pride in its night markets but for our money, the night market in Hualien is a highlight of the east coast, p225. All the western cities have fantastic night markets but in Taipei don't miss out on a trip to Shilin night market, the largest of Taipei's labyrinths, a foodie's paradise.

Taiwan grows its own coffee, and boy, are the beans good, but its true love, passion, obsession even, is tea. Yes, of course there is the traditional tea still poured all over the land...but it is in their most famous of inventions, bubble tea, that the Taiwanese have finally found their perfect drink! That's right, if you didn't know, bubble tea comes from right here. The perfect combination for a tea-, sugar-, milk- and chew-obsessed population. People's love of the many varieties of tea available cannot be ignored. So, don't be afraid to dive in and try the near-endless array of flavors and combinations on offer from the tea shops placed on every street corner.

Despite its small size the nation produces over 80 percent of its own fruit and vegetables, with the land's fertile soil and perfect weather conditions allowing an abundance of crops to have their time in the sun. Local markets and street stalls still dominate supermarkets and if you wander around any village, town or city, the sense of community really shows in the hubbub of the morning and weekend markets.

Convenience stores are another cultural center in Taiwan, despite being dominated by a certain American brand; these ever-present, brightly lit stores full of the same packaged food and drinks are essential to daily life in Taiwan. People use them for their daily coffee, to pay the bills and to post their packages. These stores are much more than just a consumption nightmare, although they are that too. Don't belittle them too much, they are a sight for sore eyes after a day riding the mountains or a much-needed break from the heat of the day along the hot, exposed highways.

Taiwan's love affair with bicycles

Taiwan, once the world's center of bicycle production and still home to the world's largest bicycle manufacturer (Giant), has a strange love affair with bicycles. It would appear on the surface to have a detailed network of dedicated bicycle routes and paths. In reality, this infrastructure is often little more than signposts and faded road markings. Bicycle rest stops once littered the island offering free water, bathrooms and tools at many locations. Sadly, this network has also been allowed to fall into disrepair. Gladly, police stations still remain great locations to get free drinking water, pump up those tires and ask for accommodation advice. Don't be afraid to enter a station and ask to fill your bottles, often the police there will be excited to see you.

Road cycling is popular around the big cities and Taiwanese riders are everywhere on the weekends. Most of the world's most trusted carbon frames are still produced in Taiwan and the lycra community is massive in Taipei and beyond. Mountain biking, gravel, and BMX are burgeoning communities, still with few facilities or opportunities compared to North America or Europe. But with new events, great stores and social media these sports are starting to have a real presence.

Due to the bicycle's historical significance as a tool for transport and recreation, cyclists are seen as a valid member of the road community in Taiwan, and as such bicycles can use specific lanes and light boxes throughout the country's roads and highways. Cars take care when overtaking, for the most part, and cyclists have the right of way in most situations. Taiwanese have a relaxed approach to their road etiquette and are happy for cyclists to use the roads and pavements as they see fit, just be safe and respectful. Just try to stop the auntie or uncle as they ride their rusting three-speed across a busy intersection and up over the pavement. Watching all road traffic pause is a delight, but perhaps don't try that yourself.

What's in a (road) name

Roads in Taiwan have complicated names, and while there is plenty to be said about their distinctions among provinces, counties, cities and districts, we have simplified their use for ease of the book. Luckily the transport department uses a very easy-to-follow road sign system for recognizing types of roads, making navigation straightforward.

Taiwan highways are by far the most common roads used on our tour. The distinct blue triangle sign is easily recognizable and a Taiwan staple. We often ride along county roads and district roads and there are only a handful of unnamed roads on our route.

If you illegally enter a freeway or red highway you can be fined 10,000NTD. This is especially prevalent on the east coast between Yilan (宜蘭) and Hualien (花蓮), where the new tunnel network often catches people off guard and the police are strict with the fine.

Taiwan has very few toll roads outside of the freeways. There are occasional fee-paying roads to national recreation parks: for example, at the entrance to Alishan village (阿里山), Shitiping Recreation Park (石梯坪) and Zengwen Dam Road (曾文水庫). The dam road in Tainan County is the only paid entrance on our entire route.

F5   Freeways – number inside a green formosa flower – these roads strictly do not allow bicycles.

R6   Red Highway – red rounded triangle – these roads strictly do not allow bicycles.

T7   Taiwan Highway – blue rounded triangle – bicycles allowed – most used roads on the bicycle networks. Popular online map services use the simplified tai character when referencing these roads (台7). These roads are open to cyclists.

101   County road – three numbers in a white rectangle with black border local roads open to cyclists.

南63 District road – local prefix or suffix with two or three numbers in a white rectangle with black border. The character represents the county it is situated in – for example, 南63 is in Tainan County (台南).

Lost in translation

Pīnyīn is the modern Romanization of Mandarin Chinese, implemented across all of China. However, Taiwan has not implemented a single, unified policy for its use. As a result, different spellings appear all over the island. While pīnyīn is employed by the central government and is the most commonly used, there are many versions in use throughout the country and the English-speaking world. The name of the capital city is a great example. Taipei, in English, comes from a more traditional Romanization T'ai-pei, whereas Táiběi is the pīnyīn and used for road signs in parts of the country. There is also Tai-pak and Taipeh, derived from other traditional Romanization forms that can be found among certain communities. Don't be surprised to see the different spellings of place names throughout the country. We have used the modern pīnyīn, most commonly found throughout *Roads above the Clouds*.

Arrival & Departure

So, what to do right out of the gate, so to speak? If you haven't brought your own ride or already organized a rental then there are lots of bicycle stores in Taipei that will rent you a bike and some basic gear to get you around the island. Assuming you have brought your own bicycle, there is a host of choices upon arrival.

The main international air hub at Taoyuan is the arrival point of most visitors. This airport is the main gateway to the country's north and Taipei. Riding straight from the airport is tricky. If you arrive at one of Taiwan's other two international airports in the west or southern cities of Taichung or Kaohsiung, riding out from the airport arrivals is a much simpler and easier affair.

There is one international ferry port to the west where ferries arrive from China. If you arrive from this route then you will be set to go as soon as you land. Sadly at this moment there are no ferry routes to the Philippines, Korea or Japan.

Usually we wouldn't have made a note on this subject, for many seasoned tourers the joy of unboxing and riding off from the airport is part of the experience but sadly Taiwan's main international airport doesn't allow it.

Taoyuan's international airport has a fairly strict no-riding policy from arrivals. Over the years we have heard mixed reports of people achieving it but in our experience, it isn't possible as the main exit from the airport leads to a freeway that does not allow cyclists. But there does appear to be one road from the airport you could attempt.

From either of the two arrival terminals follow the flow of traffic, pointing yourself eastward and looking for signs for highway T4. From here T4 South heads directly for central Taoyuan city. After 12km it becomes road 110 that leads all the way to Sanxia. See our *To the Start* map on the next page.

Here are the alternative ways to get your bike out of Taoyuan International Airport.

Shuttle bus

There are shuttle buses to Taoyuan city and Taipei city. To use these, you can just throw your bike in the cargo hold, but we would recommend keeping the bike in the box for now and assembling at your destination.

Take a taxi

Certainly the priciest but also the most convenient, consider this one if you arrive late and have a night booked in Taipei city. Taking a taxi all the way to Taipei is expensive in and of itself so adding a large box shouldn't cost you anything more.

MRT train

The good news, bicycles are allowed on most Taipei metro lines and can get you to almost anywhere in the Taipei area. The bad news, you cannot take a bicycle onto the metro at either of the two airport stations. Why this is, we do not know but it is a situation that does not make unboxing at the airport any easier. Joining the MRT line from Taipei to the airport has been no trouble with a large box, but the airport staff have stopped us several times from taking the MRT with our bicycle boxes.

Kaohsiung Airport

The large port city of Kaohsiung in the south is Taiwan's second largest international airport, with flights from nearby regions, so this could be a great option if arriving from other parts of Asia. This simple small airport is right on the edge of the city and unboxing here and riding into downtown couldn't be simpler.

To the Start

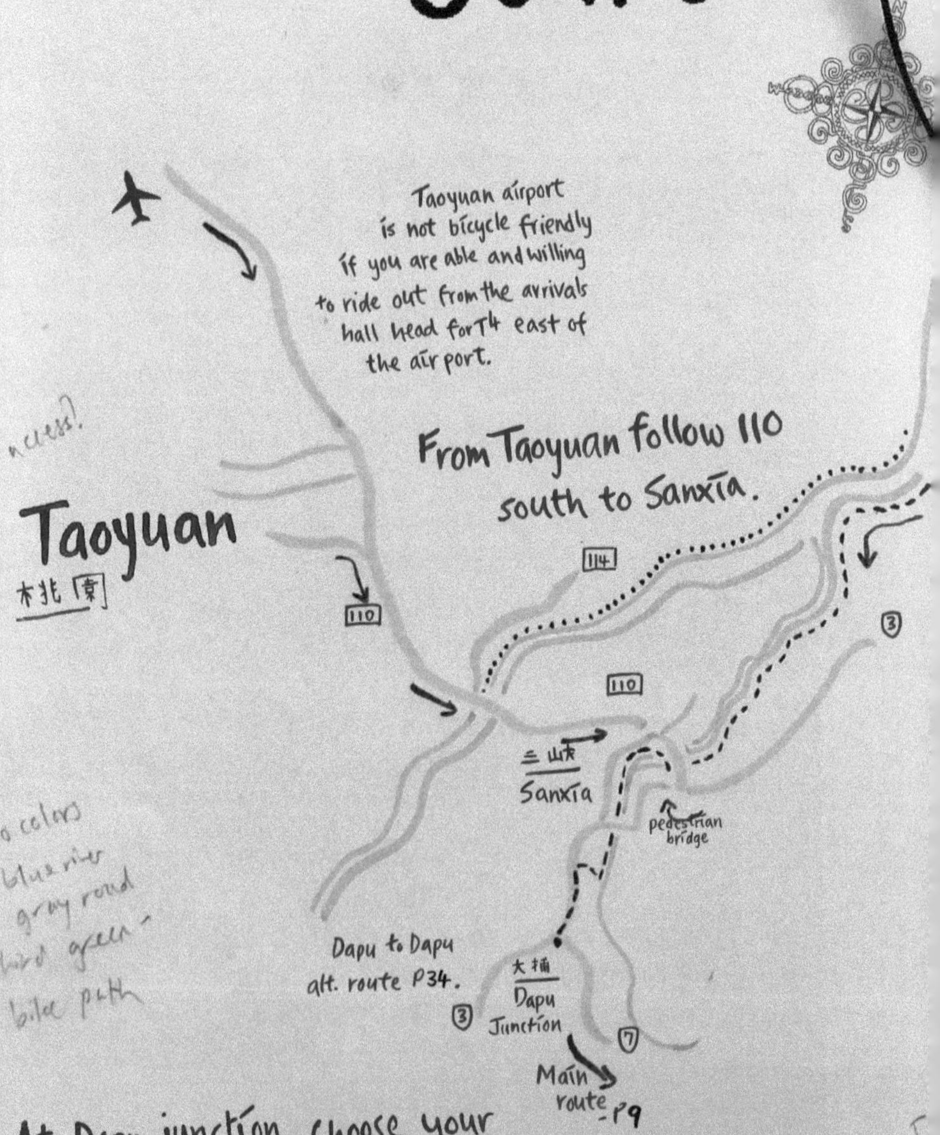

Taoyuan airport is not bicycle friendly if you are able and willing to ride out from the arrivals hall head for T4 east of the airport.

Airport access?

Taoyuan
台北市

From Taoyuan follow 110 south to Sanxia.

110

114

110

3

三峡
Sanxia

pedestrian bridge

two colors
blue river
gray road
third green -
bike path

Dapu to Dapu
alt. route P34.

大埔
Dapu
Junction

3

7

Main
route P9

At Dapu junction choose your route - the high mountains or our alternative along the western hills.

- Sanxia riding

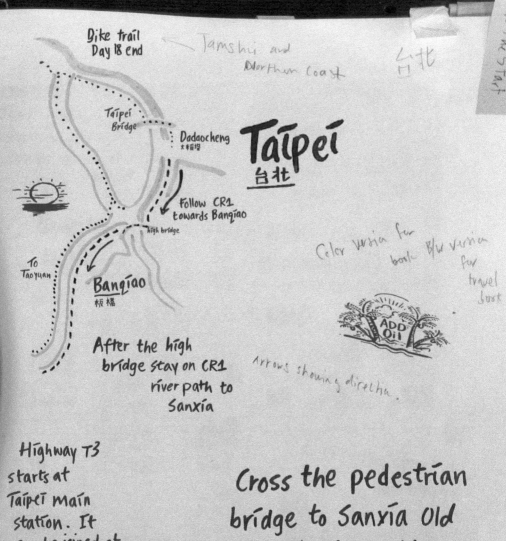

Dike trail
Day 18 end

Tamshii and
Northern Coast

台北

Taipei
Bridge

Dadaocheng
大稻埕

Taipei
台北

Follow CR1
towards Bangiao

high bridge

To
Taoyuan

Banqiao
板橋

After the high
bridge stay on CR1
river path to
Sanxia

Color version for
book B/w version
for travel book

ADD
Oil

Arrows showing direction.

Highway T3
starts at
Taipei Main
station. It
can be joined at
Dingpu MRT
station.

Cross the pedestrian
bridge to Sanxia Old
Street alternatively
stay on the T3.

From Sanxia Temple
cross the small red bridge,
south. The start of our
tour - P6

- Taroko
- Yushan hike national park
- Tainan old streets
- Food + drink (bubble tea)
- Fast food beauty
- Sat life
- Taipei 101 +
  nightlife

37

around the island

High mountains dripping
with atmosphere, hill towns
overlooking vast national parks,
and sleeping under
clear starry skies.

Our remote start
through Taiwan's
interior,
an
enriching
challenge
for the mind,
bicycle and soul.

Roads above
the clouds
indeed.

Taiwan Spine

When the sun is low on a warm, clear morning, and with the heat already rising, we stand at the riverside bike path leading south from Sanxia's old cobble streets. Facing directly toward the hills, the soft light silhouettes the low peaks ahead, focusing our eyes on the world duly being revealed. This is how we start our tour of Taiwan, and over the next few weeks this feeling of illumination and wonder rarely leaves our minds.

As we climb up into the mountains we become initiated to the sounds of the island. Monkeys bicker in the trees; cicadas, crickets and insects of all types play their tunes in our ears. Thunder rumbles overhead as water drips down through canopy, hillside and road alike. Our eyes are overwhelmed with the near constant mountain vistas cloaked in mist. The sounds of far-off temples echo around and the sweeping force of rivers rush below.

As we make it up higher the air cools and the high mountain farms start to cover the hillsides. Crates of produce line the road or trundle past in the back of blue trucks. Small towns sit on ridges and the trail dips and curves ever higher as we wind our way up past the tree line and out the other side to Taiwan's highest road pass.

The Northern Cross-Island Highway takes us away from the industrial cities of northern Taiwan. Up and out of the populated areas we are swept across valleys and along hillsides as we climb toward the first remote region on the map.

If you have come straight from the airport you would be forgiven to think that Taiwan is a wild and untamed land, as there are few people or buildings up here in the hills, save for a few small villages and stores. You need perseverance and strength as we spend three days climbing up to the peak of Taiwan's interior.

It is a glorious ride, and an absolute achievement. Get ready to view the real power of this small island as its high mountains bring disbelief and wonder. At the end of it we descend south into the heart of Taiwan, not quite the western ride you were imagining but, thankfully and as is usual with Taiwan, nothing turns out as you expect.

Sanxia to Linsen

Here we go. We start our adventure by the market town of Sanxia (三峽), northwest Taiwan (台灣). Sitting on the bank of a river, tucked away at the back of the crossroads between Taipei (台北) and Taoyuan (桃園). A bustling meeting point of old and new worlds, as well as high-rise freeways. Sanxia is squeezed between these metropolises and the mountains that rise up into the clouds beyond. It's the perfect place to plot our escape from the concrete jungle up into the lush green canopies.

We spend most of this first day traversing the mountain highway, T7. A peaceful and remote start, whereas all other routes are busy and heavy with traffic. From Sanxia to our road's end we travel over 85km and so the day needs to be started early.

If you are unsure of your fitness, consider breaking this day in two by taking an extra night at Baling (巴陵), some 50km into the day's ride.

Our round-island adventure starts on a picturesque bicycle path that leads dead south out of Sanxia and away from the hustle and bustle of life. You can find the river by heading south behind the old temple or market road. If you are coming from Taipei along the river bikeways then the CR1 passes along this spot on the T3, see our *To the Start* page.

As you follow the river path, rolling hills come into view. We stick with river-tracing roads for the first half of our journey. As we ride the T7甲 our journey starts with a climb that in the summer sun can be a little daunting, but it's a great early morning ride and in the cooler months it is a fairly comfortable affair.

After reaching the midway town of Baling the road really starts to arch up as we weave along our first cliffside road in Taiwan. Moss, ferns and creeping jungle vines cover the edges of this narrow mountainside road. Quiet and almost devoid of traffic, this road comes alive after an early afternoon shower. Wet asphalt shimmers as clouds rumble overhead, water gushes along rivers below and trickles down the loose cliff walls as mountains loom large off in the distance.

At times, we glimpse our first vistas as we roll coolly toward the mini summit, passing out of Taoyuan and crossing into Yilan (宜蘭) County. From this point, the quiet wild road heads deeper into the mountains.

As we seemingly pass through a crack in a cliff, dark shadows creep in and high cliffs block the sun; thick forest and running streams abound. This area is stunningly eerie; be glad the heavy climbing is finished for the day.

Eventually emerging out the other side of the mountain's forest, now heading along an altogether different mountain ridge with stupendous views we descend on toward a wide farming valley and the end of the first day's ride. This descent is long, sweeping, full of mind-bending views of the mountains ahead. This is an adventure in and of itself and a great introduction to the mountain region.

This is a road that truly enriches the senses, pulling you straight into Taiwan's remote interior; we start as we mean to go on. The adventures lie ahead, you can almost see them all in the distance. As the mountains glisten you feel that the whole world is just up over the other side. Bliss.

Warning: steep climbs ahead
Our spirit is always: Jiāyóu (加油)! Every road is for every rider and we truly believe that anyone can cycle tour, practically anywhere. But having said that, the start of our tour comes with a warning.

The first stage in our journey *Taiwan Spine* is a truly mountainous route. It is a difficult challenge for any rider, especially at the start of a tour. We don't want to discourage, and we believe the challenge is worth it. We have ridden this route with experienced and first-time tourers alike. We have met people of all physical conditions who have traversed these mountains.

However, If you think this route might just not be for you we advise to take our alternative Dapu to Dapu route, p34. This western hill ride is perfect for those wanting a more relaxed beginning to their adventure while avoiding the dull industrial zones of western Taiwan. Along the way there are still plenty of workouts for your legs, and once you get underway, you can always switch back to our main route for the climb to Tatajia (塔塔加) and Alishan (阿里山), p87.

If you do decide to take our mountain route, take your time, split your days up if you need to. Don't underestimate Taiwan's roads, but equally don't underestimate yourself! And most importantly, when you need to, just quietly tell yourself... 加油!

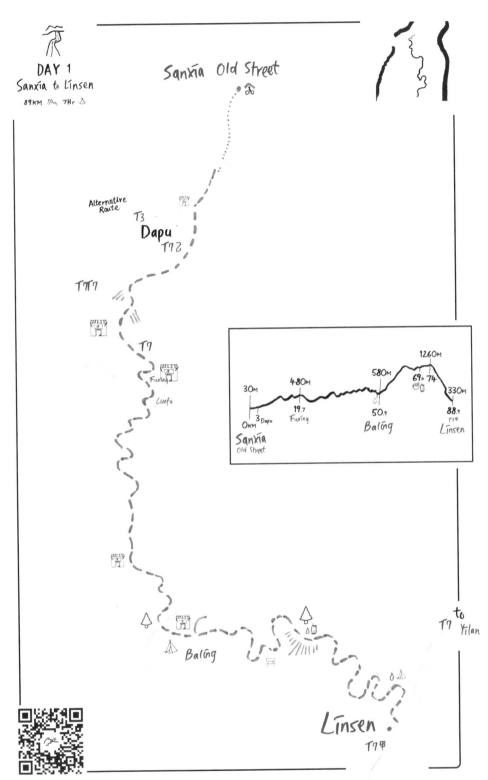

DAY 1
Sanxia to Linsen
89KM 🚴 7Hr ⛺

Sanxia Old Street

Alternative Route

T3
Dapu
T72

T77

T7

Fuxing
Luofu

Baling

Linsen

T7甲

T7 to Yilan

T7甲

30M
0KM
3 Dapu
Sanxia
Old Street

480M
19.7
Fuxing

580M
50.9

69.4 74

1260M

330M
88.9
T7甲
Linsen

Baling

DAY 1

89KM 🚶 7Hr ⛺

0.00 Start at the Sanxia (三峽) Old Street temple! Beside the pedestrian bridge is the Sanxia river bicycle path. The start is marked by a bright red arched bridge. Face your bike south toward the hills, pass through the barrier and across the small bridge; the path drops down onto the grassy bank. Travel along the riverside, heading south. If you can't find the bikeway just follow the highway T3 heading south from here.

1.75 Turn right after passing along a bridge, the path comes to an abrupt end. Follow signs for CR1 through what looks like the entrance to a private residence. The small lane brings you out onto the T3.

1.80 Turn left onto highway T3. Here the central road barrier prohibits a simple crossing; pass down to the closest crossing and turn, heading southbound on T3.

3.00 Turn left onto the T7乙 at Dapu (大埔) junction. Follow signs for T7乙 and Dapu Road.

Just before the junction, at the post office, there is a turning onto a bridge. Crossing the river leads to a side road that runs parallel to T7乙 and offers a quaint alternative for a few km, reconnecting with the main highway a little farther along.

Dapu to Dapu alternative route
If you are planning on avoiding the high mountains then lean right, keeping on the T3 heading south. From here follow our multiday western hills alternative route from Dapu, Taoyuan, to Dapu, Chiayi. See p34.

7.20 Now on the quiet T7乙, a long, stiff climb for the next 7km with no stores as you ride alongside a river that traces up and around hills.

15.2 Reach the top of the climb, wipe your brow. Phew! Head down the descent toward T7, our main road for the day.

17.1 Turn left onto the T7 at the roundabout junction and head south on the highway. There are stores here and if you are riding in the hot summer sun, there is more shade on this next section before you reach the top of a short climb.

Turn right for the T3 and Daxi (大溪). If you want to avoid any more climbs this is the last chance to join the alternative route along the T3.

20.8 Head straight at the top of the hill and the small indigenous village of Shuiyuandi (水源地). Here is a wide junction with a convenience store on the opposite corner. When you leave stay on the T7, keeping the store on your right, heading straight into the descent.

25.3 As the road levels off there is a small parking lot at the edge of the Fuxing (復興) suspension bridge you can cross with your bike and rejoin the highway on the other side of the river.

After the river crossing, the road climbs again. From here the next 25km undulates and climbs, a fairly easy road but without any rests or stores so make sure you start with plenty of water and snacks.

48.3 Access to 桃113 and 竹60. This stunning, but exhausting, route leads up over a steep climb before descending into Hsinchu County. At the end of this ride you rejoin the western hills route, picking up highway T3 at Hexing (合興). See p43.

50.0 Just before the red arch bridge at the outskirts of Baling (巴陵) is a cute cave museum and old suspension bridge. Turn off right just before the main bridge, you can walk your bike through the museum tunnel before crossing the suspension bridge. Beautiful views of the river, gorge and surrounding hills.

50.9 The town of Baling is our last town with stores for the day. This is the lower town, the higher town up on the mountain's higher plateau is a tiring and steep ride up. So, use the lower local store with plenty of supplies. It is a great place to sit with fun locals to interact with. There are also a couple of hotels with restaurants here if you need.

From Baling the road climbs for our second and longest ascent of the day. An afternoon rain shower, the heavy tree coverage as well as some higher altitudes should provide you with a cooler ride while adding to the atmosphere.

Stop over at Baling
If you want to break up the day then staying in Baling is a great option. There is a private campground 1km south of the village along Yeheng Road (爺亨道路).

After staying in Baling for the night then on your second day you could reach the village of Nanshan (南山) p18, before arriving at Lishan (梨山) on your third afternoon.

62.4 The top of the climb crosses through a ridge that marks the county lines. There are several pull-ins and trailheads along this section of road. Often people will park their cars, vans and bicycles here for the night to sleep and prepare for a sunrise walk or ride.

The next few km drops before gently climbing through a beautiful narrow gorge area with streams and forest. It is a truly stunning area of the country. And as remote as Taiwan ever feels and a good warm-up for the next few days of riding.

69.4 Mingchi (明池) resort, hotel and forest recreation entrance. There is a toilet and vending machine here in the parking lot for a quick break. This sprawling complex has walking trails and a relaxing outdoor café.

The road finally flattens for good here, with only a few sharp corners before the descent.

70.3 Get your camera ready. After a few sweeping corners, you are on top of the mountain road. Comfortably snaking around the long cliff edges, giving you incredible views of the surrounding peaks. On a good day, you're able to see the full mountain ranges ahead and it is truly breathtaking.

77.3 The last bend before the steep descent really starts, from here it's downhill all the way. This is one of the quietest and most twisting descents you will have on the trip.

87.7 At the bottom is the tiny village of Linsen (林森), with two private campgrounds open year-round and one small, often closed roadside shop. This is the end of the ride for the day. With no obvious signage or entrances, ask at the indigenous stall for a place to camp.

88.9 Finish at the junction with the T7甲 at the bottom of the descent. A T junction splits the highway and T7 heads north to Yilan while the T7甲 heads south toward the high mountains, tomorrow's ride.

For alternative places to stay, there is one larger hotel 4km further down T7甲, just before the bridge. After 3km on the roadside there is a large rest stop with benches. 2km later cross the long bridge and turn left off the highway to find a large rest stop with a closed police station and the well-preserved yet defunct Tuchang train station (土場車站).

Taiwan's cross-island highways

Due to Taiwan's extremely mountainous center its main road networks and railway lines are kept to the coastal regions. But there are three cross-island highways that attempt to connect the west and east. These three mountain roads crisscross Taiwan's difficult landscapes and are all steeped in history, intrigue and for cyclists, frustration.

台7 – Northern Cross-Island Highway
This highway connects the western city of Taoyuan (桃園) with the northeast county of Yilan (宜蘭). We make full use of this road on Day 1 of our tour. It rises up and then quickly descends to Yilan's eastern cabbage fields. It is a good warm-up of things to come. Of the three cross-island highways this is the most reliable, and shortest. It is usually fully open. With little chance of road closures or landslides. The others are a different story.

台8 – Central Cross-Island Highway
Originally taking you from the edges of Taichung (台中) in the west to Taroko (太魯閣) and Hualien (花蓮) on the east coast. This magnificent mountain crossing is prone to landslides and rockfalls. The route up east from Hualien is, perhaps, Taiwan's most famous road, kept open all the way down to Lishan village in Taiwan's core. Sadly, the western portion of the highway from Guguan (谷關), in Taichung, p48, up to Lishan has been closed to traffic for years with no sign of reopening. Constant landslides have made this road unusable it seems. Instead, to make any cross-island route to the west you have to combine the T8 and the T14甲, using Wuling Pass (武嶺). See p26 for information on descending to Taroko Gorge and the east coast.

台20 – Southern Cross-Island Highway
This infamous highway has only reopened in the last year after being closed for over a decade due to unbelievable landslides. Crossing from Tainan (台南) in the west to Taitung (台東) in the east this mammoth road has faced huge reconstruction work hampered by bad weather and further landslides over the years. For sure this stunning highway is perhaps Taiwan's best individual road ride. The eastern route is also home to the entrance point for the wonderful multiday mountain hike to Jiaming Lake, an important marker on any Taiwan adventurer's map. Sadly this highway remains closed to cyclists. For information on the Southern Cross-Island Highway, see p126.

There is a government website with up-to-date road closures. It also tracks maintenance work or temporary road closures on these mountain routes. Worth checking out before you head out on your journey at 168.thb.gov.tw.

Linsen to Lishan

Cabbage fields spread out across the dry riverbed at the T junction of the T7, marking the edges of the flat farming area and the entrance to the high mountain ranges beyond. From here the T7 splits and we leave the main highway road as it turns north toward Yilan (宜蘭). The T7甲 is our road for the day, as it heads south down the spine of Taiwan and up into the central mountains.

As we travel toward the peak of the country don't expect heavy traffic. Instead, you meander along quiet, well-maintained roads that follow rivers, valleys, forests and pass though farming communities. This is rural Taiwan at its best, peaceful and atmospheric.

Nowhere feels more dramatic than the day's finishing point at the mountain farming town of Lishan (梨山). A temple stay awaits us in the chilly mountain surrounds set to a backdrop of Taoist chimes, hillside lanterns and smiling faces that peek through the mist.

The day starts out heading uphill on the T7甲. The road climbs nearly all day but the first section is undulating, with sweeping bends and wide views. Once we cross the river and pass through crop communities, we really start to feel the climbs with some deceptively persistent road. The town of Nanshan (南山) is our first stopping point and a marker for the end of the day's lower farm landscape.

After Nanshan, an even stiffer climb awaits through a narrow section of mountain road that heads up and over an equally narrow forest pass. Water drips from farming pipes all along the roadside here, making a great soundtrack to your climb. The pass, a straight strip of road at Siyuanakou (思源埡口),

has an eerie air to it. As you pass through mist and pine trees, feel the air becoming decidedly cooler out the other side. A mesmerizing descent has you edge toward the town of Huanshan (環山).

Then, like the opening of stage curtains, a short climb past the entrance to the Shei-Pa National Park (雪霸國家公園) lifts you up over a ridge to reveal an awesome mountain vista. A scene of great life and scope. You are now in the middle of Taiwan's high mountain ranges. Rolling ridges and peaks spread as far as the eye can see, valleys and rivers burst with life, the road snakes around remote farming communities, the air is markedly cooler as you drop down a second and longer descent to a small market town of Huanshan perched on a ridge. Even the convenience store boasts incredible views from its upstairs windows.

After leaving Huanshan, one last climb for the day awaits us. Tired legs and empty lungs have to push here, with the sun edging toward the back of the mountains you equally creep closer to the finish line. At the top of the climb after a dozen tiring km's you reach the outskirts of Lishan. As the T7甲 ends you stumble onto T8 and into the bustling mountain town.

Your end-of-the-day reward is panoramic views of mountainsides as the sun sets off in the distance, and the hillsides light up with the dots of night lights. A stay at the town's plush hotel or in the ramshackle temple, nestled up close alongside other road travelers; choosing either luxury or the cheap and clean private accommodation of the temple adds to the atmosphere up here. Walk the streets of this small but entertaining place as the market winds down and the evening clouds roll in. Grab dinner from the local eateries, you can even eat yummy homemade pizza as you stare out at the now shimmering night scene.

Local foods and produce of all kinds can be found in this proud mountain community. Strolling past the stores here in the evening is a delight, tension lingers in the air as you maintain your excitement for one more day of climbing in this unique and quiet world.

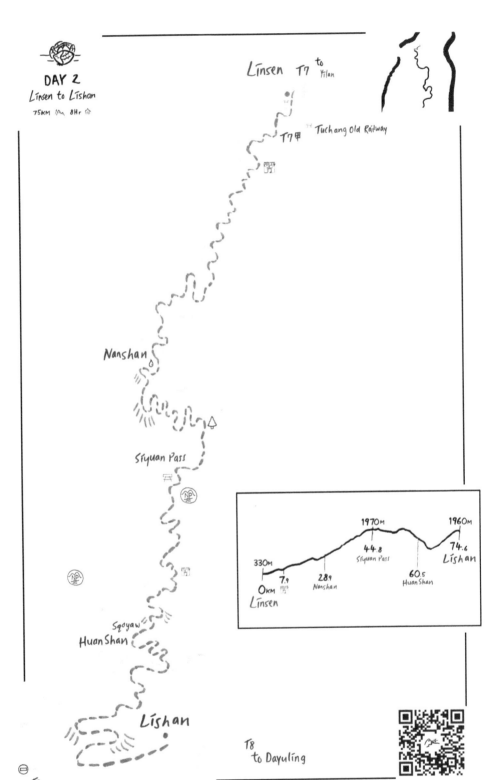

DAY 2
Linsen to Lishan
75KM / 8Hr

Linsen T7 to Yilan

T7甲 Tuchang Old Railway

Nanshan

Siyuan Pass

Sqoyaw
Huan Shan

Lishan

T8
to Dayuling

Elevation profile:

330M
0KM
Linsen

7.9

28.9
Nanshan

1970M
44.8
Siyuan Pass

60.5
Huan Shan

1960M
74.6
Lishan

T8

DAY 2

75KM /⚡ 8Hr 🏠

0.00 Start at the junction with the T7, turn right onto the T7甲. The T7 turns north and races quickly toward the northeast city of Yilan (宜蘭).

3.00 Cute roadside rest stop with garden, benches, water feature, and monkeys in the trees.

3.20 Cross the bridge.

3.58 Turn right after the bridge following signs for the T7甲. Turn left to visit the open-air museum of the Tuchang train station rest stop.

5.00 Pass a beautiful but locked park with pond and school.

7.90 Stop—local store! This is such an important local store. It is your only chance to grab food, snacks, and water for the next 20km of uphill road. Make sure you have supplies. The little *āyí* who runs this place opens up early and she is always happy to meet weary travelers.

　　The road climbs and undulates for the next 14km running along the river in shade, passing indigenous villages and farms along the way.

21.5 Cross the bridge. Take in the views of the river flowing back down the valley. The next 7km can be tough, especially on a hot day as you are passing out of the mountain shade.

　　After the bridge crossing, the road climbs steeply to leave the riverbed, eventually heading along a hillside.

　　From here your legs will tire on this stretch of road through a farming community; it doesn't look steep but it is energy sapping with zero shade. So, relax into a slow ride and soak up the amazing atmosphere as you pass through the cutest farm area with crops growing all around. The sounds of locals riding homemade tractors and rushing water escaping pipes fill the air. The locals will cheer you on and the road will force you to contemplate your senses as they are overloaded.

29.0 Finally you have reached Nanshan (南山). Restaurants, public toilets, stores and sleeping options in the heart of the community. We have heard about people camping at the local sports park. Ask at the elementary school or the police station. In Taiwan, these are usually great places to ask for help in finding a place to set up camp for the night.

Once we leave Nanshan we ride up a long 15km climb that while energy sapping is almost entirely in shade. As we reach the top of this climb we are in another world, truly. The pass takes us away from the low farms as we climb into a much mistier atmosphere and crops are replaced by ferns, bamboo and pine trees.

44.8 Siyuan Pass (思源埡口), turn the corner at the small shrine to an amazingly eerie straight stretch of road. Surrounded by pine forest, the road is chilly and the upcoming descent even more so.

52.9 The bottom of the fun descent. Cross the small gorge bridge, and now just one small 3km up to the second part of the descent to the pic-

turesque region of Huanshan (環山) and views of Shei-Pa National Park (雪霸國家公園).

53.5 At a large local shop and café is a turning for the entrance to Wuling Farm (武陵農場) and the main road into the national park, home to Taiwan's second highest mountain, Xueshan (Snow Mountain 雪山). Instead, we carry on, up the hill.

Lots of farm dogs are tied up along the roadside here. Sadly, a common sight in rural areas in Taiwan. Don't be afraid of their bark but don't approach these dogs either.

55.8 Top of the climb, take in those views and enjoy the descent.

61.4 Center of Huanshan. The temple here has basic accommodation and a convenience store (with incredible views). Our day has one more climb, but first a descent out of the town.

65.0 A narrow gorge where the river weaves its way between two cliffs, a stunning little spot where the gap nearly bends in on itself.

The last climb of the day starts here. Don't worry, as the sun starts to get low the views are incredible and you will forget your burning legs.

73.8 Turn left onto the T8. The end of the day's climb. Enter Lishan (梨山) at the end of highway T7甲.

After turning left at this junction, you briskly climb to find stores, restaurants, viewpoints. The local information center is in front of the town's only hotel. The center can help you call ahead to the temple to confirm your room.

Turning right at this junction, you will ride down west and meet a Closed Road sign at the closed-off section of highway T8. Do not head this way, unfortunately it won't reopen any time soon.

74.6 Finish in central Lishan. Lishan is short on accommodations. There are a couple of small guesthouses that are overly priced, and this area does not have any campsites. Instead there are two almost polar opposite options for the night. The Lishan Guesthouse is a stunning centerpiece to Lishan's skyline; the entrance is a beautifully large traditional building. But don't let the name fool you, this is a pricey affair with hotel rates and service. It might be worth splashing out for the night.

Luckily the town's Taoist temple (寺廟) offers the perfect alternative. Perched at the north end of the main road, it has rooms for the night. Simple, and run-down perhaps, but with clean, warm, private rooms with communal bathrooms and showers that work. It is a relaxing, quiet and safe place to spend the evening. Those who work there are always kind and helpful, as are the other guests. Women are welcome too and will find a safe environment if alone.

From the large viewpoint in front of the hotel the highway winds up through the village. Local restaurants and stores line the roadside.

The lights to the eastern edge of the village mark its end. The temple complex is perched just on the next bend, with mountain views. We start the next days' journey from this junction.

Lishan to Renai

You will notice that our notes on this third-day ride have far fewer turns than most. Have no fear, this is no humdrum day, in fact quite the contrary. This is simply the best day of Taiwan's mountain roads and perhaps the highlight of your entire trip.

In fact there are only two along the whole route. There are not a lot of towns or coffee shops along the way, in fact just one of each. What this day does have in abundance are jaw-dropping mountains, high peaks and wild landscapes of forest, grassland, boulders and sky. All at the top of Taiwan. Oh, did we mention the country's highest road pass, its last section proving to be the toughest challenge on two wheels? But for good measure it comes complete with the most awesome of downhill rides. You'll be left utterly bereft of words and full of life.

Leaving Lishan (梨山), we head out on the T8 as it heads along the dazzling mountainside. For now, we fix our gaze on the day's only tunnel and junction at the crossroads some 28km up ahead. The first 8km are a joy, flat and rolling, you hardly have to kick the pedals. But then, just as you get relaxed, surrounded by stunning views of the high mountain vistas the road starts to climb along ridges and forest edges, not too steep but a good warm-up for what lies ahead. Hopefully you made an early start and the sun should just be peeking up over the horizon ahead as you edge toward what seems to be an impossible ridge line no road can cross. Don't worry, the tunnel at Dayuling (大禹嶺) will help you out.

After passing through the tunnel you come out to a junction where your attention turns right. High mountains that peak much higher than anything seen so far. We leave T8 here and join the T14甲.

Next up is the gloriously tiring and tough summit ride. This last 10km of climbing forms the peak of Taiwan's internationally revered KOM bike race. This road leads us up to Wuling Pass (武嶺), running alongside and around the peaks of Hehuanshan (合歡山), a popular short hiking trail to one of Taiwan's highest mountains. The road is challenging, no section more so than the first 3km. But with the last section in sight, a brief descent and a warm mug of coffee at the newly renamed H2 café (formerly 3158 Cafe) will have you all set for the last 2km of struggle. A morning of drama, mind-blowing views, a bit of torment but, ultimately, wonder and a sense of achievement.

The views from the pass on a clear morning are indescribable. Blue-hued mountains stretch off in the distance, nearby peaks and their lush green caps contrast with a clear blue sky. The three rolling hilltops that the road runs down, like knuckles on a fist, striking up into the air. The rocky spike of Wuling providing some shade and support as the wind whistles through and over the grassy, fresh landscape.

The sense of achievement is palpable at the pass; people throng here on good- and bad-weather days. Even as the clouds roll in, masking the views below, you can't help but feel you are above the world. The equally exhilarating ride down is a chance to take flight and really ride through clouds. Nothing in life should come easy but every hard-fought win should come with a reward. Luckily this peak offers such great food for the soul. Soak it in.

Waiting for us on the other side of Wuling Pass is one of Taiwan's most vibrant and enjoyable descents. We will drop 2500m of elevation in little over 30km. With a sweeping, well-paved road that, at points, narrows down to tight lanes and single-car-width corners as it turns past cliff edges and switchbacks. The adrenaline coursing through you, your fingers bitterly cold, gripping the side of the bars as you train your eyes on the mirrors that show you around the blind corner.

As you get a little farther away from the top the road starts to head straight, passing through forest, over ridges and around peaks as the mountains that were once below you come into your eyeline. This ride demands concentration, asking you to reach your comfortable limits, but the joy you feel, the sheer euphoria, keeps your mind present, on the moment, the road ahead, the world around and the bike underneath you.

By the time you arrive at the mountain tourist town of Qingjing Farm (清境農場), you will feel you can accomplish anything. This hillside sprawl of stores, hotels, guesthouses and tourist attractions spans for some distance along the mountainside above the town of Renai (仁愛), plenty of options for places to stay. With jaw-dropping views aplenty.

Bike touring in Taiwan has reached its literal high already. From here you start to wonder what other surprises are in store. The roads ahead will appear even more tempting, perhaps even more enjoyable. As you have reached the peak of difficulty, the peak of endurance and the answer to the question *Just what can I achieve?* Well, now you know your limits and it seems they are near endless.

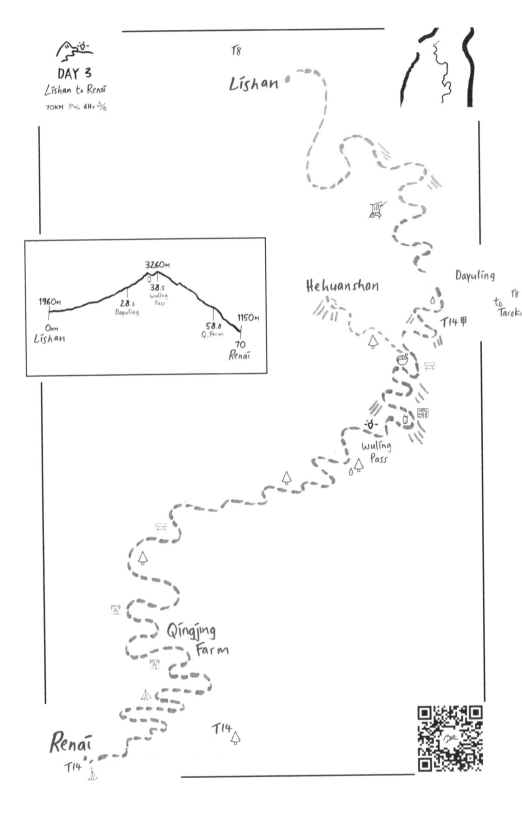

DAY 3
Lishan to Renai
70KM / 6Hr

T8

Lishan

3260M
38.5
Wuling Pass

1960M

28.3
Dayuling

0KM
Lishan

58.8
Q.Farm

1150M

70
Renai

Hehuanshan

Dayuling

T8 to Taroko

T14甲

Wuling Pass

Qingjing Farm

Renai

T14

T14

DAY 3

70KM /ᴧᴧ\ 6Hr ⊿/⟨

0.00 Start at the Crossroads, at the far end of Lishan (梨山)! Head south east for Hehuanshan (合歡山), along the T8.

There is one alternative route option here. At the lights turn right onto the 中131, which after a steep climb becomes the 投89. This alternative road leads down to Renai (仁愛) in Nantou, completely skipping the climb up and over Wuling Pass (武嶺). It is a wild ride with some steep descents through incredible farming villages and breathtaking vistas. It does cut time but the initial climb is as steep as it gets, so don't go thinking this is a simpler affair than the high pass. We would only recommend this route if you have completed the Wuling route before and want a different challenge. After all, you have come this far, would be a shame not to reach the top of the world.

0.20 Pass the Taoist temple at the edge of town, stunning views from the off. The first 8km of the ride is super relaxing and easy enough. The road winds flat and down, twisting past mountain homes, farms and along an epic trail until we arrive at a small river crossing nestled in the crack between two high peaks.

From here it's 28km until you reach the tunnel and changing of the road. A relatively short ride in distance but tackling the long, sloping climb takes time; come prepared with water and snacks to get you to the pass of Wuling. The first location to buy anything comes just 5km from the top of the climb and there is no guarantee it will be open.

8.20 After crossing this mountain river, we start to climb. The first section of the day, on highway T8, is a simple and not overly exerting ride, with no stores but plenty of views worth stopping and gawping at. Go slow and take breaks, store some energy. The road stays cliffside and so wide vistas of the surrounding ranges are on offer on a clear morning. The earlier you take this ride the better.

28.0 Enter Dayuling (大禹嶺) tunnel. Here at the tunnel, wait for the lights as it is narrower and deceptively longer than it looks. Once you pass through, you will be transported to the end of our ride along the T8 and placed in another world once again.

28.3 Turn right onto the T14甲 at the end of the tunnel, you will find yourself at Dayuling. At this junction of Taiwan's central mountain roads, turn right, following signs for Hehuanshan. There are public toilets here at the junction, but no stores.

I won't lie, the next 10km of riding is some of the toughest around and is truly a challenge for the body and mind. Famed as the last section of

---

Central Cross-Island Highway to Taroko Gorge and the east coast
From Dayuling junction the T8 races down the mountains and through to Taroko Gorge (太魯閣) before eventually out to the east coast near Hualien (花蓮). If you want to travel to the east coast, or perhaps you're on a time limit, consider this route. For more information on Taroko see p226.

It is an incredible journey and the best of Taiwan's long descents. After the euphoria of the first 6km descent you get hit with a soul-sapping 4km uphill section that will, temporarily, take it out of you. The top of the climb is marked by a tunnel. As you exit, set yourself straight, tighten those straps and prepare for the longest of ways down.

What lies ahead is a 45km thrill ride, as you cascade down the mountainside. Around cliffs, through tunnels of stone, gliding above clouds and forest before passing like a bullet through both. Weather, light, seasons and life will change as you continue your drop. Get ready for sun, rain, fog, heat, chills and sweat to fill the senses. The road is safe with rail guards all the way, plenty of lights in the tunnels and well-maintained asphalt.

The only real place of note to stop along the way is the beautiful Bilu Giant Tree (碧綠神木), Taiwan's oldest recorded, over three thousand years old. Right by the roadside this stunning tree glistens in the sunlight. There are public bathrooms and a small café here that usually serves ginger teas and coffee.

All the way down the descent you will find rest stops, pull-ins, restrooms, and viewpoints to stop at. Gawp at the views, rest your fingers and your limbs. Have a lunch in the middle of a mountain forest and snap away.

The last section above the gorge provides some incredible switchbacks, and views as the mountains narrow together and hills jut out of the mist. Spectacular.

While not strictly the bottom of the descent, the village of Tianxiang (天祥) marks the top of Taroko Gorge. Here you should take a long rest, fill up on everything before you complete the descent through the gorge and arrive at the ocean. See p243 for more information on this section of the ride.

the internationally revered KOM race from the ocean to the summit, this section of road is steep and takes a long time to complete.

By far the first 3km are the hardest. So, once you start don't get too dispirited, the whole road is not entirely like the first few switchbacks. Take your time and rest, heck walk, where you need to. Plenty of passing cars and motorcycles will cheer you on and all cyclists struggle up this mammoth of a climb. Don't be afraid, you can do it, make a morning of it, revel in the views, your pain and the mental struggle. It will all be worth it, we promise.

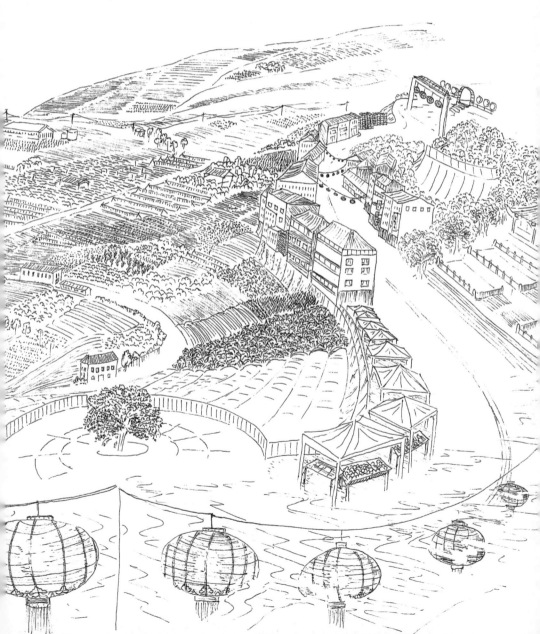

31.7 The road straightens a bit here, with wide switchbacks raising you up above a plateau, opening up the dramatic views.

32.9 Hiking trails for Hehuanshan peak start here.

33.4 Phew! A rest stop at a large parking lot, toilets, free water, a small store and seats, mountain panoramas abound.

    The next section of switchbacks starts tough but the road relaxes with wide grasslands opening up. A look back down all the dotted road fills you with a sense of achievement.

35.7 The first pass, reach this point and you really have made it, almost. Take in those views though! A small descent is ahead, and just in time too.

37.1 At the bottom of the short downhill, just before the last steep climb is a parking lot, viewing platform, public bathrooms and the H2 café. Well worth stopping for a high-altitude coffee served in real mugs. Take in the views from the platforms. You can even take away the mugs to celebrate your achievement if you don't mind paying a little extra.

    Hotels are in short supply in this area but if you want to spend a night up here and you don't have a tent, consider the Ski lodge. A simple but clean and warm night's stay. It is the second of two small lodges at this junction, the first, Songsyue, is a much pricier affair. Both are found on the side road that runs down the hill, opposite the parking lot.

37.2 The last 1.5km is a stiff, sharp climb to the top, with incredible views all around on a clear day. There are bicycle warning signs as this section of road randomly narrows around corners and provides you with a couple of really mean gradients just for the added pain.

38.1 Top of the climb, just a couple of pushes to the pass!

38.5 Wuling Pass! You made it! Here we are at the top and highest road pass in Taiwan, 3275m above sea level. The spellbinding views here are often gone by noontime. But in any case, with the weather up here being so unpredictable, soak in the atmosphere, chat to other riders and people who have made the pass that day, smiles and laughter abound. The descent now is perfect, astounding views and beautiful switchbacks, downhill paradise. Just one note of caution, until the top of Qingjing (清境) some 20km away there are few to no stores or bathrooms and few pull-ins or rest stops. Luckily you should make light work of that distance as you descend.

40.7 A great viewpoint, with amazing vistas back up to the pass and of the road to come as it snakes though the central mountain range.

52.5 The start of three small bumps in the road. Even these little uphill jaunts are nothing too daunting but they do make you engage your legs for a few hundred meters.

58.3 Arrive at the top of Qingjing. Here is the first convenience store, group of hotels and a gas station.

59.5 Large entrance to the private, gaudy amusement-parklike setting called Swiss Garden. Here is where most tourists concentrate their time.

62.3 Qingjing Farm main rest stop.

    After passing down a few switchbacks there is a double rest stop either side of the now narrow highway. Here is the main hub of Qingjing.

A large parking lot with a food hall, as well as viewpoints and a small relaxing park near to the area's information center, which is across the road at another store and open-air food hall. Here you can take your break at the end of the day and find fast-food restaurants, coffee shops, convenience stores and the such. From here take a well-earned rest and find out your lodgings for the night, this hillside town is sprawling, with homestay and hotels dotted all over the mountainside for km's. If you are looking for camping for the night there is one paid option, farther down the hill at the giant orange boat.

If you are looking for a good stop away from crowds for a free camping night, there are not a lot of free quiet spaces around here. Head down the last few km of descent and past Renai (仁愛) onto the T14.

65.6 At a tight left-hand turn is the southern entrance to the 投89, the other end of the alternative route that connects to Lishan (梨山) cutting out the high mountain pass, see p25 for more.

66.3 From here you can clearly see the emerald reservoir up ahead, and the views stay great all the way down to Renai.

There is a private campground here; difficult to find the entrance but you might have noticed the large orange boat from the hilltop above, well that's its main building.

66.6 Rest stop convenience store, also has fruit stalls on occasion.

69.7 Turn right onto the T14, at the end of highway T14甲. As we merge right we arrive almost immediately in Renai.

A left-hand turn here would take you up the T14, which heads into the nearby hills. There are plenty of private campgrounds along this road as well as the Chunyang (春陽) natural hot springs, some 5km up the highway from Renai.

70.0 Finish in central Renai village! A police station, convenience stores, local restaurants and free rest stop campground. There is little in the way of accommodation in this village so if you want to stay in a hotel, we recommend higher up in Qingjing. If you are camping for the night, head 300m further down the road; just outside the village is a gas station, immediately after is a left-hand turn into the Wu She Daba (霧社大巴) rest stop with 24hr bathrooms and a small camping area just beside. There are often campervans in the parking lot for the evening. It is a basic space but the bathrooms are well maintained.

Heading farther down the highway, the T14 carries on down the mountain 25km to the center of Puli (埔里). There you can find plenty of hostels, restaurants and stores. From there you can make the ride up highway T21 to Sun Moon Lake if you wish. See p65 for turning to Puli.

We have ridden Day 3 and Day 4 itineraries together to make it all the way to Sun Moon Lake in one day. But we don't recommend it. You will be tired once you reach Qingjing; instead find a good guesthouse, or pitch your tent, and enjoy the late afternoon's views.

Clockwise Notes
Taiwan Spine

Climbing to Wuling, across the central range, back to Taipei

So you're here huh, ready for the ride of your life. Climbing from Renai up to Wuling is the most popular route for cyclists aiming for the famous pass. There are few steep sections, and the well-used highway has smooth grades and comfortable space, for the most part, there are some very narrow spaces nearer the top, but the climb ends with spacious area to ride.

From the top of Qingjing Farm area to the pass there are no locations for water or food so make sure you have supplies for the climb. The views are stupendous, but the road is quite exposed and as such the sun can be hot in the summer and it is very cold in the winter months. If it is raining or foggy make sure you are visible on the narrow descent and wearing warm gloves. Ending the ride with frostbite is not nice.

The descent down from Wuling north is sharp and steep, so take the corners easy as there is always traffic around. Make sure you don't fly past the junction at Dayuling. Turn left at the junction and enter the tunnel, you are now on the T8 and a very comfortable ride down to Lishan. If you want to head to Taroko and the east coast of Hualien turn right at the junction, head east on the T8.

From the bottom of Lishan turn right onto the T7甲. The ride from here down to Linsen and the junction with T7 in Yilan is wonderful, sweeping and gentle, there are two short climbs but the day's ride is fun and comfortable in the most part. Once you are at the junction with the T7 turn left and head up the mountain once more. This climb is long and steep, so try to hit it by lunch. After the climb you can descend down to Baling where we recommend you spend the night.

If you are tired and really don't want to take the climb up the T7, as an alternative you can ride the fairly simple ride north along the Yilan portion of the T7 and head for Luodong; from there you can catch a train back to Taipei, the descent from Lishan to Luodong is a comfortable day's ride.

There is only one small store between the village of Nanshan to Baling, you will need to stock up before the long climb, see p17.

From Baling the road flows along a riverbank before two short climbs and two long descents. At the end of the final, long descent you will arrive back at Dapu and the junction with highway T3, see our *To the Start* pages for our route from Sanxia to Taoyuan and central Taipei along the river path. The ride from Baling all the way to Taipei can be done in a day and the last stretch of nearly 40km will be along simple flat river bike paths back to the built world and the life within.

Dapu to Dapu

Dapu Junction in New Taipei to Dapu village in Chiayi. This route to the south takes us away from Taiwan's hectic metropolises, leaving the world behind in search of an alternative way.

Rural life, remote indigenous
     villages and cultural history.
Quiet jungle-lined roads, cobble
          streets and country lanes.

Dripping with intrigue, cloaked in mist
and surrounded by spectacular nature;
Taiwan's mysterious western hills.

Alternative Route

Dapu to Dapu

Our alternative route between the two villages of Dapu (大埔), in New Taipei (新台北) and Chiayi (嘉義) offers a less strenuous trip than our ride through the high mountains and a much-needed antidote to the dull and uninspiring ride of Taiwan's official Cycle Route 1 (CR1) western section.

Don't go thinking this is also a dull, flat meander either. The ride through the western hills takes us past some of Taiwan's oldest towns, indigenous communities and beautiful, quiet, atmospheric scenery. We pass towns with crumbling cobble streets, temples packed with ceremony as well as vibrant market villages selling local produce and treats. There are rural farms, wild jungles, stunning mountain vistas and misty mornings by the riverside. Slow bike paths down country lanes take us to rolling highways with quiet, wide spaces. Climbs up through the hills offer views of the high mountains as we wind through to the country's heart of Sun Moon Lake (日月潭).

While there is a lot less climbing compared with the mountain route, the coming days still offer a few sections where your climbing legs will be put through their paces. As well as the choice to add in one of the best climbs in the country, up through Yushan National Park (玉山國家公園).

Utilizing the T3 highway for much of our route, we will be hugging the fringes of Taiwan's central mountain ranges. This highway has a few sections of fast, heavy traffic flow but for the most part it acts as a single, laid-back hill road.

Occasionally we leave the T3 to explore quieter alternatives, avoid major metropolises and seek out some smaller communities and cultural treats. The km's away from the main highway offer up a taste of the atmosphere found in the high mountains. Fern-lined jungles dripping with rain climb into remote and atmospheric areas with the sounds of monkeys in the trees. We pass through hills strewn with farms of tea, bamboo and betel nut as well as rice fields alongside wide riverbeds and the near-constant sounds of nature hiding by the roadside. The cultural high of visiting Taiwan's often forgotten rural communities as well as popular areas teeming with unique experiences of life, community and hospitality.

After five days, we arrive in the warm surrounds of Taiwan's largest reservoir where we link back up with the main route through to the southwest and beyond. Having successfully navigated perhaps the best route down the island's

western region, you might want to have a break from riding. From here you can easily roll along to one of the southern cities of Tainan (台南), Kaohsiung (高雄) or Pingtung (屏東). From Dapu you can avoid a lot (not all) of the traffic-dense routes that plague the industrial western region.

Day one is an exploration through the lush lower hills and traditional villages of Taiwan's four northwest counties: New Taipei (新台北), Taoyuan (桃園), Hsinchu (新竹) and Miaoli (苗栗). After departing Sanxia (三峽) we pass first by Daxi (大溪) with its old street and pretty park, and cross the ornate pedestrian bridge. Then along quiet farm roads before we arrive at Beipu (北埔) beside the highway. Before long we leave the main highway and snake up through a quiet forest road, lined with jungle, hiking trails, tea cafés and an information center. After a deserved descent through jungle and beside hills we arrive at the cute and enticing town of Nanzhuang (南庄). This riverside town, with its babbling waters, suspension bridge, and old street leading to an atmospheric hilltop temple, is popular with local tourists. A nearby free campground and sweet guesthouses ensure we have a restful night by the waterside.

On day two, after leaving Nanzhuang, we carry on south, heading first up and over the Xianshan (仙山) hill road. This is our first real climb on the route. It boasts amazing views from its peak, passing a large temple complex and market along the atmospheric pass. After our descent through some smoky dense woods, we land back on the comfortable, fast and wide T3 as it continues to trundle south. Passing through the strawberry town of Dahu (大湖), then a glistening reservoir, we have a lovely, bright descent into Taichung's (台中) northern valley region. We end the day by the banks of another river at end of the lovely, shaded Dong Feng Bikeway! This bike path stretches along some lovely quiet old railway line, avoiding the now busy and hectic highway.

Day three starts on the bikeway before turning south, briefly, onto the Central Cross-Island Highway; we are in search of the T21. This pivotal stretch of road travels south through Nantou (南投), taking us all the way to Sun Moon Lake (日月潭) and, if you join the main route, up and across to Tatajia (塔塔加) Pass. We will certainly be riding this road a lot during the course of the day and beyond. The stiff first 8km is as beautiful as it is challenging for a late morning ride.

But it's all rewards here on our western route. After the climb comes a quite stunning, long descent into the belly of a rolling mountain range. After which, we take a side route around to Puli (埔里), avoiding more climbs. This city is the hub of the region and sits at the base of the large lake's plateau. From here we rejoin the T21 and push for one last uphill, along a wide highway. It is such a rewarding end to stand at the shores of the popular and refreshing mountain lake having just ridden up to it.

Day four starts beside the lake. Perhaps, take a morning, or an extra day to unwind and ride the shoreline paths that snake around the water's edge. There are three southern routes out, whichever one you take we eventually link up with our main route here as the two routes cross paths on Sun Moon Lake.

There's a choice to make here. You can join with the main route as it starts to follow the T21 up to Tatajia Pass, with views of Taiwan's tallest mountain.

Then visit Alishan forest and savor the high tea plantations as you enjoy the longest descent on the trip, down to Dapu, Chiayi (嘉義).

Staying on our alternative route, we head down and out of the hills in search of the T3 once more. After leaving Sun Moon Lake we head to Shuili (水里) before taking a wonderful downhill trip across the 131 all the way to Linnei (林內), where we hit mainline train stations for the first time. Finally, highway T3 heads largely downhill and flat around Chiayi, where we can find a night's rest in Douliu (斗六) or the village of Meishan (梅山).

Day five, the last day before reaching Dapu, is a simple affair with no turning off the highway. The T3 snakes its way down through Chiayi. It becomes a simple, pretty and quiet provincial road once more, working around forest farms of pine, bamboo and betel nut. The first half of the day is relaxing and without too much strain. But before long the road butts up against the hills and a hot, long climb is required.

The ride up onto the ridge overlooking the country's largest water hole is a strenuous one, it is possibly the longest on this side trip and it does take time. Once completed, however, the views are great and the descent is a breeze. After we come downhill you can explore the Dapu area, with roadside waterfalls, perfect for a dip. The warm, quiet village is a great place to wander around, relax for the night under the stars and revel in your trip as we head further into the unknown. From here we rejoin the main route at the start of day eight as our southwest trail gets underway.

DAY 1
Dapu to Nanzhuang

<u>0.00</u> Start at the Y junction on Dapu (大埔) road! Follow the T3 highway as it bends south. The road dips, rolls and climbs, toward our first historical town of Daxi (大溪). For now, we are riding along Taiwan's Cycle Route 1 (CR1), but we will be leaving it soon.

For directions to the start in Sanxia (三峽) see pxxxiv, following the first day of our main tour to the Dapu junction on p9.

<u>10.8</u> Lean right at the lights, keep on the highway as it rolls downhill at the large intersection. We will leave this hectic highway soon.

Daxi Old Street and park
At the large junction, a white multi-arched gate looms over the road. This is the entrance to Daxi. With its historical Old Street, as well as the cliff-edge park, it is a great place to stop and taste some of Taiwan's traditional foods and culture. The old building facades that line the street give a sense of an aged country, often lost in much of the concrete you would have faced traveling through Taoyuan (桃園).

To find the old road head straight across this large junction, turning off the highway. Cross in front of the looming white gate hanging over the town entrance before heading down the small lane that is directly opposite, this is Daxi Old Street. Head down the old narrow road past stalls and stores, as well as local tourists.

At the very end of the road, you come upon an old temple, turn left at the junction and you immediately hit the town's cute park. This charming green space hangs on the edge of a cliff overlooking the bridge, and river, below. Sadly, there is no easy route for you and your bike down to the bridge from here. The staircase is steep and slippery and the only elevator has a seemingly strict no-bicycle policy.

<u>11.3</u> Turn left at the traffic lights, before the large bridge. At the bottom of the hill turn off the T3 and down a lane that runs along the base of the cliff. You are heading for the beautiful white suspension bridge. Weave a route through the green leafy area.

<u>11.7</u> Cross Daxi Bridge. Otherworldly in the daytime, dazzling at night, cross this unique, splendid structure, very unlike most bridges found in Taiwan.

12.1 Turn left off the bridge, then almost immediately turn right onto the bike path. Avoiding the main road at the end of the bridge, head almost back on yourself under the bridge. Just after the parking lot, turn right heading south along the bike trail; the river is now on your left-hand side.

13.6 Stay on the bike trail. It will head underneath the overpass of a large highway. The bike path turns into a farming road, keep heading south. At any small intersection follow old bicycle signs.

14.9 Cross a stream over a small old bridge, you can take in the surrounding farming area from up on the now slightly elevated lane.

16.2 Turn right after the small old bridge as the farm road twists and turns, beautifully through fields. There are no signposts here, you are now directly facing the hill in front.

16.9 The road climbs along three switchbacks, taking you onto the side of the hill, before turning south again as it flattens out. Ride along the now flat hill road back into farms and a bamboo-lined road.

19.3 Turn left toward the temple front as the road hits a T junction in front of a brick wall.

19.4 Turn right into Sankeng (三坑). Head down the lane that runs directly away from the temple. This cobble lane has some great steamed buns (包子), worth stopping for.

19.5 Turn right (forward) merging with the main road at the end of the lane.

19.8 Turn left onto the T3甲 highway, southbound, at the end of the Sankeng road, after passing under the green archways.

   The highway is now wide and flowing through the countryside there is plenty of space with an occasional scooter/bicycle lane.

Hillside staircase adventure
Opposite this junction you can notice a staircase that heads up into the lush green hill. If you have the strength, you can carry your bike up through a pretty hillside park that leads you up to a road that can connect to the T3. It takes out some dull highway, but be warned, both the path and the connecting roads are steep.

21.6 Lean right at the junction, stay on the T3甲.

26.3 Turn left onto the T3 here at the main junction, heading directly south. This highway also has plenty of space. Ride the T3 for some time, as it dips, climbs, and flows south though Hsinchu County (新竹).

53.3 Traffic lights at the edge of Beipu (北埔).
   Another sweet historic town along the northern hills. Turn left at the junction, using the box under the lights. The temple and surrounding old streets here are great places for a stroll to find some of old Taiwan still in action. You can also find Taiwanese treats, grab a lunch or perhaps a bubble tea and peruse the market that is often in full flow.

57.7 Stay on the highway as you pass through this intersection junction with a gas station. Go slow, our turning is coming up soon.

58.5 Turn left up a small side exit, leaving the highway. Before the overpass at Emei (峨眉) see the large mural of birds beside the highway underpass.

58.6 Turn left passing under a teapot archway onto the 竹41. Now heading away from the highway for the remainder of the day we follow the quiet back roads and head into Miaoli's (苗栗) rural region.

Shortly after leaving the village the road starts to softly climb, becoming a lush jungle route with no shoulder, or cars, with a quiet natural atmosphere.

63.0 Rounding a corner underneath the tea house. Take a break here, either leaving your bike at the foot of the steps and walking up or riding around the corner to the parking lot entrance higher up.

The tea house with good drinks and food along with the large information center and beautiful pond gardens surround an old indigenous school building lovingly renovated and restored. Well worth a break just on the edge of the jungle before the hot steamy climb continues.

63.5 A small and very lovely café with astounding views from its back garden.

66.4 The top of the short climb as the road rounds the pass and crosses into a different valley.

68.1 Turn left at the small junction.

68.6 Turn left under the gate onto road 124. Heading south, pass through a village before a short tunnel.

71.0 At the junction beside the long bridge, carry on forward, staying on the 124.

71.5 Turn left, heading for Nanzhuang (南庄). At the lights use the box leaving the 124.

73.0 The turning on your left heads uphill to the town's old post office, temple and end of the long network of food alleys.

73.5 Turn left after following the one-way road system through the town turning at the T junction next to the fire station.

73.7 Nanzhuang information center. You can leave your bicycle here and explore the rest of the village, including the food streets and pedestrian suspension bridge that hangs over the river.

Soak in the atmosphere as throngs of people visit this sweet region, famous for its indigenous communities and crisp, clean air.

73.8 Lean right, crossing the bridge just after the information center. We now cross the river to the town's southern end.

74.1 Finish at the edge of the town! The T junction at the end of the bridge marks the end of our first day, here in the heart of Nanzhuang. This charming village sits along a river network in the foothills with looming mountains overhead. A restful morning here by the river or in a café feels like the right way to spend your time at the start of an adventure.

There are several options for accommodation. Turn right after the bridge and find the lane at the end of the suspension bridge for some small hostels and guesthouses, such as the charmingly relaxed Mountain Lodge Hostel.

Alternatively, you can turn left and travel up the 苗21 for 5km to the equally charming but much quieter remote village of Donghe (東河), where there is a free local campground by the river. For paid campgrounds, you can carry farther along on the 124 as there are several just outside of Nanzhuang.

If you feel you have the legs the large Taoist temple at Xianshan (仙山) has great views and lovely cheap rooms to rent for the night. But while this climb is not too taxing, after a long day of riding it might feel a step too far for most, see p46.

Nanzhuang to Dongshi

0.00 Start at the edge of Nanzhuang! At the junction, at the end of the bridge, go forward, staying on the 124, south. There are convenience stores at this junction, it is the last store before the climb's end in Xianshan (仙山). The first few km's are peaceful and quiet along this lovely, tree-lined road.

8.60 As you cross a stream the road leaves the river and starts to climb the hill toward Xianshan.

11.2 Alternative route on your left, this road leads to other remote indigenous villages and it is a beautiful ride, but with some steep climbs and tough turns; only take this route if you really want to explore the region further.

11.4 The road climbs stiffer here as it nears the pass.

15.0 Top of the climb here at the large temple complex and market. You can find some yummy food stalls including a locally made almond milk coffee here.

　　The temple has some comfortable cheap rooms for the night, complete with Wi-Fi and TV. The reception desk will help you get settled in, don't expect too much but these rooms are comfortable and clean. A short hiking trail to the peak of Xianshan can be found here too; on a clear day it has some amazing views.

15.1 The descent starts underneath the market, follow the 124 as it skirts in front of the complex and starts to descend toward the western flats again. Take it easy on the switchbacks as you first head into, then out of, a very eerie, foggy forest.

21.0 The bottom of the descent, enter the village of Shitan (獅潭).

21.1 Turn left at the first junction with lights, staying in the village, don't enter the highway just yet.

21.4 Large convenience store at the edge of town. This store has a lot of bicycle memorabilia from days gone by of the Tour De Taiwan passing through the town.

21.5 Merge onto the T3, heading south. We rejoin the highway here, heading toward Dahu (大湖).

33.3 Head straight. Large junction with the village of Wenshui (汶水) and access for freeways.

The left-hand turning winds up to the rear entrance of Shei-Pa National Park (雪霸國家公園). There are some wonderful hikes and new cycling trails accessible from this rear entrance to the park but all need to be reserved in advance, and the routes start high up in the mountain range.

36.4 Strawberry town of Dahu. Here you will find pick-your-own strawberry farms, a large strawberry museum, giant strawberry statues, strawberry ice cream and drinks available all year round. Stay on the main highway as all the attractions are by the roadside.

The road climbs and dips along small hills for the next few km's as it widens with lanes.

48.3 Start of the short climb to the top of the hill, surrounding the large reservoir.

51.0 Top of the climb beside this lovely large pagoda rest stop, overlooking the huge body of water and surrounding hills.

51.9 Turn left, at the T junction, staying on highway T3. The road widens here as the full view of the valley below opens up, the descent is fast and comfortable, the views are great!

52.5 Consider stopping just as the descent starts at the little coffee stand on the side of the road. With bicycle parking!! This cute truck has made some wonderful viewing platforms with sofas and comfy chairs on the hillside, offering uninterrupted views of the wide valley floor and rivers below.

56.0 At the bottom of the descent cross the river along the long, flat bridge.

60.5 Turn left onto 中44 to Shigang (石岡). After a short descent at the traffic lights beside the convenience store leave the T3 highway.

62.1 Lean left, heading onto a long flat bridge, crossing the river. The road is wide here with lots of lanes, great views on a clear day of the high peaks off in the distance.

62.9 Turn right heading straight down a small lane. Shortly after the bridge the road bends left, we turn onto the residential street straight ahead. No signs.

63.1 Shigang old train station. Welcome to the Dong Feng Bikeway! This delightful path stretches all the way from the edges of Taichung city at Houfeng (后豐) across the Shigang region to the town of Dongshi at the edges of the central mountain range. This flat, well-maintained and well-used bike trail uses an old rail line; trees line the path and it keeps riders well away from roads and junctions.

If you turn right and head west it will take you to Taichung, Taiwan's second largest city. Travel that way if you intend on staying in that city or if you want to keep on highway T3 and avoid any hill climbs. But be warned the route around the metropolis is long, dull, hot, and full of traffic.

63.2 Turn left onto the bikeway, heading east toward Dongshi (東勢).

70.6 Finish in Dongshi! End of the bicycle path at Dongshi. All along the bikeway there are places for camping, as well as some local guesthouses. There are several paid campgrounds and hotels in the area.

DAY 3
Dongshi to Sun Moon Lake

0.00 Start at the Dongshi Hakka cultural station! Head west toward the T8.

0.80 Turn left onto T8, heading south on the highway. It is a wide road as it exits Dongshi.

    This is the starting point of the famous Central Cross-Island Highway that heads up into the central mountain range before traveling back down to Taroko Gorge (太魯閣) on the east coast. Sadly, the road is not open across the island. The western half of the T8 is blocked at the village of Guguan (谷關). Due to landslides and poor road quality there are no plans to reopen this road in the near future. See p12 for more information on the spectacular eastern portion of the road.

6.50 As the road narrows to a single lane it starts to head uphill. Find a large convenience store here, it is the last for some time.

13.5 Turn right, onto highway T21. We turn off T8 here as it heads into a tunnel and off into the hills. Crossing the river at the start of the T21 our ride up this first mountain is special as it takes us into the region of Nantou (南投), bringing us closer to the famous Sun Moon Lake (日月潭).

13.7 Small village here with local shops. The road starts to climb up a sharp but beautiful incline, take it slow and soak in those views.

20.9 Top of the climb. As you round the corner of the pass, there is a large bicycle and coffee mural as we drift into Nantou. The mountains stretch into the distance and all we can see are clouded peaks, forest, farms, jungle trees and green, green, green.

21.0 The descent starts here, your reward for that climb, nearly 14km of constant, refreshing, downhill forest riding. Enjoy.

35.0 Turn right at the Y junction, toward Guoxing (國姓). There is a large convenience store as we leave the T21 here.

    You can follow the main highway all the way to Puli (埔里), but it climbs a couple more times and takes you to the far side of the large sprawling town.

38.5 Pass through Guoxing as the road stays flat and fast.

40.6 Cross the river along the green bridge.

40.8 At the crossroads turn left around the last piece of the village.

41.3 Turn left onto the T14 at the traffic lights turn left and start heading

south along the main highway. This quiet route takes us up toward Puli passing through tunnels, underneath a raised freeway surrounded all the while by green rolling hills.

56.0 Turn right at the Puli junction onto the T21, for Sun Moon Lake. If you need a break you can turn left across the river into the town of Puli. This large town is an interesting spot and convenient if you need a place away from the lake to stay for the night. But with bicycle stores and restaurants at the lake, there is little need to stay here.

59.2 Convenience store at a junction. Keep on the T21 as it climbs more. The highway is wide with multiple lanes but the traffic is always heavy on weekends and during national holidays.

64.5 Turning on the right for the great 131. This road heads downhill and skips the great lake. See p75 for more information.

65.1 Lean right, staying on the T21 as you get ever closer to the mountain lake. A left turn here takes you to the village of Yuchi (魚池).

69.2. Finish at Sun Moon Lake! The T21 hits a junction as it heads in two directions, looping around the beautiful and famous Sun Moon Lake, Taiwan's largest natural lake.

Turn right and head counterclockwise to reach the town of Shuishe (水社), the largest development on the lake with hotels, hostels, restaurants, shops and bike stores. There is a lovely boulevard on the water. The loop bicycle path largely starts here; be warned, this path does not travel completely around the entire lake.

Turn left and clockwise around the lake for the more secluded, quiet and natural side of the eastern shore. After passing the impressive Wenwu Temple (文武廟), you will find little else than the trees and the monkeys that reside in them. On the southern end of the lake you have the smaller town of Ita Thao, which also has some hostels, restaurants and stores but is a much quieter place for the evening. Its jetty is a beautiful spot at night to sit out and people-watch, along with stargazing.

If you want a paid campground, the southern shoreline near to the Ropeway Station gondola lift is your best shot. To reach here quicker, travel clockwise around the eastern shore. See p73 for a map of the lake.

DAY 4

Sun Moon Lake to Meishan

0.00 Start at Sun Moon Lake's northern entrance on the T21! Head counter-clockwise around the lake with the water on your left.

    For the alternative, remote and frankly better downhill ride, follow our main route out from Sun Moon Lake, down the 131 to Shuili (水里), p75.

1.73 Following either the road or the bike path you arrive at Shuishe (水社). Here you will find a large bicycle store and repair shop, plus a waterside promenade with restaurants, ice cream stands and hotels.

    For the next few km you can ride either the bike trail or the road; they are side by side around the water's edge.

4.90 Stay on highway T21. Once you arrive at the large information center, the highway leaves the lake and heads up into a tunnel. You need to leave the bike path here and follow our route along the T21 south.

5.30 Head uphill through the short, well-lit tunnel.

5.75 Small junction with crescent moon sculpture, turn left here for an old road tunnel that leads back to the lake's loop road. From here we leave the lake and head south out.

8.00 Lean right at the junction keeping on T21 heading for Shuili.

8.50 At the end of the village the road starts a short climb.

10.0 Top of the climb, our real descent starts here.

15.7 Turn right onto T16 at the end of the descent at the T junction.

    To stay on the T21 turn left. The road heads toward the climb to Tata-jia and an alternative route option. See the box on the following page.

18.9 Turn left onto a bridge crossing the river on the 131. After the T16 heads downhill it curves into the outskirts of Shuili. This sweet little town doesn't look its best from this angle, but at the crossroads there are coffee shops, large convenience stores and restaurants.

    Venture into the town by heading straight. We cross the river on the long, flat bridge and onto the old 131. Here the ride is largely flat and pretty as it heads into the rural farming area.

20.3 End of the bridge, we are now on the southern banks of the river, stay on the quiet lane.

23.0 Lean left at the four-way junction and stay on the same road. There are no signposts, just keep left.

Ride through Taiwan's Yushan National Park versus a gentler ride to Dapu
Here you have a choice to make; you can follow the remainder of our Dapu to Dapu alternative route or you can add in the climb and ride our original route up through Yushan National Park to Tatajia, Alishan National Forest and the southwest beyond.

This route is wonderful in good weather, a truly incredible area to explore. With wide, stunning ranges with views of the highest mountains in the distance. If you think you have one long climb in you, now is the chance to give it a go. Turn left here at the junction and follow the T21 to Tatajia. It is a two day ride from here to the pass and a third day to Dapu and beyond.

Stay on the Dapu to Dapu alternative route
Turn right onto T16 toward Shuili. This route avoids the high mountains, instead it flows along to the T3 where, from here, you also have three days of riding to Dapu in Chiayi.

25.5 Lean left. At the outskirts of a small village the road bends both left and right, you can head right through the village but it is easier to follow the main road left for a few hundred meters.

26.1 Turn right onto the 139 heading north on the four-lane, quiet highway.

27.1 Turn left off the 139. It is important that you don't ride all the way onto the large bridge crossing the river. Instead you want to turn off the high-way here.

At this junction take the diagonal slip road, not the small bridge. If you miss this slip road just turn left at the next small lane, eventually you will hit the same road.

27.7 Turn left onto the unnamed dam road. Now with the main river on your right you should be traveling at first south and then west as the road climbs up level with the water. The large dam should be up ahead and the bridge crossing the river behind you.

29.5 Views of the dam on your right just before you enter the long, well-lit tunnel.

30.2 Cross along the red arched bridge.

30.5 The road slopes down and merges with another river road on the other side of the dam, careful for merging traffic here. We want to take the first left to join the highway we just passed over.

31.0 Turn left down a small farm lane.

31.3 Turn right onto highway T3丙, heading west in search of the T3.

36.0 Merge left, onto the T3. The side highway finishes here as we go south along the T3 heading for Linnei (林內). Turn right here for Ershui village.

42.5 Head straight along the T3 as it passes through Zhushan (竹山).

44.8 Left-hand turn for highway 149 that heads up into the beautiful Meishan

(梅山) mountain region.

46.6 Cross the wide river along the flat, and at times windy, bridge.

48.4 Watch out for roadside monkeys here.

49.0 Turn left off the highway, through the village of Linnei. You can stay on the T3 and skip around the town, but it is simpler and more relaxing to pass through it, plus you might need a break at this point.

   Here there is a good train station, a helpful police station with bike tools and plenty of stores and local restaurants.

53.4 Merge left rejoinging the T3 at the end of the town's main road, heading south toward Douliu (斗六).

60.8 Turn left at the large junction, staying on the T3. At the outskirts of Douliu the T3 becomes a ring road for the large town. Head straight here if you want the train station.

63.3 Turn left, sticking with the T3 as it splits off from the multilane ring road. Follow signs for Gukeng (古坑). Turn right if you want central Douliu.

65.5 Keep on the T3 as we head south toward Gukeng and Meishan. Follow signs as the highway bends and turns. The road stays largely flat for some km until we reach the edges of Meishan.

67.1 Head under the large freeway, heading south on the T3.

69.6 Keep on the T3, south for Meishan.

75.2 Pass under freeway 3, staying on the T3.

76.8 Turn left, staying on the T3, heading into Meishan at the light junction.

78.7 Finish, in central Meishan village! This small set of streets sits at the base of the famous 36 Bends mountain road to Taiping (太平) and the gateway into the Meishan and Alishan ranges. Here are some of the best, hidden mountain regions in the country. Full of tea plantations, mountain vistas, wet tropical jungle and cool, clear air. It is well worth exploring if you have the time, see p95 for more information.

   Accommodation is not in abundance off the mountains. Consider continuing down to Chiayi (嘉義) or earlier up in Douliu. There are paid campgrounds in the area and you could combine days four and five together to get all the way to Dapu, but this becomes a grueling day with the extra-long climb at the end.

DAY 5

Meishan to Dapu

0.00 Start at crossroads in Meishan village following the T3! We simply follow the highway south as it works its way around the outskirts of Chiayi city.

11.9 If you want to head into Chiayi, turn right here, shortly after the bridge following signs. The city with its important train station is just 10km from here.

24.3 At this junction carry on the T3, from here we start our climb up and over to the reservoir.

27.2 Stay left at the Y junction as the now small, quiet highway enters a mini pine forest. Here the real climbing begins, it's a tiring uphill climb of 16km to the top.

Guanzhiling Hot Springs and Dongshan Coffee Road to Tainan
The road to the right is the 172, a beautiful climb and then descent to lower Guanzhiling (關子嶺), a hill-hugging hot spring town. This junction also marks the start of Tainan's Dongshan Coffee Road, a beautifully sweeping road that heads south along coffee-lined hillsides.

This is a wonderfully remote and quiet route to take if heading for Tainan or if you want to have a day of hot spring soaks. Just be warned there are three climbs, including one through the town. Needless to say, from the start of the 172 to upper Guanzhiling is a tough challenge in the heat.

43.6 Top of the climb. Finally, you have reached the top of the long 16km climb, from here it's a rough and steep downhill ride to the reservoir's edge with panoramic views of the wonderful landscape.

57.6 Bottom of the descent as you enter the reservoir edges and jungle-strewn loveliness.

63.4 Cross the bridge, staying on the T3. Here we finally rejoin our main route as we head along the last 5km to the village of Dapu (大埔).

Consider turning up the 嘉129 here and riding the 1km to the delightful Qingfen waterfall (情人瀑布) for a cooling dip.

67.9 Turn right onto Dapu Road. Here at the edge of Dapu (大埔) just before the gas station at the sign for Dapu Visitor Center.

68.3 Turn left onto Datong 1st Road (大同一路) just before the concrete arch.

68.8 Turn right down the park road at the town's main crossroads, in front of the convenience store. Head for the water's edge and the free campground. Most of the town's stores and restaurants are concentrated around this junction.

69.3 Finish, central Dapu and the entrance to Lovers Park! We have done it, our five-day alternative ride through Taiwan's western hills has ended in Dapu beside the reservoir waters. There are lots of places to view the reservoir and wander around a peaceful evening, unwind and bask in a trip well undertaken. From here we rejoin the main route as we head south into Taiwan's flat west and the southern shores of the Taiwan Strait. Turn to p110 for Day 8 and our route out of Dapu, through mango country.

Dapu free campground and accommodation
This is a free camping area so please respect it and keep any area clean. The locals are sweet and very friendly, if a little curious. If the campground is closed for any reason, camping in the area should still be OK; there are other viewing platforms and flat areas for a place to pitch for the night. During national holidays, it can get manic here, but it is a huge area, there will always be space for a cyclist; it is very quiet midweek, you can often have the entire place to yourself.

If you are not camping, Dapu has one sweet guesthouse on the highway opposite the gas station, and the holiday park situated just before the entrance to Lovers Park has a wide range of lodging options.

Nantou

The heart
in the heart of Asia.

Giant lakes, tea plantations
   beside soaring peaks, hidden Japanese villages,
snake kilns, waterfall-draped tunnels,
   hot springs in pine forests, and winding roads
through a never-ending choice of side trips.
This and a whole lot more in Taiwan's
                              remotest region.

Nantou

D escending Taiwan's highest mountains to the region of Nantou is a joyous exploration of quiet, hidden valleys. Engineering feats and the perseverance of nature help to find ways through the maze of rivers, hills and rural farms that run in between the rolling mountains.

The island's lush interior is in full view as we head to Sun Moon Lake via remote, quiet and laid-back roads. Taiwan's largest lake, and our first taste of Taiwan tourism, is a stunning hue of greens and blues, surrounded by mountains of shimmering jungle. Lit up in the day by bright sunshine and glistening at night under the gaze of a full moon, you might just get lost in a trance to the hypnotic waters here.

As our tour of Nantou continues so do the roads through magnetic nature and picturesque backdrops that pull us along breathless rides. We pass through teapot villages, alongside some off-track towns and into valleys below. There are so many adventures to be had here, it's hard to imagine simply riding through and not stopping off at one or two.

We end up in a valley underneath Taiwan's highest mountain, Yushan. The hot spring town of Dongpu and the indigenous village of Wanxiang offer us splendid evenings to relax, in the smoky haze of rural life. Perhaps to take a soak in the warm sulfur waters or a stroll to view the highest peak sitting beneath a nightshade sky of stars.

The last day of our Nantou trip asks for one last mountain climb up into the country's must-see national park of Yushan. The home of East Asia's highest peak, also known as Jade Mountain. This climb is long, but with stunning views of the high mountaintops and a more comfortable climb than those we have tackled so far it is a must-have adventure. The prize at the end: the best night's sleep you can have as we camp among fresh pine on the comfortable mountainside pass of Tatajia. The views from up here are surpassed only by the joy as we dream of descending once more.

Renai to Sun Moon Lake

Our journey from the central mountains of Taiwan to Sun Moon Lake in the heart of Nantou (南投) makes use of one of the least known routes in the country, helping to maintain the remote beginning to our adventure. The destination, a lakeside jewel that is our first real populated location since leaving Taipei.

Happily, unlike the metropolises of the far north and the hectic, traffic-clogged west, this popular spot is a surprisingly quaint, pleasant location despite the throngs of people. Reaching into the island's remote and quiet veins to arrive at its most touristy center brings you, once again, an altogether different Taiwan experience.

Leaving the high mountain town of Qingjing (清境) behind, we head down toward a hidden valley region deep inside Nantou. We are not out of the hills yet and this day does require some small climbs, but it is a short ride and its end point is a must visit for any traveler to Taiwan.

Of course, in a country so small, the true feeling of remoteness is elusive. But Nantou, placed centrally on the island, is segregated by its mountain ranges. Broken up into hidden pockets of hillside slopes, valleys, farms and rivers. They are just perfect for exploration and getting away from the monotony of highway life.

After the last section of the Wuling descent down to Renai (仁愛), we leave the T14 and travel around a wondrous emerald reservoir before dropping into a quiet and otherworldly region. This adrift area can be reached from the south only by an old series of tunnels, and from the north a single narrow pass. It's a very peaceful and beautiful part of the country. The communities that live here have eked out a rural life for generations.

Once we reach the edge of the valley floor we climb out, first passing along water-dripping tunnels, then up along waterfall cliffs and finally up and through a mountain and out the other side before we cascade down into the outskirts of Puli (埔里), the largest town in the region.

One of our favorite roads in all Taiwan, the county road 131, sees us safely avoiding any major highways and traffic. This beautiful backdoor road is a treat for the senses. Traveling up the mini gorge, past the rice paddies and farms, is an attack on the senses as the lake draws us closer. Avoiding the main car-heavy routes to the lake we head up a winding lane past giant ferns and a creaking bamboo forest, eventually arriving through the back door at Taiwan's largest natural body of water, the famed Sun Moon Lake (日月潭).

Perhaps Taiwan's most developed natural landmark, this lake sits in the heart of Nantou County and is a must visit. There are campsites, rest stops, tourist villages, ferries, a gondola taking you across the hills to cultural parks. The cute bike paths that loop and dip along the water's edge are more for day-trippers, but a short hop along it adds to the fun.

The temples that dot the hills and local stalls selling dried fruits and other treats are staples of modern Taiwan life that up until now our trip has rarely seen. All of this, surrounded by hills and peaks covered in tropical forest that casts green shadows on the road, pathways and waters, adding a dramatic looming effect.

The shoreline bikeway was supposed to offer unbroken path all around the lakes' circumference; in actuality, this isn't the case. On the eastern shore, it abruptly ends and throws you onto the main loop road and to the southwest; many day riders have gotten lost in the odd twist and turnings of the lake road. In any case, the main road running around the eastern shore, T21甲, is a comfortable and relaxing ride. Even cars seem to adopt a more leisurely pace along these parts.

Despite its fame for being oversubscribed and somewhat developed, the stunning waters still have plenty of natural, quiet charm, producing a relaxing atmosphere rarely seen on the island's western half. The area really comes into its own during a sunrise and sunset; don't miss a sunset seen from the eastern shores or a sunrise walk along one of the waterside promenades.

Sadly, the glistening lake, inviting as it seems, does not have any beaches. It is forbidden to swim in the blue waters, apart from during a once-a-year swimming event. So, take a walk along a hidden section of path, eat yummy treats or an ice cream at one of the jetties overlooking the waters. Enjoy a camping experience in the trees, cooking dinner and soaking in the evening's atmosphere as the sun sets over the hills and the moon hangs, reflected in the ripples below.

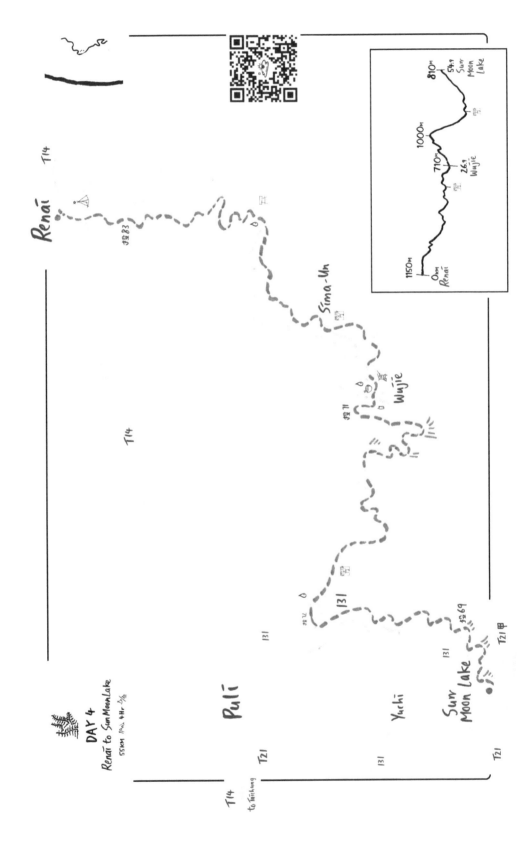

DAY 4
Renai to Sun Moon Lake
55km 17km 4Hr ⅗

Renai

T14

T14

霧83

Sima-Un

Wujie

投71

T14

Puli

131

T21

T14
to Taichung

131

Yuchi

131

霧69

Sun
Moon Lake

T21

T21甲

Elevation profile:
1150m
0m Renai
710m
26.9 Wujie
1000m
810m 54.9 Sun Moon Lake

DAY 4

55KM /⋀\ 4Hr △/冊

0.00 Start in central Renai! There is a police station, convenience store and other useful shops. By the time you leave here make sure you have supplies, as these are our last chances to fill up for the next 30km as we head into the secluded valley.

0.60 Turn left onto the 投83 as the T14 bends sharply right. Leave the highway and turn left at the mini junction with the entrance to route 投83, our road through the hidden valley. Be careful of traffic on the blind bend.

To Puli and main highways to Sun Moon Lake
The T14 races south from here, keep on that road if you are heading for Puli (埔里) or the city of Taichung (台中). This is also a more direct route to Sun Moon Lake if you are in a rush. It is a further 25km downhill to the center of Puli and a further 15km up the mountain to the lake, linking up with the T21 in Puli.

0.65 The start of the 投83 is marked by a large wooden placard proclaiming the Aowanda National Forest Recreation Area (奧萬大國家森林遊樂區).
      The 投83 starts warmly as it snakes, largely downhill, around the reservoir that during high water levels shines a deep emerald green. It's a beautiful winding road with great tree shade and views of crisp waters while monkeys play in the canopies above, very relaxing.

6.50 Side road that runs down to a jetty by the water's edge.

7.28 At the end of the reservoir the road passes around a rocky edge and drops into the valley beyond. A pretty rest stop has an information board and views back along the water.

9.02 At the bottom of a short downhill in a narrow valley the road passes beside a small village that sits in front of the hydro dam. This indigenous village has a small store, usually closed, the word *sleepy* comes to mind.

9.14 A short, sharp climb to reach the pass out of this valley, followed by a fun if short-lived descent to the river.

10.8 Turning on the left to the Aowanda National Forest. This mountain road winds up to a dead end at this spectacular setting, as a high suspension bridge sways over the riverbed below. Not for the faint of heart but this plateau is a great camping spot for the night.

10.9 Cross the river along the flat bridge. This next section of road climbs and dips beside the river, along the valley floor and through farming villages. The air is fresh and quietness prevails. During the heat of summer these climbs get tiring; luckily, they are not long climbs, but it's certainly not a flat ride.

11.8 Here the road splits, and no map will help you. For some reason, the river road has been omitted from them. But keep right and follow the river road as it crosses a bridge and runs in front of the small farming town around a few bends. The left-hand turn climbs sharply up into a quiet indigenous village.

13.9 The two roads meet back up. Either road from the previous junction will bring you to this point. Keep south passing a bridge on your right, don't cross.

Another small village. The road climbs shortly after you pass through, leaving the river.

19.6 Sima-un, of the Wan Feng (萬豐) tribe. This village has a small store for drinks and snacks if needed. The road climbs again after passing the store.

23.3 The last farming village. At the far end another small climb awaits before a short, dusty tunnel.

25.5 The end of the road, as the reservoir butts up against the dam. The path appears to stop right in front of a sheer cliff wall. But as you approach you see it shift to the right, eventually finding the entrance to a long, old, dark, wet tunnel. Travel through and feel as though you are being transported to another world. We are now traveling along the 投71.

As the tunnel ends you come out to the rushing sound of a waterfall. Green ferns and hanging trees line this wet and narrow exit. Momentarily you feel like you are in the heart of a mountain before the road races down and takes you into the Wujie (武界) valley below.

26.9 Passing through Wujie town you quickly reach the main bridge across the wide river. There are some small eateries and shops around here, as well as a lovely suspension bridge. To the south of the main river crossing, on the eastern side of the river there are also some small commercial campgrounds. Take a break before tackling the day's largest climb.

While not an overly sharp incline it does climb for some time. Luckily shrouded in jungle, the route is well shaded from the sun and plenty of

small waterfalls line the route, cooling the air. Once you arrive at the top, you face a long tunnel to pass out of the valley.

27.4 When ready head straight. The road climbs as soon as you cross the bridge. The first sharp corner feels steep but the road mellows a little, a fairly painless event from here on out.

On this climb there are great views of the town, river and valley below. If it's a hot day, you are in luck, mini waterfalls line this next section of road and you can easily cool down by dunking your whole body without leaving the road. Just watch out for falling rocks if just after a heavy rain-fall.

32.9 On a hidden corner you reach the top of the climb and the entrance to the tunnel.

Bringing you out to a long, super fun and fast descending road as you race down toward the outer edges of the Puli region. Look out for those views of the town and the dipping sun in the distance.

36.6 The last of the switchbacks. The road heads dead straight here and rides fast on a well-made surface. Be careful for slow-moving farming vehicles emerging.

40.6 The road bends right. Now we are heading through a farming area with schools and occasional stores.

42.1 Turn left onto the 投72 at the set of traffic lights. Follow signs for the 投72, southbound.

If you head straight here, the 投72 moves north, and arrives eventually in central Puli.

43.2 Turn left onto the 131 at the first crossroads.

43.9 Enter the well-lit tunnel. Out the other side, the road enters a narrow gorge and follows a fast-moving stream.

Carry on south along the 131 as it passes beautiful fields of rice, fruit farms, campsites and rolling hills.

50.1 The 131 hits a small bridge where there is a delightful wooden pagoda as the road splits. Keep to the right and cross the small old bridge. Here is a short 300m climb rising away from the river, ending on a left-hand bend.

50.6 Turn left onto the 投69 immediately around the bend. Follow signs for Sun Moon Lake, leaving the 131. Don't worry, we find it again tomorrow.

52.0 Turn left shortly after passing by a temple. Keep on the 投69. There are no signs for Sun Moon Lake, but you can follow the sign for the Formosan Aboriginal Culture Village (九族文化村).

52.4 Head straight at the crossroads. No signs here at this junction. Go straight, we are almost at our destination.

53.2 All of a sudden, this dead-straight road narrows and bends around farm buildings, follow it, first left then right. Narrowing to a small lane. Look out for the water buffalo sculpture.

53.6 The last km climbs from here to the lake. It's the penalty to pay for such a quiet and beautiful arrival. The giant ferns on the roadside are mesmer-izing.

<u>54.9</u> Finish at Sun Moon Lake's eastern shores! The lane throws you up and onto an odd open parking lot area. From here you can see the lake edge, cross over the lake loop road to the wooden bicycle path and take in your first view of the calm waters and jungle below.

Heading counterclockwise, the northern exit away from the lake on highway T21 is just 2.5km to the north. And the southern exit just a further 10km after. Head clockwise around the lake on the T21甲 lake road for a further 20km to find the southern exit away from the lake on the T21.

From this observation point at the quiet eastern edges of the lake you could be forgiven to think this place is as quiet and as remote as the rest of the day's journey. But don't be fooled, a few km in either direction are the central towns on the lake road, and on weekends throngs of tourists descend on this picturesque area.

Now you have reached the waters of Sun Moon Lake (日月潭). There are plenty of options for sleeping, camping and eating around the lake. The campsites nearer the cable car, in Ita Thao, are actually the best. On the western shores there is a lot of development around the town of Shuishe (水社). You could consider a night of wild camping, keeping to the eastern areas.

Assuming you arrived in the early afternoon, have a look around, gain your bearings. A complete loop of the lake on the T21 (and T21甲) takes two to three hours with rest and stops along the way. There is a more detailed map of the lake on p73. We will start the next day's ride from this point, departing the lake from the northern exit.

Sun Moon Lake to Heshe

After a rest beside the great lake of Taiwan, it's time for a nice hot soak and the chance to see Taiwan's highest peak. Perhaps even hike it too! Today's ride takes us from the heat of Sun Moon Lake down and then back up to the hot spring town of Dongpu (東埔) at the foot of the Yushan range, in the shadow of Jade Mountain.

As we travel through Nantou region we are now in the dead center of the country. There are several exit points from here to the western flats and the metropolis of Taichung (台中), as well as the chance to join our alternative route that makes its way to Dapu (大埔) via Chiayi (嘉義), avoiding the climb to Alishan (阿里山) see p51.

While today is not an entirely flat route it is a relatively simple one. Most of the day can be taken at a relaxed rate. Hidden away from the afternoon sun the temperatures ease around here, making for a comfortable journey.

Nestled underneath mountains at the northern point of the Yushan National Park (玉山國家公園), the valley at the base of Dongpu Mountain is home to several little-known hamlets with their own indigenous cultures, languages and an abundance of farms. There are stunning views of the mountains above from trhe hot springs. Here you can find the gateway to one of Taiwan's longest hiking trails that cuts north to south through the country's largest national park. We take in the atmosphere of this cute little place and soak our bodies in the natural warm waters as clouds cling to the cliff walls overhead. It's a good rest for body and soul before tomorrow's final mountain climb up to Tatajia Pass (塔塔加).

The options for leaving Sun Moon Lake heading south would appear clear cut and obvious. The T21, which entered from Puli (埔里) in the north, travels around the western shore of the lake and runs, heading directly for Dongpu Mountain. The T21 is our main road for the next two days of riding as it heads all the way up past Dongpu and finishes at the top of Tatajia Pass. Due to the size of the lake, where you have spent the night might determine your exit point. We use this main road in our Dapu to Dapu alternative route, p50.

But there is another way out of Sun Moon Lake, avoiding any climbs, a straight descent from the lake that takes on a very fun and adventurous side trail. Counterintuitively we first head north out of the lake, until we find the 131, turning south we travel along this quiet, stunning road. This route doesn't add any great distance to our journey but offers a much richer assault on the senses and avoids some of the climbing required along the main route from the lake.

From Sun Moon Lake to Shuili (水里) the 131 is a quiet backcountry descent that is a pure joy to ride down. The road is lined by jungle, banana groves, village homes, a pretty reservoir and an enjoyable Japanese-era village, perfect for a drop of time travel. When you arrive into Shuili it will feel like no time has passed as you zip down this near-forgotten route. A lush start to the day.

After you have finished exploring the little railway town, we climb up the T16, past the snake kiln, to reconnect with the T21 as it steadily travels south along a wide valley floor and river that flows out of the Nantou ranges.

From here the T21 travels through the center of Nantou, cutting between two giant mountain regions. This part of the country is picturesque, with areas begging to be explored and plenty of side trips to be had. Narrow hill roads branch off in all directions up eye-watering gradients into the canopies above.

The T21 can be a little narrow and busy with traffic during holidays, but like the 131 it is lined by jungle, and has stunning views across the valley as you pass time-trapped homes, with near distant wildlife as your soundtrack for the day.

When the road eventually crosses the wide valley riverbed, you are lifted, with ease, up onto a stilted road that gives panoramic views of the mountain ranges ahead. On clear days, as well as stormy ones, it's dramatic to feel yourself, small as we are in this world, riding below these giants as they tower over you.

Shortly after crossing the river, the T21 really starts to weave up toward the day's end and the base of the mountains ahead. Like most of the route so far, the path is shaded and pretty, remaining comfortable even for tired legs. Just as the road threatens to make you work too hard and before the real climbing begins, you arrive at the village crossroads of Heshe (和社). From here we leave the T21 for another day. As the afternoon gets long it's time to find your bed for the night at one of two delightful villages nestled at the base of the lofty Yushan range.

The delightful indigenous village of Wangxiang (望鄉) just behind Heshe has some lovely homestays for the night as well as views of Taiwan's highest peak, Jade Mountain. Higher up on the other side of the river is the delightful hot spring town of Dongpu. Nestled in shade by sheer mountain cliffs, this charming village is the entrance to the Yushan National Park. Both locations offer atmospheric evenings to relax in before the next day's tackling of the climb through Yushan to the pass at Tatajia (塔塔加).

Sun Moon Lake's Eastern Shores

Counterclockwise along the lake's eastern shores the T21甲 makes up two-thirds of the loop road. These markers are from the starting point at the northern entrance to the lake along highway T21. For markers along the western shore see T21 route on p50.

1 0.00 Northern junction of lake with T21. Start of the T21甲 east.
2 1.50 Grand entrance to the Wenwu (文武) Temple and views of lake.
3 1.80 Public bathrooms and entrance to secluded natural park.
4 2.08 Parking lot and entrance of road 投69, end point Day 4 ride. Access to east section of bike trail.
5 3.50 End of east section of bike trail.
6 3.95 Sloped entrance down to parking lot and secluded water.
7 7.00 Entrance to cable car station.
8 6.60 Slope side road to waterside campground and local restaurants.
9 7.10 Ita Thao village with hotels, shops, restaurants and waterside promenade.
10 7.35 Left turn up mountain road 367 to Dili and highway T16.
11 11.5 Viewing platform, temple entrance and local produce stores.
12 13.9 Switchback corner with parking lot to ferry port and views.
13 17.8 Entrance to western lakeshore bike trail. Take this route if staying on the lake and avoid climbs.
14 17.9 Tunnel marking the end of the T21甲 on the lake.
15 20.8 Southern junction with T21. Turn left to Shuili and Heshe for Tatajia Pass.
Turn right to loop north, up to the lake along highway T21, p75.

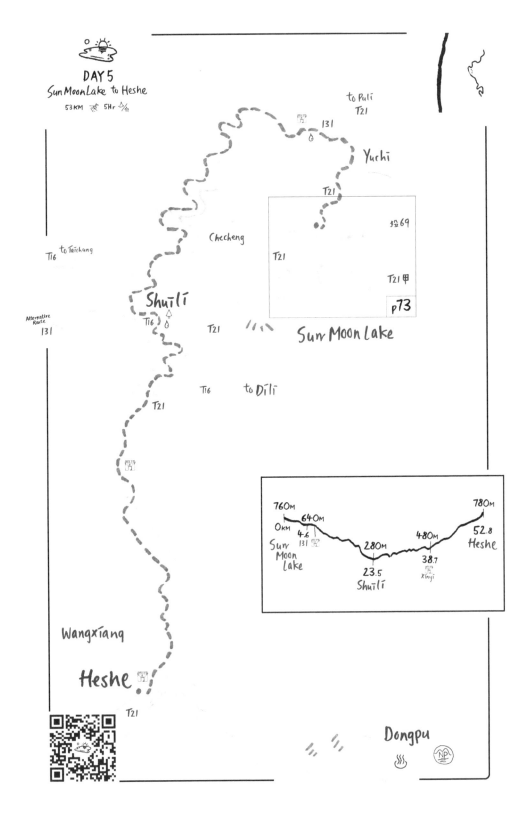

DAY 5
Sun Moon Lake to Heshe
53 KM 5 Hr

to Puli
T21

131

Yuchi

T21

盆69

Checcheng

T21

T21 甲

to Taichung
T16

p73

Alternative
Route
131

T16

Shuili

Sun Moon Lake

T21

T16   to Dili

T21

760M   780M
0KM   640M   52.8
Sun   4.6   480M   Heshe
Moon   131   280M   38.7
Lake   23.5   Xinyi
           Shuili

Wangxiang

Heshe

T21

Dongpu

NPL

DAY 5

53KM 🚴 5Hr ⌂∕俞

0.00 Start at Sun Moon Lake's northern entrance! Turn north along the T21 toward Puli (埔里). Our starting point at the northernmost exit from the lake probably doesn't match where you stayed for the night, don't worry, from any point on the lake road you can find either the northern or southern exit along highway T21. From here we ride briefly north, toward Puli to find road 131 as it heads south, for the best descent out of the lake to the town of Shuili (水里).

   If you want to travel along the T21 south until you leave the lake and rejoin later, just head south, either way around the water, following signs. Eventually you will find yourself on a descent south away from the lake joining our route, south of Shuili, see p77.

0.20 The T21 widens and hurtles down the hill. It's fast but in the early morning the road is usually all yours, enjoy!

4.00 After a short climb the turning on your right for the 131 heads east; do not take this turn.

4.60 Turn left onto the 131 just after a convenience store and gas station at the lights. This is our route to Shuili, follow signs.

5.90 Lean right through the cute village on a stream. Local stores, whitewashed walls and murals abound. Cute, cute, cute! Keep right at the teapot.

   The 131 is lovely as it descends through a pretty and quiet area. The road is lined by tropical vegetation, as well as small farms and homes. Apart from the odd farming van you shouldn't see too many vehicles through here.

17.0 Tunnel at the reservoir.

20.0 The dam at Checheng (車埕).

20.3 Turning for Checheng village and railway.

Checheng village
This small historical village is well worth a stop. The Japanese-era train line that runs from the town of Ershui (二水) through Shuili and up to the terminus at Checheng has been repurposed as a tourist line with sweet old trains, alas no space for bicycles. The town has a beautiful train station, well-preserved old streets, as well as a stunning museum and cute wooden shop fronts. The Japanese carp pond in beautiful surrounds with original buildings is reason enough. Checheng is one of the best-preserved villages in Taiwan we have seen.

23.0 Arrive at the edges of Shuili. The town has a train station and regular buses that run up to the mountains and cities. There are local stores, restaurants and the usual markets.

Notice the slalom course set up in the river. The town hosted the Asian Canoe Slalom Championships in 2013. Taiwan is not known for its water sports but you will find companies that run activities all over the island, including white water rafting, SUP and surfing, not to mention diving and river tracing. Most of these activities are best accessed on the east coast, Kenting (墾丁) and the outer islands.

23.0 Head straight as you enter Shuili, cross over the first and second crossing in the town. The crossroads is the main junction in the village.

23.5 Turn left onto the T16 toward Dili (地利), southbound, following signs. The park along the riverfront is a great little place to take a break. There is a bike trail that runs along the river here but unfortunately doesn't really take you where you want to go; ignore maps that suggest otherwise.

23.9 Crossroads with large convenience store, coffee shop and gas station. Carry on across the junction, staying on T16 as it heads uphill. This is where we cross paths with our alternative hill route to the town of Dapu. If you take this turning here you will follow the 131 again toward Chiayi, skipping the climb up to Alishan. See p51 for directions along that route.

If you are looking for a train station from here then head this way and follow directions to the beautiful little stations at Ershui or Linnei (林內) for bicycle-friendly trains heading north and south. p51.

24.4 The road curves left underneath an elaborate pedestrian bridge. Here the road climbs. Stay on the T16; this is your only route option as it snakes up to join the T21.

27.0 Head straight to join onto the T21 at the traffic light junction atop the hill's brow. Here the T21 joins from Sun Moon Lake. The two highways merge momentarily heading south as one.

27.7 Stay on the T21 at the top of the climb and here we say goodbye to T16, which turns east toward Dili and Dongpu.

After a short descent, the next 10km is a fast slope with few tough sections. The highway has no shoulder here and it can feel claustrophobic, especially in bad weather.

Side trip! Qi Cai Hu
Follow the T16 to Dili if you are taking our off-road, once-in-a-lifetime mountain adventure. See our Nantou side trip section for details on the Qi Cai Hu (七彩湖) ride. P82.

38.7 A large convenience store at the bottom of Xinyi (信義) village. You are in plum country now.

41.5 The start of the network of long, high bridges that take you over this beautiful, wide valley. Breathtaking on both a sunny and stormy afternoon.

45.5 The end of the bridge network is marked by a short descent onto the other side of the river. The road climbs for the next 7km until we reach the town of Heshe (和社).

Now the road weaves between some very cute farms and a moss-covered cliff. The air is chilly as the walls drip with moisture and the mountains cast afternoon shadows.

50.5 Right-hand turning for the beautiful indigenous village of Wangxiang (望鄉).

Notice the deep red sign for the GO Bill homestay, follow these signs all the way up the little hill road. The village is 2km along this fun farm lane. This is the best route up to the village, a great alternative night's stay to Dongpu if you don't fancy the ride up to the hot spring town or if you are arriving late.

52.3 Main turning up to the village of Wangxiang. This is a short ride up to the community on the plateau, but it is steep at points, and when we say steep, we mean it. But the route is short and you are up in the village in no time.

52.8 Finish, at the junction in the center of Heshe! Just as you enter the village of Heshe is the one convenience store in the region. This store will be invaluable for the next day's journey as the ride up to Tatajia is bereft of stores, water or places to buy food. If you intend to cook your own meals over the next few days then stock up in Heshe. While Dongpu does have stores they are all geared toward its tourist trade, but there are fine local eateries and restaurants up there so perhaps give yourself the night off from cooking. Either way, this is the last convenience store until you are halfway down the mountain in Alishan.

From here highway T21 climbs straight away up into the clouds in search of Yushan peaks, high mountain roads, monkeys, forests and the pass of Tatajia.

But don't worry, that's for another day, for now we are in search of a relaxing evening of towering peaks, clear starry skies, aromas drifting on a breeze, soft grass under feet and, perhaps, a nice hot soak. The two nearby villages of Dongpu (東埔) and Wangxiang offer up a perfect night's rest in the chilly shadows of the mountains.

Mountain villages of Dongpu and Wangxiang

Dongpu
Higher up on the other side of the valley, perched on a hillside and nestled underneath the Yushan range, is the hot spring village of Dongpu. The climb up to this pretty place is not too exhausting apart from a couple of tiring switchbacks nearer the top.

With the promise of an atmospheric village, complete with local restaurants and outdoor hot springs as well as tea plantations all under the shadows of some impressive cliff walls to tempt you up the hillside, you will reach it in no time when you think about the warm soak in natural sulfur waters above.

After crossing the arched bridge behind Heshe, it is a 7km ride that zips and winds up the mountainside. There are beautiful views all the way up as the mountains of Yushan sit high in the distance and clouds wrap around them in front.

Just before the town is the start of a mini switchback section. Here there are some small tea farms and expensive hot spring resorts that have camping and guesthouses. There is a large Dongpu (read Tongbu) Entrance sign at the town's information center and a parking lot marking the start of the town's main street.

The impressive suspension bridge here marks the start of the hiking trails up into Yushan National Park (note this is not the start of the hiking trail to the peak of Jade Mountain, that trail starts at Tatajia). You are allowed to spend the night camping here and in such a beautiful surrounding area, who could resist? The town is just a short walk further up the hill. The suspension bridge is well worth the walk, and hot springs abound.

The center of town has some great little restaurants with inexpensive local dishes, and some hot spring resorts as well as local produce on sale for any wide-eyed tourist. There are also hotels here that offer a plusher night's sleep, should you need.

The hot springs at Dong Guan Hotel are not attached to the hotel, but their traditional-style outdoor hot springs sit close by down a lane. This spot is great because as you lean back and soak you can peer up at the high mountains looming overhead. If you are lucky, you might see a bit of snowdrift on the peaks above, helping you to dream of high mountain hikes and the wilderness drifting on distant skies.

Why not take a day off and explore the area? You can even take in the first few km of the trail into the national park from Dongpu without a permit. Expect truly colossal views, fun narrow cliff paths, giant waterfalls and fresh, clear air, perhaps even a drop of snow in winter.

Mountain villages of Dongpu and Wangxiang

Wangxiang
Right behind the highway just before Heshe is the village of Wangxiang. This sweet little indigenous community is perched upon a plateau with views of Yushan Peak off in the distance. Nestled among vegetable farms, the area has one small main street where the community gathers for the evening, and the community center, local eateries and stores are a focal point.

Spread out from this street, hidden between small farms are a few lovely homestays and campgrounds offering an authentically local vibe, in equally lovely surroundings. The pick for me has to be hikers' choice of GO Bill B&B (GO北爾民宿). This family-run little homestay at the back of some farms has a very comfy feel with traditional bedding, a courtyard garden and rooftop tables with astounding views, homemade breakfast included. Note that the two routes up to the village are short but very steep.

The turning 2km before Heshe is a more comfortable and prettier ride, whereas the turning just before the police station at Heshe is as steep as they come but offers quicker access from the convenience store.

A stay in either Dongpu or Wangxiang after a fairly soft, relaxing ride will really set you up for our tour's last, long climb. No matter where you stay make sure you are in Heshe for an early start the following day, typically leaving on the highway before 8am so that you can be at Tatajia Pass by lunchtime.

Qī Cai Hu
multiday gravel adventure

ucked away, high up on a peak in the central mountain range are the lakes of seven colors. This mysterious place has become something of an adventurer's obsession over recent years as old electrical service roads have been opened up to hikers, and now even cyclists can get in on the act.

The trip to Qi Cai Hu (七彩湖) is a spectacular one. A very different adventure to anything cyclists can experience in Taiwan. Crossing rivers, up rocky rubble road with sheer cliff drops. Riding through long grass, sand tracks, pine forests and high mountain plains. Offering jaw-dropping mountain views and completely clear skies. It really is a special part of the island's interior.

The route can only be accessed in the winter and spring months as a river needs to be traversed, with waters needing to be low enough to cross on foot. Once the path is deemed open, usually by early January until the plum rains arrive in late April, enthusiastic hikers and intrepid riders make the challenging journey up the 3000m ascent.

A truly off-the-beaten-track mountain adventure here. The road is brutal on your bike and your body. A mountain bike, gravel bike or perhaps touring bike with wide tires is recommended and you shouldn't take all of your touring weight.

The ride up the trail and back is a minimum three-day affair, with a night prior to the trip needed at the village of Dili (地利) to get permits signed by the local police office.

From Shuili (水里) ride highway T16 south, following signs for Dili, staying on the T16 when it turns east diverging from the T21. Permits for the trail are arranged through the police department. You will need to visit the police station in Dili to to confirm your hike. This cannot be skipped as the permit is

confirmed at the guard house on the route. To apply for the trail search for Mountain Entry Application System 七彩湖. Sadly the police department's main webpage is broken, nv2.npa.gov.tw, but you can navigate to the right page.

From the village, with your permit in hand, carry on east leisurely along the now tiny highway to the road's end. There are private campgrounds in Dili and along the road toward and after the village of Gugushan. Alternatively, you can ask in the village.

Delightfully the road crashes to an end at a washed-away bridge. Thunderous mountains rise straight up all around you, as you take a gravel track down to the riverbed; the feeling of entering an unknown world is palpable.

The river crossing is simple, shallow and comfortable during the low season when the trail is open. But the tough uphill ride starts immediately after. The road levels out after the first scramble up but it is an ominous sign of challenges ahead. This section of the road is at least asphalt all the way to the police checkpoint where, when the gate is open, you need to produce your permit to pass.

The ride up to the lake is a two-day undertaking, with most riders arriving early afternoon on the second day. There are no campgrounds to speak of on the route, and plenty of hikers and riders mistreat the route so please make sure you take all your trash with you when leaving the trail. There are minimal water sources besides the stagnant lake water on top and one dripping stream 30km up the mountainside; you have been warned.

The first 35km of terrain climbs along rough gravel, rock and stone. The yellow chalk and dust along this mountain edge add to the intense ride and there will be points where you consider walking the bike to conserve energy. The views are stupendous and the path is magnificently arduous. At the top of the climb the landscape changes completely as you cross into woodland, giving you relief from the exposure to the sun, welcoming the feeling of your bike doing more work than you.

There is an obvious camping area beside a helipad and an old, abandoned building just after this pass where the mountain momentarily plateaus. These are some 35km up above the end of the first, and main, climb. Most hikers and riders seem to camp here for the night. Personally we liked to camp in the forest a little further along.

The second day's ride twists and turns with the contours of the mountainside, crossing streams and passing giant felled trees. After a couple of sections of descent there is another roadside abandoned cabin, you can rest here for the night should you need.

The third section opens up to a wonderfully open-sloped plateau where tall grassy plains stretch out with views of the region's mountain peaks all around. After passing through a fantastic, deep wet wood, several ingenious tunnels take you through to the final section, the last push. A rough, undulating trail of sand, rock and gravel weaves and climbs its way up, the grades are simple but it is a challenge for tired legs. Once you reach the peak shortly before the lake, your body will be spent.

There is a large flat grass area adjacent to the largest lake perfect for camping, but expect a lot of people vying for space when attempting the route on a weekend. The lakes are beautiful, sitting exposed on the mountaintop. The views are unparalleled, the sky is wide and by the time the sun sets splendidly you will have gotten over your ordeal and feel life is good once again.

There are plenty of trails around for exploring in the afternoon should the weather, and your body, permit. Some people even come up here for extended days riding and hiking around the area. The warmer months of March and April, with rising heat and clear sky nights, are when the route is at its best. Very few people get to see this part of Taiwan and when we spent nights up there, it truly felt like a new perspective, and those clear night skies reflecting in the lake waters—spellbinding.

The ride back down from the lake all the way to Dili can be done in a morning but be aware that although a fast descent, the rough terrain and sheer cliff edges require a measured ride so take your time, it is tough on the wrists and the tires, don't tumble.

This trip is not for the faint of heart: You will need good fitness to complete it in anything under four days and you will need to take all provisions with you, but for those of you looking for the edge-of-it-all adventure, then this multiday off-road ride is for you. It lingers in the soul.

Heshe to Tatajia Pass

After a relaxing evening in the chilly surrounds of Dongpu (東埔) Mountain, soaking it up in the hot springs or exploring the village of Wangxiang (望鄉), who's ready for the second-longest climb on our tour?

Our last day in Nantou (南投) also sees us on our last day climbing in the high mountains. The road to Tatajia Pass (塔塔加) is one of this island's most incredible journeys. Most of the road is simple with no real steep sections apart from a 3km push after 35km; it is nowhere near as taxing as the ride up to Wuling (武嶺) Pass. This green, shaded climb brings you right alongside, and offers incredible views of Taiwan's peak, Jade Mountain (Yùshān, 玉山): East Asia's highest mountain, beating even that of Japan's Fuji. If you were not previously interested in the two-day summit hike, you will be more intrigued after viewing the magnificent peaks from this adjacent highway and watching plenty of hikers prepare their gear at the trailhead.

Steadily climbing up to 2600m the road is 45km of, well, up. There are no food or drinking options along the way. Expect to take somewhere between four and five hours to complete the climb, adding in breaks along the way.

Riders that have skipped around the high mountains so far by taking our Dapu to Dapu (大埔) western route should consider joining the main route here as it offers a great challenge with an incredible reward.

Start the climb early during the cooler hours, nothing beats you down more than the rising sun. It is our last day in this kind of environment and the beauty of the area should not be missed. Take your time, camping up top among pine forest and mountain vistas allows you the freedom of all day to reach it, bring plenty of food. Equally an early start gives you the option of adding in part of the descent on the other side, down to a homestay near Alishan (阿里山).

Riding along a farming valley at the beginning of our climb, the road snakes around a hillside until you launch up and over a sharp ridge. This eventually brings us out opposite Dongpu village, with panoramic views of its nestled position under the shadow of mountains.

As we cross into Yushan National Park (玉山國家公園) the flora and fauna start to change. Pine trees overtake the lower bamboo plantations as the sounds of the forest envelop you. Monkeys play in the trees; cicadas echo and screech all around. The area is still and quiet in the morning and apart from the odd car and motorcycle group you are left on your own to wander in this simple, evocative space. As you climb higher the peaks of Yushan come into view across the road, at points where the trees part you get full vistas of the north and main peak.

Years of earthquakes, typhoons and landslides keep this road on its toes and there is always a section or two being reconstructed. Once you reach the sections of long, open-sided tunnels the tarmac begins to stretch up high and, for some, the effects of the altitude gain start to slow you down as energy levels get sapped.

At 38km there is a road sign warning of 12 percent grades with higher degrees of steepness to come. This marks the beginning of a 3km section, which has been newly reconstructed, with sharp inclines on the corners. At least the tarmac is smooth and the top is within reach.

At the top of this section the road passes across another ridge, over to the western slopes of Dongpu Mountain. A couple of twists and turns before vast mountain ranges come into view across the valley. The road is magnificent as Taiwan showcases its lush green peaks. The route from here to the top is fairly easy climbing, well shaded with the last 2km proving very simple, almost flat. Once you spot the 143km road marker you know you only have a few meters to go.

Tatajia Pass is a long, flat section of road that runs along the western slope of Dongpu Mountain. The road has two parking lot areas, each with public bathrooms and wide-open views. The first, at the crest of the pass, is beside the entrance to the large information center with museum, restrooms and restaurant. The second parking lot, further along the now changed highway, is at the mouth of the Yushan Peak trailhead, a fantastic two-day return hike to the peak. If you arrive in the late morning you will see hikers preparing their gear for the start of the walk ahead; arriving after lunch, see those who have just returned from the trail.

With lots of viewpoints, short hiking trails and a great information center, let alone atmosphere, spending the afternoon and night up here is one of our Taiwan highlights. There are limited options beyond camping but the fast descent down the other side to the villages in Alishan offers more stupendous views and homestays aplenty. Make sure you have some time to spend up here, our last day in the high mountains is breathtaking. Soak it in, for tomorrow we descend and start our ride down to the heat of Taiwan's western flats and the ocean beyond.

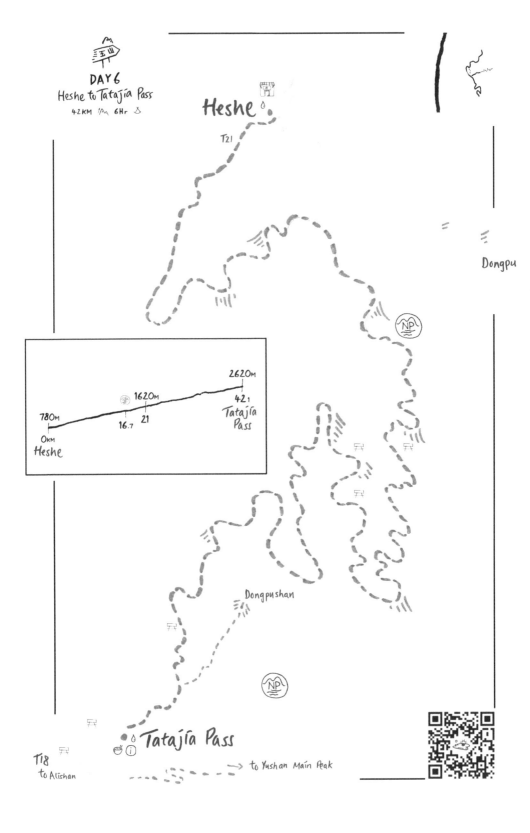

DAY 6
Heshe to Tatajia Pass
42KM 6Hr

Heshe

T21

Dongpu

2620M

1620M
42.1
Tatajia
Pass

780M
16.7   21

0KM
Heshe

Dongpushan

NP

Tatajia Pass

T18
to Alishan

to Yushan Main Peak

DAY 6

42KM / 6Hr

0.00 Start at Heshe junction, facing south! From either village of Dongpu (東埔) or Wangxiang (望鄉) head back down the hillside to the junction at Heshe (和社) and rejoin the T21.

Stock up here at the convenience store if you need. There are no, repeat no, food or drink stores until Alishan (阿里山) entrance some 20km into the following day. If you are sleeping at Tatajia (塔塔加) Pass then have all your provisions ready now. The information center does have free filter water and a small restaurant, which cannot be relied upon. Outside of opening hours there are water sources at the public bathrooms, which you can boil to cook with, but make sure you have enough for the climb.

The first section runs along a wide riverbed until finally turning and heading up the mountainside. The ride starts fast and doesn't feel like much of a climb; this soon changes, as the road crosses the river it starts to climb up and over a ridge before another short, flat section that runs along the mountainside.

8.55 Traffic gate and junction for tea farm area. This gate opens at 7am so no need to be here earlier. The temple here has been used by campers eager for an early start.

16.7 Yushan National Park (玉山國家公園) entrance sign, we cross into the national park here, it's where we stay for the rest of the ride.

Shortly after this point the climb starts to pass along some open-walled tunnels and incredible vistas. On a clear day expect stunning views of the Yushan mountain range as well as close-up views of the road as it twists and turns around the mountain above.

19.4 Rest stop with information board, picnic table and great open grass camping area overlooking the mountains, and public toilets, no water.

28.3 Shortly before a tunnel there is one pull-in that gives the last, but best, view of Yushan's peaks.

28.6 Tunnel here.

29.0 Parking lot rest stop, no bathrooms but a beautifully atmospheric, moss-covered picnic area.

30.2 Start of steep 3km-long exposed switchback section recently recon-structed.

37.2 Pass over a ridge to reenter forest and head out onto the western slopes of Dongpu Mountain.

38.5 End of the tough climbing, almost there, notice people stopping to pho-tograph the famous Couple Trees of Tatajia (塔塔加夫妻神木).

41.3 Trailhead for Dongpu peak, by the roadside.

<u>42.1</u> Finish at Tatajia Pass, highway T21 ends! Tatajia Pass, information center, bathrooms, rest stops, Yushan Peak hiking trails, oh, and did I mention incredible mountain vistas, cool, crisp air, top-of-the-world feeling. You made it!

At km marker 144.3 the T21 transitions onto the T18. For now the road stays flat, maintaining its altitude for 1.5km before descending toward the pass at the top of Alishan.

Along with parking lots and restrooms there are viewing platforms, long wooden walkways that line the highway as well as the short hiking trail to the peak of Dongpu Mountain. This short 20-minute trail brings you to a near-360° panoramic view of the mountains on a clear after-noon. It is a simple and worthwhile afternoon activity.

The small Dongpu Lodge is the only bed here on the mountainside. It is managed by the national park. To sleep here for the night reservations need to be made, often months in advance. Reserve through the park's website, see p93.

While there is no official camping site up here, most nights see a few campervans and hikers pitch up in the parking lots. Wait for the after-noon tourists to leave and find a nice place to put your tent. On a clear evening the uninterrupted views of the star-filled sky and silhouetted mountains fill the soul.

If you don't want to spend the night up here, feel emboldened to glide down the other side to the villages of Alishan and Shizhuo (石棹). Shizhuo has lots of small guesthouses and hotels dotted along the mountain ridge that runs down from Alishan. The descent through the Alishan Na-tional Forest Recreation Area (阿里山國家森林遊樂區) is as equally stun-ning as the climb up to Tatajia. The road is fast and comfortable and with few uphill sections you should make light work of the extra distance. If you started the day's ride early then, for even modest riders, it can be completed with enough time to be up to the pass and down to Shizhuo before the afternoon sunsets. See p105.

Yushan Peak Trail: two-day return hike to East Asia's highest, 3952m
For a great side adventure off the bike, Yushan National Park's two-day return peak trail is a real highlight of Taiwan's outdoor activities and a pilgrimage for Taiwanese hikers. A simple enough hike if you are moderately fit, with a clear, comfortable path and a large sleeping hut near the summit.

The first day sees you walking along comfortable forest trail with wide vistas of the surrounding peaks, ending at the lovely Paiyun lodge nestled among trees underneath the peak. The atmosphere is electric as your fellow hikers chat about the following day's challenge and the weather closes in. This hut provides reserved bed space and food for your dinner.

The hike to the peak starts before sunrise. You pass beyond the tree line and walk up comfortable switchbacks before the final, tiring piece of ascent up jagged cliff. This portion of the trail has several guard rails and covers to protect from rock falls. The views from the peak are indescribable as the sun rises up over the Pacific, cloud and peak. The andscape's changing colors and hues will keep you on the peak for hours.

This trek is highly coveted and to apply you need to do so way in advance. There is a handy weekday quota allowing access to foreign nationals. But this option is only available if reservations are made at least one month in advance. Permits, reservations and payment must be made in advance. It is much easier to be in-country to arrange as the website is tricky to navigate and payment for the accommodation, while inexpensive, must be made promptly and in advance though Taiwan's banking system. For more information and application process visit npm.cpami.gov.tw/en.

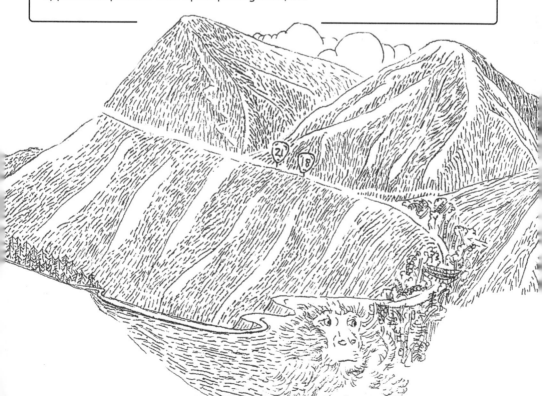

Nantou Side trips

The area around Sun Moon Lake is a large, wild region, parts of which you will have ridden through on our main route down from Wuling (武嶺) and across Wujie (武界). But there are even more areas to explore to the south of the great lake in this sprawling mountain landscape.

Of course, there are a lot of trails and hiking opportunities, not to mention the multiday adventures that cross through Yushan National Park, which we also cover in another section of our journey up to Tatajia (塔塔加) Pass. The off-road gravel biking route up to the mountains of Qi Cai Hu (七彩湖) is one truly out-there ride that is unique in Taiwan.

There is plenty more to discover and uncover in the near-endless side roads and mountain paths that reach out from the valley. We are only scratching the surface here. As a remote, explorers' region, Nantou really doesn't disappoint.

Jiujiufeng / 99 hills

The famous 99 hills (九九峰) situated to the west of Sun Moon Lake are a geological marvel that only rose up after the large earthquake in 1992. This quake literally transformed the region. The country took a long time to recover from the trauma of that event but the resulting new landscape added another fascinating hill hike to this central region. Not quite on the level of the Philippines' Chocolate Hills. But on a certain day the view of these sharp hills all tightly packed is alluring. Add in their easy access without crowds (for now), and you can easily spend a day or two in awe at the power of nature and its ability to constantly reshape our world.

To access the hills, take the T14 from either Taichung (台中) or Puli (埔里) and turn north into Caotun township between km markers 28 and 29; head north following the occasional sign for the hills. The short hiking trail starts behind the village. It is difficult to find this trail that offers good views.

If you want to hike into the hills proper, you need to find the narrow Shizhuoxiang Road that runs north from the T14, further east of Caotun. It is very hard to notice this unmarked lane. After crossing the river, turn up the narrower left-hand lane. Follow the extremely small brown bicycle signs for the main peak route. It's a tough hike up a dry riverbed before a steep but well-trodden path up to the narrow peaks of Jiujiufeng.

Note that the Nantou County government recently bought this land with intentions to increase its tourism with some ambitious plans, so get here before this well-kept secret is let out.

Dalunshan tea plantation lookout
To visit the epic tea plantation views at Dalunshan (大崙山) you need to be comfortable riding up, steep. But when has anything worth doing been easy? Once up here you will experience incredible mountain vistas, tea plantations with narrow winding lanes perfect for exploration. You really are treated to some of Taiwan's best tea views, and that's saying something. First sleep down in Lugu (鹿谷) for the night, just 20km up from Shuili (水里), and then ride up on a clear day for some epic views and fun descents. The ride alongside paths through bamboo forest and across to the Tianti scenic area suspension bridge is an incredible ride that is barely known on the cycling scene. If you have to do one trip that will be just for you, then consider this one. Even the ride to Lugu via highway 139 is up quiet, beautiful lanes that are devoid of traffic and full of wide, jaw-dropping views.

Ride the 149 to Caoling (草嶺) into the epic Meishan township (梅山鄉) and Alishan mountain regions.
Now, the eagle-eyed of you might notice that, strictly speaking, Caoling is in Chiayi County, but the road up to this region from Zhushan very much is in Nantou and it's a wonderful ride up. Once you cross through the mountain tunnel and arrive in the inner mountains of Chiayi you will feel transported into another land.

Starting from Zhushan, which is along the T3 route to the west of Shuili (see p51), head south along the 149 before turning onto the stunningly quiet and rural Lixing Road. This region is quiet farms of tea and all manner of fruit that sit alongside a beautiful, wide riverbed. Hints of Taiwan's Moon World are exposed at cliff edges of this deep valley. Rejoin the 149 just as it starts to climb. And boy on a hot day does this climb feel tough. But perhaps after no more than an hour you reach the top, and the views back down are wonderful. At the mouth of the tunnel, check yourself as the ride through starts your descent into the hidden valley of Caoling. This secret region then connects back up into Meishan region and across to Alishan. The climbing up and out of the Caoling valley is tough and if you are not into riding uphill on your bike then don't consider this trip. But for those seeking alternatives to the Alishan route or for anyone looking for a couple of days of epic hidden routes then this is the area for you.

The region climbs up to over 1000m and the roads that connect Caoling with Fenqihu are incredible, if steep. The reward is a unique trip through Taiwan's interior and out to the high tea regions above. If you know the weather in Alishan will be cloudy consider this as an alternative; there is much to explore in the Meishan region, such as the famous 36 Bends road, the tea plantations and the back roads that connect to Shizhuo and Fenqihu and the Alishan mountain railway, see p106.

Clockwise Notes
Nantou

Dapu, Chiayi to Renai and the base of Taiwan's highest climb

Riding through Nantou is a wonderful experience, proudly showing some of the island's most picturesque views. But heading north does feel like a near constant uphill ride. From Dapu up to Alishan and to Tatajia beyond is a two-day climb. If tackling this route, then spend a night in the wonderful tea village of Shizhao before you take on the long climb up to the pass at the edges of Yushan National Park.

The descent from the high pass of Tatajia is splendid but sadly not as long as the climb up, it will feel over all too soon. Then the soft uphill ride along the T21 to Sun Moon Lake is a fun and simple one, but the long climb up at the end of the day to the lake will feel draining. If you choose to skip the Alishan climb follow our alternative route and travel along the T3 to Linnei before reaching the quiet 131 to Shuili and then up to Sun Moon Lake.

Riding from the great lake to Renai in the center of the country you can retrace our Day 4 route; the climb up the hill from Puli to reach Wujie and the hidden valley route is tough but quicker than you think. There is only one really tough climb just as you reach the dam at the north end of the valley ride. Once you reach the top of the dam the last few km through forest-lined reservoir is a lovely, simple journey. Riding highway T14 all the way from Puli to Renai is pretty but still strenuous and very heavy with traffic.

If you are not planning to ride the central mountain route up to Taipei then head out from the lake along the T21 north. Once you leave the lake the fast descent will take you to the edges of Puli, turn left joining the T14 toward Taichung before turning off right for Guoxing. This 6km ride along a quiet country road will take you back to the T21 at the Y junction. From here the T21 climbs a stiff, long 14km climb, sorry, before descending to the T8 and eventually highway T3 where you can head north along this route retracing our Dapu to Dapu route back to Taipei.

Ride like the wind down through pine forest and
tea hills to perfect waterfall swims. Sleep beside
the island's largest reservoir, where coffee,
pineapples and mangos grow.
Explore moonscapes, the nation's oldest
city and hidden bicycle trails.

South West

Pass under the shadow of
Taiwan's southern mountains through paddy
fields cut by the audible thrill of canals,
gushing waterways and village life.
As we descend leisurely towards the tropical south.

South West

Grip your handlebars and relax your elbows, your mind becomes transfixed on the road ahead. The euphoria you feel as your senses try to keep up with the views around, and the sounds that whistle in your ear. It's instinctive, that's what's so alluring about this simple machine of metal and rubber. Sometimes you forget the bicycle is even there as, together, you roll, downhill, with the world shining all around.

Our arrival into Taiwan's southwest region starts with the longest descent of the trip. From the top of Tatajia Pass we travel through the stunning region of Alishan. First we wave goodbye to the high mountains as the sun rises across monkey crossings, pine forest and far-off peaks. Along an incredible mountain highway, rolling down, down, down. We drop first through forest, then along cliff edge and finally through farms of tea. These green hills cascade as we glide around them, dipping ever further down.

Past idyllic indigenous life, suspension bridges and waterfalls for afternoon dips, all before hitting the water's edge of Taiwan's largest reservoir, where, for those with tents, we get another night's fantastic sleep, at Dapu's free campground. It will pass by in such a blur, you will need the evening to process what your mind and body just went through.

From Dapu we head into the southwest proper: a flatter region of the country where fruit farming dominates the landscape. You can take side trips to the island's oldest city, Tainan, or perhaps even the giant port of Kaohsiung. Our route keeps us on the fringes, where we prefer to travel lightly alongside the base of the mountain ranges. Hopping, skipping and jumping our way south most of the journey from here to Kenting is flat, well, as flat as Taiwan gets.

And the last day's ride through Pingtung County is the easiest ride of the entire trip, but luckily it is still a stunningly fun one. Through beautiful countryside we travel south along the pineapple highway, rolling ever down, to sun and sea.

This is our last section before we hit the southern peninsula, outlying island and Taiwan's famed east coast highway. Here is our last inland ride, the last chance to explore the West's giant cities and remote mountain regions. Enjoy it for at the end the world will change anew.

Tatajia Pass to Dapu

Today marks the end of our high adventures as we cross the pass of Tatajia (塔塔加), away from the central mountains, descending to the hillsides toward Taiwan's southwest. From a peak of 2600m we are now racing down through the pine forests, tea plantations and mountain villages of Alishan (阿里山). At the end, we find ourselves beside the shoreline of Taiwan's largest reservoir and the waterside village of Dapu (大埔) just 200m above sea level.

Nestled on the border of Chiayi and Tainan counties we end the day on the edges of the southwest region. Taiwan gets hot from here as we travel through fruit farms, badlands, across dams and suspension bridges, over rivers and beside rice fields as we begin our ride to the ocean.

Sixty-eight km of our day is a near-continuous downhill ride. Aside from a couple of uphill kicks just after the mountain town of Shizhuo (石棹), we descend 2000m through the pine forests of Alishan National Forest Recreation Area (阿里山國家森林遊樂區). This beautiful forest region is nestled on a broad mountain area with some incredible day hikes if you want to take the time.

This downhill matches that of Wuling (武嶺). It is the perfect plunge down a mountain road. With a nice, smooth grade and few switchbacks this road passes different landscapes and towns, enough options to pause and rest without feeling like you have lost momentum. Pass through and around fresh pine forests before gliding along tea-strewn ridges. There are perfectly located rest stops along the smooth highway, great views and plenty of options to take a break off the bike. The smooth grades and quiet morning traffic will ensure that this ride isn't too hard on your hands, or legs.

Our first stop is across another pass that offers us one last look back at Yushan (玉山) before we cross over and into dense pine forest as the descent begins. In the middle of the ride we arrive at the entrance to Alishan mountain village and hiking area. This stunning wooded region was the height of Japanese logging activity in Taiwan. The vegetation has been allowed to regrow over the last fifty years or so, producing incredible results. The transformation has been astounding with the reintroduction of vital species of tree, insect, animal and bird alike. There are many walks available, from small hour jaunts through thick forest to multiday excursions across ridges, cliffs, following old train line trails in search of mountain lakes and quiet forest glades.

After leaving Alishan the road becomes even more spectacular as our cliff-hugging highway exposes us to quite breathtaking views of mountains all around. The road wraps and weaves, but stays wide and has plenty of space for passing vehicles. After descending for what feels like forever we arrive at the village of Shizhuo, a crossroads for the region's tea manufacturing that marks the end of the initial descent. From here the pine forests make way for tea fields, bamboo and cliffside cafés. This is one of Taiwan's most famous tea growing areas as the fresh mountain air around here is said to blow extra life into the dark green leaf. The oolong tea here is delicious and there are stores in Shizhuo that will happily invite you in and offer tasters.

From Shizhuo the traffic builds and on the weekends, it becomes more impeding. Luckily after a few more villages and tea plantations our route turns off the highway, quite literally sliding off the T18 and racing down a mountainside to the river village of Shanmei (山美). Entering a beautiful, remote valley, vegetation closes in as we pass small indigenous communities, ride around rivers, suspension bridges, waterfalls and monkeys. At the road's end we cross a river passing a great roadside waterfall, perfect for an afternoon dip. All that just before we reach highway T3, by the water's edge of Taiwan's largest reservoir. This impressive water is surrounded on all sides by jungle-strewn hills, and the sweet village of Dapu sits lovingly by its quiet, lapping waters.

At the back of the village, by the waterfront, we find one of the best free campgrounds on the island. Situated in Lovers Park, the locally run free camping area has 24hr toilets and a well-maintained grass area. We pitch our tents at the water's edge on the lawn that overlooks the hills, under big, clear skies.

There is a real increase of heat as we descend, and the temperatures at the end of the day are far higher than the mountain regions as we head into Taiwan's tropical south. So, soak up the close smell of pine, silent skies and crisp air while you can. Enjoy the cloud-soaked vistas one last time. We are leaving Taiwan's high mountains and with it our long climbs and longer descents.

The southwest is much more populated than the central mountains and tomorrow we pass through many towns and villages, but our route still skips the major cities and built-up areas. Instead we take a tour through the quieter fringes of the farming communities, minimizing the amount of climbing we do, a stark change to the last two days. With the choice to add in a break to one or two of Taiwan's great southern cities, perhaps it's time to take a day or two off the journey. Whatever you choose, there are plenty of fun routes in Taiwan's southwest to keep you interested and to get you where you want to go.

But for now, prepare for a comfortable night under the stars, reminiscing on the journey taken so far, in the company of a very friendly community.

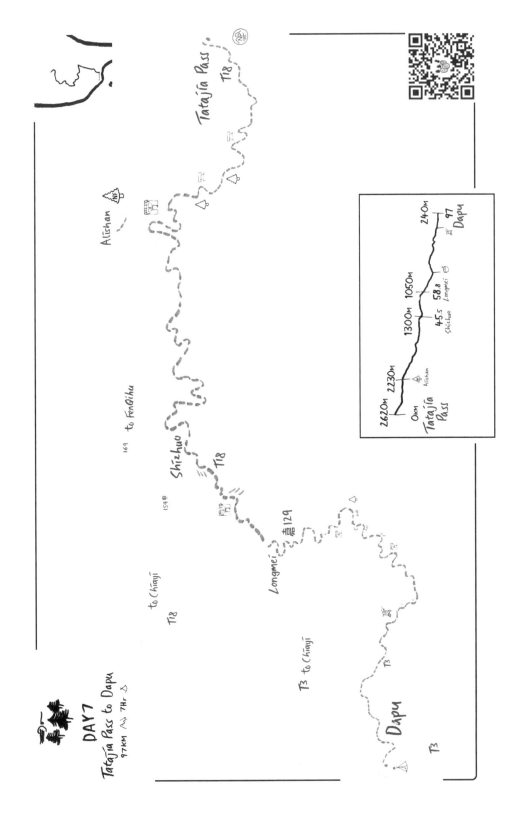

DAY7
Tatajia Pass to Dapu
97km 7Hr

Tatajia Pass

T18

Alishan NF

to Fenqihu 169

Shizhuo

T18

159甲

Longmei

吉129

to Chiayi
T18

T3 to Chiayi

Dapu

T3

2620m
2230m
Tatajia Pass
0km
Alishan

1300m
45.5
Shizhuo

1050m
58.8
Longmei

240m
97
Dapu

DAY7

97KM 〽 7Hr ⛺

0.00 Start from the lofty heights of Tatajia Pass! Outside the entrance to the information center, at the beginning of the Alishan Highway T18, we head south. The road starts beautifully with wide mountain views. Parking lots and bathrooms here.

1.07 Entrance down the slope on the right for the Dongpu hotel.

1.60 Pass the last of the parking lots, the road starts to descend from here. This is the start to the famous Yushan (玉山) Peak trail.

Viewpoints, platform walkways and trails that head up and down the mountainside are scattered along the road as we wind west along a ridge. The first 3km are, on a clear morning, quite simply epic. As you pass monkey crossings, old train stations and thick foliage you will be afforded grand views of the world below. Turning the last corner of the furthest ridge we cross into Alishan National Forest Area (阿里山國家森林遊樂區).

12.5 The last viewpoint at Zizhong (自忠), one last chance to stare back at Dongpu and the eastern mountains, including Yushan.

Just around the corner the next few km are flat and rolling as we head around a mountainside, before a fast-downhill section takes us quickly to the entrance of Alishan town. Watch out for erratic traffic if visiting on the weekend. From there the road passes through pine forest and across mountainside. It is a happy, relaxed ride.

20.4 Just after a couple of sharp, long corners we drop beside the entrance of Alishan. The bus station, store and restrooms here are situated just to the side of the T18. Carry on down the mountain when ready to leave, following signs for Shizhuo (石棹).

105

You might see an abundance of traffic parked up on the roadside here. Entrance to the town is managed and ticketed. The bus station, convenience store and information hall are right at the entrance; beyond this point the road winds along to a small town of hotels and trailheads into the scenic area.

The multiday hike from here down to Fenqihu (奮起湖) tracing down the old train line is a beautiful and historical journey. It is super popular with day hikers too. If you want a taste of Taiwan hiking but don't have time for multiple days, a half-day hike around here is well worth it.

See recreation.forest.gov.tw/en for information on short day walks and longer hikes.

From here the road's longest descent starts. With sweeping corners and open-sided tunnels, the views are, of course, mesmerizing and the ride is near perfect, there are not too many technical sections and it is a comfortable ride.

34.5 Little village of Shitzulu (十字路), literally "crossroads," where you can access the old railway trail, just off the main highway.

The vegetation changes from here as pine trees make way for tea plantations that scatter the roadside. The tea from Alishan is famous and the industry covers the landscape where it can.

45.5 Head straight, staying on the T18. The arrival into Shizhuo is marked by a crossroads with traffic lights.

Shizhuo, while small, has lots of restaurants, convenience stores as well as homestays and tea plantations that dot the hillsides. There are

---

Fenqihu and Meishan region

Turning right at the crossroads will take you to the village of Fenqihu. This route is the gateway to a fantastic mountain range of soaring tea plantations and hidden roads tucked away in the heart of the mountains. It is also the final station stop for the Alishan Forest Railway that runs once daily up and down the mountain from the city of Chiayi (嘉義). This repurposed section of the old logging railway is a lovely journey and Taiwan's highest train route still in operation. Free shuttle buses also run from this station up to Alishan, sadly no bicycles allowed.

The Meishan (梅山) region just beyond Fenqihu is well worth exploring if you have an extra few days. The route links up into Chiayi's fabulous mountain range and central Nantou (南投). The other routes into this area include the Meishan 36 Bends road and the Nantou climb to Caoling (草嶺). Both of these routes up the mountains we pass along Day 4 of our alternative Dapu route, see p52.

no campsites here. For the next 10km you pass through small tea villages with plenty of store options and great vista viewpoints.

50.8 Longtou (龍頭) roadside village with convenience store and views.

51.8 A right turn onto the 130, a beautiful alternative route down the mountain if you are heading for Chiayi, but be careful of those steep corners halfway along.

52.8 Xiding (隙頂), stores and viewing platforms of those lush tea plantations and surrounding hills.

<u>58.8</u> STOP! Turn left onto the 嘉129 at Longmi (龍美). Here we leave highway T18 and turn south; this road will take us to the waterfront village of Dapu (大埔). Turn down the first left at the amber lights. Do not take any other road. Make sure you are on the 嘉129 to Shanmei (山美).

The road drops sharply but comfortably through mountain farms and it is beautiful to be in this environment. Watch out on this narrow mountain road for blue farming trucks at the occasional bend.

All the other side routes from this junction will leave you on narrow rough roads, thick with danger and intrigue; maybe worth the risk, up to you, just don't blame us if you descend thousands of meters and then have to ride up due to a blocked path or landslide.

If you want to visit Chiayi or take the alternative route to Dapu then carry on down the T18. Make a stop at the bottom of the descent to the suspension bridge and temple of Chukou (觸口).

68.5 Pass by Shanmei tourist center. And here we are, finally, our descent has finished. Not the last piece of downhill for the day but with a short climb to reach out from the town of Shanmei. This remote river crossing marks the end of the long descent out of the mountains.

68.6 Cross the main bridge over the river. Spend a few moments on the long suspension bridge. There is a store, restaurant, as well as bathrooms in the tourist center across the high hanging pedestrian bridge.

<u>68.7</u> Turn right staying on the 嘉129 after the bridge crossing, following signs for Xinmei (新美) as the road heads uphill.

The left-hand turn heads to the main indigenous village and lovely local trails into the surrounding hills. There is a 100NTD entrance fee for all visitors to the village.

72.2 The top of a 4km climb. This hidden valley road is beautiful: rushing streams, small indigenous communities.

76.2 A mini descent into the indigenous village of Xinmei. Here there is a campsite and some small local stores, if they are open.

84.9 The small village of Chashan (茶山) also has a store or two if open.

87.0 After a final, steep descent cross the riverbed on the second bridge, staying on the main road.

After this crossing it is a short ride to the beautiful waterfall. This section of road does climb up a few horrid corners, but don't worry, a great reward is just around the corner.

89.9 Just to the right after a small river crossing is the incredible Qingren waterfall (青雲瀑布).

While easily accessible it is also wild and happily undeveloped. And
so close to the highway too. During busy hot weekends expect to find
some people parked up here with picnics. Walk the 100m from the main
road to the large deep pool and swim underneath the cascading water. It
is a great antidote to the heat of the mid-afternoon sun. The waterfall
dries up in the late spring but there is always a pool to swim in, be careful of rockfalls.

91.0 Turn left onto the T3 at the end of the 嘉129 crossing the bridge. From
here we join with our alternative Dapu route that avoided the mountain
roads.

Heading north, the T3 winds up nearly 800m to a peak overlooking the
reservoir before heading downhill on the other side. Head this way if you
are in search of a hot spring along the coffee road, see p111 Also from
the pass the T3 races toward central Chiayi.

95.5 Turn right onto Dapu Road just before the gas station at the sign for the
Dapu Visitor Center.

95.9 Turn left onto Datong 1st Road (大同一路) just before the concrete arch.

96.4 Turn right down the park road at the town's main crossroads in front of
the convenience store. Head for the water's edge and the free campground. Most of the town's stores and restaurants are concentrated
around this junction.

97.0 Finish at the entrance to Lovers Park, Dapu's free campground! There are
lots of places to view the reservoir and wander around a peaceful
evening.

This is a free camping area so please respect it and keep any area
clean. The locals are sweet and very friendly, if a little curious. If the
campground is closed for any reason, camping in the area should still be
OK; there are other viewing platforms and flat areas for a place to pitch
for the night. During national holidays, it can get manic here, but it is a
huge area, there will always be space for a cyclist; it is very quiet midweek, you can often have the entire place to yourself.

If you are not camping, Dapu has one sweet guesthouse on the highway opposite the gas station, and the holiday park situated just before
the entrance to Lovers Park has a wide range of lodging options.

Dapu to Maolin

Waking up at the waterside campground in Dapu (大埔) feels like a real treat. As the morning sun hits the surrounding hillsides they glow a rainbow of colors, as do the waters of Zengwen Reservoir (曾文). For us the atmosphere here was so unexpected, an arresting breakfast scene. Of course, there are bigger views to be had but it's a peaceful location stretching out on the grassy lawn. There are not a lot of official free camping sites in Taiwan and to have one that offers such relaxing surroundings, wow.

This is not a day to start too early despite the longish journey ahead. Heading out along the shoreline, we are aiming to cross the reservoir's large dam and ride south away, to find and cross Tainan's fruit farm region along bridges, through mango crossroads, unique moon landscapes and past art deco towns, all to end up in the lush hill surrounds of Pingtung County's tropical environs.

The dam road doesn't open until 9am. If you are in a rush or worried about your arrival time you can skip the side road and stay on highway T3, just be warned it still has one large climb in store once you cross over into Tainan (台南) County. The Zengwen dam road is a lovely, downhill ride that runs fast, flowing with the river, so stick with it if you can.

Depending on how your body is feeling, the first few km today will either be a comfortable wind around the country's largest reservoir or a bit of a tiring slog. This section of the T3 highway is stunning as jungle creeps onto the edges of the quiet road as it rises and dips around the water's edges.

Once you turn onto the dam road the downhill begins, so let the wheels roll and stretch out those legs. We have added a couple of local ice cream stops along the way to guarantee a hot day is full of icy, fruitier treats—and it will be a hot day.

175 – Tainan's Coffee Road

The 175 is Tainan's beautiful coffee road, hugging the western edges of mountain range with views of the rolling hills to the west rather than the reservoir. The road runs north from the hot spring town of Guanzhiling (關子嶺) down to the region just north of Yujing. This area is popular with weekend riders due to its fast climbs and sweeping descents; dotted with small coffee farms and rustic cafés, it's a great day adventure, and a fine alternative to the Zengwen Reservoir route. See p54 for directions to reach the start of the road from the T3 between Chiayi (嘉義) and Dapu village.

At the far end of the small village of Zhaoxing (照興) is a collection of farmer stalls that congregate around the suspension bridge. These stalls offer some great local produce and a chance to rest under orchard trees. After crossing the wide riverbed along the pedestrian bridge, and a bit of navigation, we find our way back to the T3. Now transformed into a wide and busy highway, very unlike the quiet country road we encountered earlier. We quickly trundle through to Yujing (玉井), Taiwan's mango capital. This small town is hidden behind a mass of crossroads, as the most essential, traffic-heavy routes that head all across the county of Tainan pass through here.

From here there is a chance to turn off our route and take a direct path west to Taiwan's oldest city, Tainan (台南). This might be the best option to explore one of Taiwan's western cities, as the old narrow lanes of Tainan are a foodie's heaven. The crumbling temples and tucked-away guesthouses give it further charm. It is fairly comfortable for cyclists to navigate around as the old center is compact and central compared to a lot of the sprawling cities on offer.

After leaving Yujing the T20 and T3 travel east together along a flat ride for 5km. After they split, the T3 is hot, humid and energy sapping. This section of our day bridges the two regions and is certainly not the highlight. Relatively fast on the downhill but slow going on every uphill section.

Just south of Yujing in the heart of Tainan's countryside is the fascinating, and interestingly named, Moon World badlands. This unique landscape of dry rock formations jutting out of arid jungle is one of the few badlands found around the world. These arid landscapes usually feature very few trees or shrubs and minimal water sources, but Taiwan's unique fame is it just happens to have the only tropical badlands in the world. This coming together of opposing lands creates a wild, seemingly impossible landscape. A maze of miniature mountains, forest, streams and local farms. You can, and will, get lost for days in here.

If you want to break up the day consider a night here: a wild side trip that offers a peek into one of Taiwan's more curious landscapes. Stopping here splits this long day into two more manageable 60km rides, with a glorious sunrise when you wake up. But be warned the roads around here are not for the faint of heart, see p118.

There are glimpses of the Moon World landscape, providing the only real relief from the heat and frustration of the rolling hills.

We detour off the T3 just before Qishan, skipping the sweet art deco village; for an alternative ride through Qishan. Instead we ride on the 121 provincial road, a small climb that rewards you with a beautiful descent at its low pass. At the top, drink in the scenery of Tainan County before heading toward the tunnel on the 181. A simple downhill ride with, and dare I say it, a fun tunnel that runs under the dragon mountain and lands you in Meinong (美濃), an alternative rest stop to Qishan.

As the day starts to get long our scenery begins to markedly change. The last section of road is an inspiring and lush, flat ride past paddy fields and wide riverbeds along the east heading of highway T28. We are in search of the mountain-hugging region of Maolin (茂林). The road is fast and simple from here, with a single 1km hill just before you cross the wide river bridge and end the day's ride at the foot of some monstrous hills.

Maolin is a small town nestled at the mouth of a high mountain valley. The mountain road leads up to some small indigenous villages, if you want to explore the region you can take an extra day and head up the river road.

At the mouth of the valley is a small cluster of shops and a couple of camping options. There is even an excellent bakery selling everything from French baguettes to cinnamon rolls. Perfect post-ride treats, dinner supplies or maybe even the next day's breakfast.

This day tops 100km and it certainly is a big ask. Luckily right near to the mouth of the valley are several campsites and plenty of rest areas that don't require you to venture up into the hills. Consider an early ride the next morning, or heck a whole day, up into the beautiful mountain valley; the indigenous mountain area of Maolin has lots of beauty and incredible surprises.

Our Day 9 ride is the simplest, most restful of the whole trip, so push on through today and you are rewarded with a fun, comfortable ride through Pingtung (屏東) County, as we finally hit the coast on our ride though pineapple country.

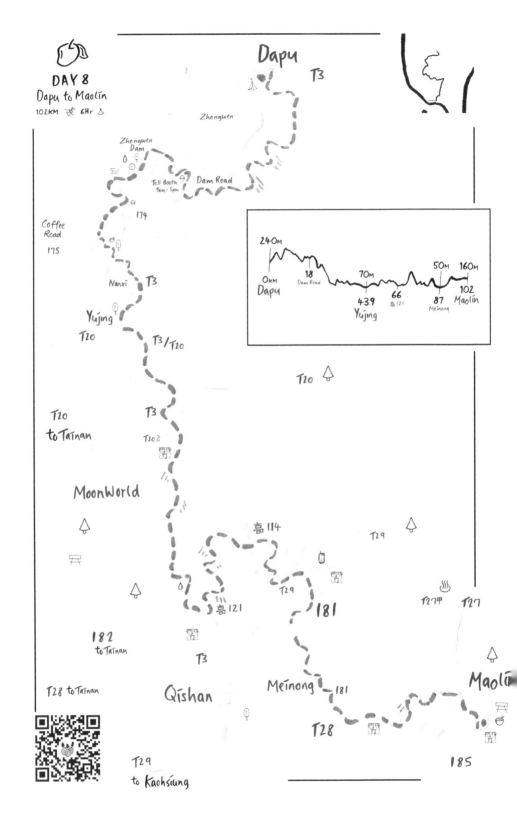

DAY 8
Dapu to Maolin
102KM 6Hr

Dapu
T3
Zhengwen
Zhengwen Dam
Toll Booth 9am-5pm
Dam Road
174
Coffee Road
175
Nanxi
T3
Yujing
T20
T3/T20
T20
T3
T20 to Tainan
T3
T20 2
MoonWorld
高114
T29
T29
181
高121
182 to Tainan
高121
T3
181
Meinong
T28 to Tainan
Qishan
T28
T27甲
T27
Maoli
185
T29 to Kaohsiung

240M 0KM Dapu
18 Dam Road
70M
50M 160M
439 Yujing
66 高121
87 Meinong
102 Maolin

DAY 8

102KM 🐎 6Hr ⛺

0.00 Start in Lovers Park, Dapu's campground! From the archway entrance of the campsite in Dapu (大埔) follow the road out, returning to the cross-roads at the convenience store.

0.60 Turn right at the crossroads at the convenience store, heading south. Follow this road a few hundred meters as it bends and gradually crawls back up to the T3 highway.

1.30 Turn right onto the T3 at the end of the road, heading south.
    For 18km undulate along a beautiful forest-lined road. The first half is a mainly uphill ride with the second being largely downhill. Once you reach the rest stop overlooking the reservoir the road feels easier to navigate, before the last short climb up to the reservoir road turning.

11.9 Rest stop, with views across the water and public bathrooms.

18.0 Turn right onto the reservoir road. Immediately after crossing the county line, at the top of a stiff little climb, follow the brown sign and turn onto the side road simply marked as Zengwen Reservoir (曾文水庫). There is an old map at the junction showing some of the highlights along the road. The road travels briefly uphill before flying down along a sweet bendy route toward the water's edge.
    Carry on along the T3 if you are in more of a rush, but there is one more climb along the way. Our main route joins the T3 again and the time difference between the two routes is minimal, while the reservoir road really is a much more pleasant journey.

21.5 Ticket entrance for the reservoir recreation area. Although a public road, this area is controlled and managed, so if you arrive before 9am or after 4:45pm expect the gate to be closed, blocking access. Entrance cost 100NTD for cyclists.

22.0 Large viewing attraction that juts out into the sky.

Several styles of large viewing platforms along the next km, some with public bathrooms. Pass through a simple tunnel just before the dam.

23.7 The dam, take in the water views on both sides, public toilets are on the other side of the dam.

23.8 The road bends left, and heads downhill fast running alongside the river out from the dam. From here the road is fairly straight as it sits with a cliff to one side and the river on the other. This is a wide, comfortable road that has plenty of space for traffic.

26.6 Information center, park and viewing platform. A great rest spot with a really cute and well-maintained grass garden. Free drinking water here, along with a small snack stall inside as well as useful information on nearby highlights and the reservoir.

27.4 Riverside park with shade, seating and a viewing platform of the river below.

28.8 Lean left, crossing the river as the road curves onto a low, flat bridge that sits on the now-wide valley.

30.0 The short climb out of the riverbed strangely widens into a four-lane road with a central partition as you pass an equally strange hotel complex on your left. The road descends again shortly after the hotel entrance.

31.4 Exit the recreation area. Leaving through the exit gate you can see a row of tollbooths, for those entering from the south.

33.6 Large opulent temple complex on your right with its outer walls adorned with animal motifs.

33.8 Turn right onto the 175 (174). The road rolls downhill and quickly hits an odd Y junction.

Lean to the right as you hit the junction and follow the signs for 174 Guanzhiling (關子嶺) and Wusanto Reservoir (烏山頭), ignore the Yujing (玉井) sign for now. Here the reservoir road ends.

34.9 Turn left onto the tiny 南183. Just before the 175 (174) heads uphill turn a sharp left, down the narrow lane to enter a sleepy village.

35.0 Turn immediately left/head straight. Head down a small slope entering the village, do not lean right, you must turn left here.

35.1 Ride to the end of Zhaoxing (照興) village road. Residents here offer local farm-produced fruits, vegetables and other delicious products.

The last store on the left just before the suspension bridge is a family-run farm, and their gardens and orchard are a great place to rest and relax in shade. Nothing beats their amazing homemade fruit ice treats. No milk just fruit, and they are so refreshing! Their passion fruit frozen pots are not to be missed. There is also an open-air restaurant serving noodle and rice dishes.

35.2 Head straight onto the purple pedestrian bridge crossing the wide riverbed, bicycles allowed.

35.8 At the end of the bridge watch out for the market stalls and hustle and bustle around the temple complex. Climb your way out and up, reaching a small town.

To Tainan (台南)

Taiwan's oldest city, Tainan is a great little stop for a city break. More easily accessible than most of Taiwan's western cities. It boasts plenty of temple relics, narrow old streets, an abundance of restaurants and food markets as well as a coastal area dotted with a rich history in Chinese architecture and colonial development. It has a strikingly slower pace of life compared to the country's other large cities. To reach it from here turn down highway T20, west.

The highway runs all the way to the city's train station and its center, about two hours' simple ride from Yujing. For a back road route to Tainan, follow the entrance to Moon World and then turn west along provincial road 168, a glorious jungle ride that leads to the eastern edge of Tainan, where you can pick up the T20 on the edges of the city.

If you spend time in Tainan and wish to carry on south after, then simply take the 182 east out of the city. This road will bring you back to Qishan (旗山); after some 15km of dull city escape roads you then enjoy 25km of pretty, undulating hill riding. From Qishan you can rejoin our route east along highway T28. There is also a semicoastal route from Tainan down to Kaohsiung (高雄), along highway T17, from the west of Tainan city.

Taiwan's best mechanic is based in the sweet little store behind the train station. Cycle Element will get you out of a jam and can order parts. Closed Mondays, details at facebook.com/cycleelement167.

<u>36.2</u> Turn right at the crossroads, shortly after passing the side of the temple complex, finding a green cobblestone street.

<u>36.4</u> Turn left in front of the small temple, following the stone path.

<u>36.5</u> Head straight at the crossroads. After the junction the road bends right, follow it past stores and homes for the next km.

<u>37.4</u> Merge right onto the T3. The highway has transformed into a larger four-lane road, with a bicycle lane. Follow it south for the next 6.5km as it enters the busy junction town of Yujing.

<u>43.9</u> Turn left onto the T20/T3. At the main junction to the southeast of Yujing we meet the highway T20. Turn left following signs for Nanhua (南化).

There are lots of options here at this crossroads. If you want to stop in Yujing and taste that sweet cold mango ice dessert then turn right here onto Zhonghua Road (中華路).

If you want to split the day and follow our side trip to the Moon World badlands then head straight and follow signs for the T20. At the next junction with the giant mango sculpture, turn left with the large flow of traffic across the bridge.

<u>44.2</u> The T3/T20 merge together and run southeast away from the town. The next 5km is an easy ride along a wide road.

<u>49.0</u> Turn right and follow the T3 south as the two highways split off. From here the road climbs through the edges of the Moon World landscape. The undulating climbs can become tiring; the road doesn't flatten out until the final descents outside Qishan.

Caoshan Moon World (草山 月世界) badlands and alt route to Tainan city (台南)
What's in a name? Caoshan simply means "grass mountain," but these are not your typical green rolling hills. A maze of small forest roads weave, climb and dip through and around this unique landscape. Spiky rock formations, streams, tropical farms and mini forests scatter a broad area, crossing county lines and sitting in a black hole between the western city flats and the high mountains to the east.

This is a natural wonder with an impressive name. While not on the scale of Badlands National Park in the USA or Cappadocia in Turkey, this is still a unique landscape. It's the only badlands located in a tropical climate, full of striking contrasts of colors and contours.

Some of the roads are incredibly challenging but luckily there are a couple that cut through and offer great views without too much pain. And getting up high really gives some great panoramic views of the moon landscape. Not to be missed during a bright sunrise.

Sitting to the east of Tainan, the Caoshan Moon World straddles both Tainan city and Kaohsiung city in Tianliao (田寮) district. This area is a great place to camp for the night if you want to break up Day 8 into two. Equally if you feel strong and want an alternative route to Qishan, head this way.

If you are heading into Tainan and want to explore some of the region's more interesting back roads this is a great route too, as the 168 is a fantastically fun alternative road to the busier and hotter T20.

Start in Yujing (玉井), follow signs for highway T20 and Zuoshan (座山). At the junction with the big mango sculpture, turn left and head south. You know you are on the right route when you see signs for Tainan.

Follow highway T20 all the way to Tainan, it's a simple journey that takes you all the way to Tainan train station. (Carry on our route to the 168 for a more interesting journey to Tainan.)

After 9km turn left onto T20乙 and head east, leaving T20. After 1km look for signs for Caoshan Moon World and road number 168. Turn right. Follow this road for 5km until you reach three route options.

308 highlands through to highway 3 and Qishan
5km along the 168 you reach a Presbyterian church. Opposite is a turning onto road 171 and the start of the 308 highlands route. This marks the road route that winds up and down through Moon World.

The route entrance is marked by a cute statue of a moon, a goat and a boy playing the flute. Turn here for a route up and through the badlands that leads you back to highway 3, eventually rejoining our main route south to Qishan.

Alternative route to Tainan

Carry on for 300m past the church and you arrive at a small junction. Turn right and carry on along road 168 to Tainan. This road has one tough climb to begin with, but after 100m up you reach the top and then it is a beautifully fun ride all the way down to Tainan. Once the road leaves the forested area you can follow main road routes that land in the east of the city after another 20km of flat riding.

Sunrise viewpoint of Moon World and rest stop

Lean to the left following signs for road 162 and Longci. This is the start of a 3km uphill ride, with some steep corners. But once you reach the top you are rewarded with panoramic views of the badlands and the surrounding mountain ranges. It's spectacular at sunrise and the rest stop is large. A new pavilion with restrooms sits alongside the older viewpoint. If you decide to camp here for the night just remember to pack up everything when you leave in the morning, and in fair weather don't expect to be alone at sunrise.

Stay on the T20 if you are heading east for the mountain climb and the Southern Cross-Island Highway, p126.

53.8 Head straight at the junction. Keep heading south on T3. If you are in need of a break turn off here. The village of Nanzhuang (南庄) just off the highway has stores and restaurants.

If you change your mind and want to visit Tainan or Moon World turn right onto T20乙 here.

54.9 Junction from the right as the road in Nanzhuang rejoins the highway. The T3 reaches one of many hilltops here.

60.8 Top of the last big hill on the T3 at this giant white temple complex.

63.3 Lean left keeping on the T3. A small village road 127 heads straight.

Tired of climbing, hit your limit of hills? The 121 and route to Meinong (美濃) is one of the day's highlights, but maybe by now the T3 has sucked all your energy. If so, consider skipping the 121 and take a break in Qishan (旗山). Just be warned the T3 still undulates and has one long climb before the final descent into the town. See below for information on Qishan and routes to Kaohsiung city (高雄).

Qishan and roads to Kaohsiung (高雄)

The town of Qishan is famed for its art deco–era buildings, although if you are expecting some grand facades think again; sadly many of the old buildings have been demolished or overrun by shop fronts and billboards. But remnants of the old structures still exist down the main old street as well as at the old train station. It is great for its street food stalls, and hill park with views over the area. The police and fire stations here are friendly places to fill up your water bottles, and there is an abundance of tea shops as well as convenience stores and coffee shops.

To reach Qishan carry on south along the T3 ignoring our turn to the 121. After 3km turn left at the main intersection, staying on the T3 following signs for Qishan. Now the road widens and climbs before eventually dipping into the eastern end of town. Follow the curving road until you pass the bus station, from here at the next junction turn right off the highway and enter the main road through the town. Once you arrive at the police station a short right-hand turn will find the old street one block west. Once you are ready to head out from Qishan head east from the police station junction. You should arrive at the river near to the beautiful pedestrian bridge.

For Kaohsiung head south out of Qishan following signs for T29. Follow this highway for some 20km until you reach the T1, which you can use to head to Kaohsiung's main train station to the city's center. When leaving Kaohsiung simply head south; use the T17 that heads south through the city before turning east, running along the nearby coastline arriving both at the port for Xiaoliuqiu (小琉球) island and Fangliao (枋寮), the start of Day 10's route, p155.

65.9 Turn left onto the 121 at the junction. Here is the end of our time on the T3. This side road has a 2km hill climb. But it is beautiful and takes you on a great side trip through farm villages and a zippy tunnel journey through a mountain.

    The 121 is fairly flat for the first 2km until a couple of tight turns through an old farm village. Then the road heads up a slow hill climb for the next 2km. There are some farm dogs that laze around during the day, but unless you run over their tails, they really are harmless. While farm dogs in Taiwan do yap if you go close to their patch, they are very docile and I have yet to experience any real trouble.

70.5 Reach the top of 121 climb. After the peak the wide road narrows on the descent, so watch out as the farm road becomes narrower and narrower.

71.8 Cross the bridge, before the road curves back up and away.

71.9 Head straight onto the 114 as the road flattens. Straight after the bridge ignore the left turn into the village.

73.1 Turn left at the T junction. Notice the quaint bridge over the stream, cross this just after turning.

73.4 Turn left onto the 117 at a second T junction. Make sure you turn left here, if you turn right you are heading all the way down to Qishan.

73.9 Turn right heading quickly back onto the 114 and follow the road as it heads south, passing a military base. This road is quiet and beautifully serene. If a little odd thanks to the high concrete wall.

77.5 Turn left onto the T29. At the end of the 114, turn down the slip road on the left and join highway T29, careful of traffic as you cross the busier road.

78.8 Turn right onto the 181 at the traffic lights, heading south again. If you need supplies desperately, carry on for 100m before turning for tea shops and convenience stores nearby. Now we are heading south again along a flat, fast road, passing rice fields and farms. We face a wall of mountain here, tunnel coming up.

82.8 The flat road curves up as it heads toward a spacious tunnel.

83.7 The tunnel ends as you enter into Meigong.

85.8 Turn left onto Tai'an Road, staying on the 181. At the Tai'an road (泰安路) junction, pass the store on your left and follow signs for the 181.

86.1 Turn right keeping on the 181, following signs. This is the last large town for the day, plenty of supplies here.

86.7 Turn left onto the 140 as it runs southeast.

89.1 Turn left onto the T28 following signs for Liouguei (六龜).

    Turn right if you want to head back up to Qishan or Kaohsiung. From here the route is pretty and uncomplicated to our day's end.

92.5 A 1km climb, a small hill but tough for tired legs. You reach the top at the 3D mural of the local highlights, hot springs, mangos and other fruit. After a short descent, the road is flat ahead.

    After the climb there isn't really much of a descent but shortly after, the views open out to the long mountain range ahead. This is the region of Maolin, we are close to the end.

Maolin mountain district
Nestled up between two mountains is the beautiful and unique Maolin district. One single road snakes its way up the mountainsides from the entrance in Pingtung County below, and what a road it is.

Often flooded with butterflies, it takes on a mystical feeling as clouds gather and the sounds of hidden villages rattle off in the distance. The road passes up above the riverbed along a high raised bridge, eventually becoming wedged between the sides of the two mountains. It is a stunning ride up here. Campgrounds are nestled by the river and on mountain plateaus, suspension bridges hang high connecting hilltops, walking paths along ridges offer striking views.

The road climbs up to a pass after an hour or so of riding, from there the view opens up to hidden ranges and valleys below. And, nestled in among it all, is the lovely village of Duona (多納). At the road's end this sweet village has kept all its charm, and the locals thrive off their traditional cultures and foods.

Tourists come from all over southern Taiwan to taste the foods and experience the atmosphere, which is especially electric during local events and ceremonies. There is a fantastic café here that serves some incredible coffee from a truly dedicated family obsessed with all things bean. Smoke from street BBQs fills the air as firecrackers and hunting rifles ring and echo across the mountain walls. The atmosphere up here is to be savored. Some indigenous areas on the island have developed tourist traps with fake events and ceremonies, but here is the real, if contemporary, deal.

The ride up to Duona and back can be done comfortably in a morning and it is well worth a half-day experience. It might be difficult to add this to a full-day itinerary of riding to Fangliao (枋寮). Either way, the side trip up through Maolin is a great use of your time.

<u>98.2</u> Turn right onto the long-arched bridge. Follow the road across the valley floor, looking for signs for Maolin (茂林) and the T28.

Carry on north up the T27甲 for the Baolai (寶來) hot spring area and the T20, as it starts its ascent up the high southern ranges.

<u>101</u> Turn right onto the T27 at the end of the bridge, facing a beautiful wall of jungle foliage, the T28 ends. Turn right onto the T27 south.

This older highway also heads north to Baolai, undulating along the river's eastern bank.

<u>102</u> Finish at the junction with the entrance to Maolin mountain road, 高132! At the junction by the bridge, stop first for yummy treats and superb breads at the Svongvong Bakery (蝶手感烘焙).

A helpful local restaurant and rest stop and entrance to the Maolin mountain area. The parking lot just by the entrance is quiet at night, and the locals are happy for overnight campers. Alternatively, the family who run the small restaurant across from the convenience store are very friendly and they have a campground and private rooms at the home complex just across the suspension bridge. Ask inside for assistance.

Maolin to Fangliao

As we enter the last day in the southwest there is a sense of change in the air. Leaving the mountains behind and anticipating the ocean ahead, your mind floods with a sense of warmth, an understanding, a feeling, that the roads ahead offer a very different experience entirely.

This day offers the best transition you could hope for. The pineapple highway through Pingtung (屏東) glides, dips and pulls us toward the south, the waters and warmth ahead. The mountains sit silently to our side, enticing perhaps, but they loom as if envious of our new path, flatter, filled with possibilities of change and the promise of the warm winds of the Pacific Ocean.

This is our first day of truly simple, flat cycling. The distance is comfortable and the road is as flat and fast as can be while avoiding traffic and traffic lights. Taking in the pineapple highway (not an official name, but you will see what I mean) is a joyful journey. After leaving Maolin (茂林) glide yourself back toward the bakery at the junction of the T27. From here look back for one last view of the mountain before turning left at the entrance of the 185.

This simple and quiet road is as peaceful as it gets. Tracing the edges of the mountain range that rises up from the western plains, heading directly south you will have shade all morning while being in the sun for the afternoon. There is no real climb to speak of on the entire 185, perhaps a couple of small inclines, but after the previous week, nothing to blink an eye at. The road glides downhill, as if traveling in a southerly direction demands a downhill path.

This route touches upon some cute indigenous towns and villages, as well as waterfalls, some to dip your toes and some to admire from afar. You will be tempted, encouraged even, to turn and ride up into the foothills, as if hypnotized by the stunning cliffs and call of indigenous villages. The first one, just as you enter the 185, is Dajin waterfall (大津瀑布); a small detour from the roadside this quiet little spot is great for a refreshing dip in the heat of a summer's day. Next up are the villages of Qingshan (青山) and Koushe (口社). We follow a quaint bike path through a little village and a road masked by trees.

After a few more km the road climbs a little as you head toward the twin towns of Sandimen (三地門) and Shuimen (水門), which straddle either side of a wide estuary that comes pouring out of the mountains. Connected by three bridges, one impressively hanging high above the river, these two towns have lots of amenities. Sandimen sits high up on the hillside and acts as the entrance to a stunning mountain road that winds up to the rocky edges of it all.

Ignoring the mountain roads, we stay on the 185 and weave through the narrow old lanes of Shuimen, passing its famous and thunderous water canal that launches out of a hole in the cliff wall, and around its sweet indigenous stores selling locally made clothing and accessories. After rejoining the 185 through a beautiful tunnel with hanging ferns and dripping side walls we pass the Liangshan waterfalls (涼山瀑布) hiking trail and tourist recreation site.

From here the 185 starts to race away, your pace picking up as you push further downhill toward the southern coast. After a short while you can shift those gears; slow down, I beg you, no need to rush. We leave the highway and follow a beautifully secluded cycle path that leads us through rubber trees and myriad fruit tree farms, fish farms and rural homes. This route makes for a relaxing journey, with some great views and a remote feel. Consider taking a small detour to visit the alluring Wanjin (萬金) church, Taiwan's oldest basilica, such an unexpected piece of Spanish architecture set in a very lively courtyard.

After rejoining the 185 at the end of the bike path the single-lane highway starts to open up into a hot dry farm area, and you start to sense that the glistening blue waters of the Taiwan Strait might just, finally, be around the corner.

After a short set of turns near to the junction of the busy highway T1 you arrive immediately at Fangliao (枋寮), a lovely fishing town by the water's edge. Here there just so happens to be the Iron Horse Hostel, a sweet, rustic, cyclist-friendly spot, just 1km outside the quaint coastal town. We rarely promote specific guesthouses but, well, the bicycle hanging from the roof and the beautiful cyclist mural show the priorities of this well placed rest stop. Fangliao is perfectly situated to host all and everyone and is really the last staging post before we enter a whole new world.

After the day has finished you can take a walk along the ocean's edge, and revel in our journey so far. One more day and you will have reached Taiwan's most southerly point. The southwest is finished and with it the end of Taiwan's high mountains and shadows of sprawling industrial cities. Instead, stretching out in front of us are the alluring waters of the Taiwan Strait.

We are halfway through the journey, and yet it feels like it is beginning anew. Now we set off in search of the island's pristine southern coastline, crystal clear waters and a new tropical atmosphere. All this before we finally change directions and turn north toward the east coast highway, where new adventures await.

T20: the Southern Cross-Island Highway
What a highway this truly is, unlike the shorter Northern Cross-Island Highway, T7, that we tackled on day one of our route, or the defunct western approach of the T8 Central Cross-Island Highway. The T20, Taiwan's Southern Cross-Island Highway, is Taiwan's true, straight-shot route over its high mountains.

A wild and epic adventure that starts at Tainan train station and stretches all the way over the high mountain ranges and down the other side to the eastern train station of Chishang (池上). It is a stupendous ride, a fairly simple climb through some of Taiwan's highest ranges, with views of Jade Mountain and Yushan National Park (玉山國家公園).

On the eastern portion the road descends past the entrance to the Jiaming Lake hiking trail (嘉明湖), one of Taiwan's best multiday hikes. Then as it heads down toward the East Rift Valley it passes along a stunning, narrow mountain road, wedged between two towering peaks.

So that's the good, here's the bad...Due to extensive damage from a typhoon in 2009 the road's high pass section remained closed for over a decade. It fully reopened in 2022 after some extensive rebuilding work on its central section. Sadly, this is a heavily controlled road with specific opening and closing times. Restricting traffic numbers and...banning cyclists entirely. As of the time of printing, there is no plan to reopen the road to cyclists.

This frustration aside, there are still options for cyclists along this road. The western approach rises up to the control point at the mountain village of Meishan (梅山). It is a worthwhile trip, there is free camping in the village and you could spend your evening persuading a van or RV heading over the pass to give you and your bikes a free ride.

Equally up the eastern approach you can ride all the way up to the entrance of the Jiaming Lake trailhead and enter for the multiday hike, just be warned the climb up will add an extra edge to your hiking trip. Check out this website for up-to-date information on road access, and let's keep our collective fingers crossed for an open cyclist route soon ysnp.gov.tw/en/highway/C001300.

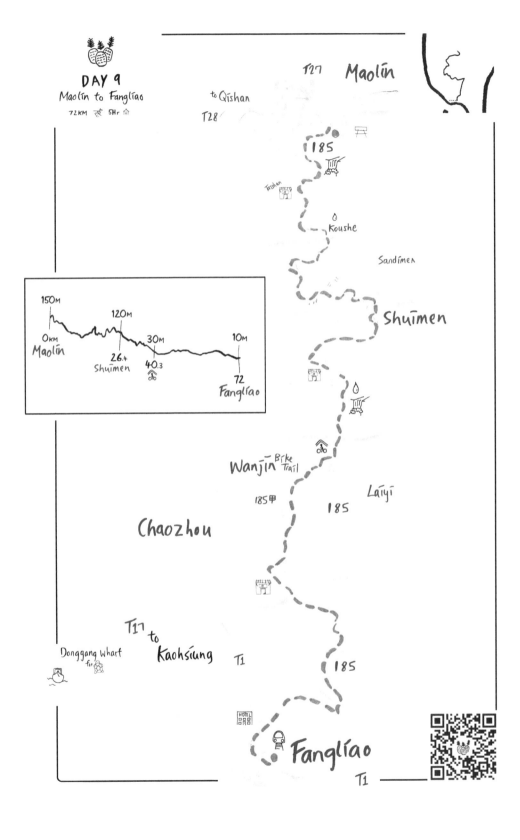

DAY 9
Maolin to Fangliao
72KM 🚲 5Hr 🏠

to Qishan

T27 Maolin

T28

185

Tsishan

Koushe

Sandimen

Shuimen

150M
0KM
Maolin
120M
30M
26.4
Shuimen
40.3
10M
72
Fangliao

Wanjin ─ Bike Trail

185甲

185

Laiyi

Chaozhou

T17 to
Kaohsiung
Donggang Wharf
for 🐢

T1

185

HOTEL

Fangliao

T1

DAY 9

72KM 🏃 5Hr 🏠

0.00 Start at the mouth of Maolin! Begin at the junction of highway T27 and the entrance to the 高132, outside the Svongvong Bakery (蝶手感烘焙).

0.10 Head straight across the bridge, keeping Maolin (茂林) behind you, we cross into Pingtung (屏東) County.

0.40 Turn left onto the 185. After the first bend the junction appears suddenly. Our road for the day starts here. Look out for the 3D mural on the stone wall just before the turning.

2.70 On your left is the entrance to the Dajin waterfall (大津瀑布). The simple walk up the hillside takes around 20 minutes to lovely shallow pools and falls nestled in the mountain's foliage. On a quiet morning it's lush up here.

   The fields of pineapple start shortly after this point. Throughout the day we pass many different fruit farms but seeing the spiky crowns of the pineapples wash over the landscape is wonderful, especially when they are a bright purple, creating a fantastic contrast to the bright green of the mountains behind.

8.05 On the left at this small crossroads you will notice a quaint old bicycle route sign, follow this route for a lovely road trail through old indigenous villages that are perched on the sloped hills. The locals are friendly here and don't be surprised to be invited in for a drink. Be warned, heading this way is tiring, hot, and turns this day's ride into a bit of a slog due to the steep roads and added km. Still lovely and worth considering.

11.7 If you need supplies, then at the crossroads with the giant yellow octopus sculpture, a handy if strange marker, turn right and travel along for 1km to reach Taishan (泰山) for stores and tea shops. Return along the same road to rejoin the 185.

14.5 Turn left under the archway onto a side village lane. At the entrance of Koushe (口社) a large concrete archway crosses the road as it curves right; turn off the highway.

Follow the lane through the village as it passes homes and a lovely little stream by the church. Leave the village over the second bridge and pass along a parallel road to the highway, momentarily lording it over those below.

15.0 Drop back onto the highway.

17.9 An alternative climb through to Shuimen (水門) and Sandimen (三地門) through an indigenous community and (even quieter) country roads, cutting a little distance off an otherwise dull piece of road. Notice the hunting scene adorning the top of the village gate.

At the turning take the smaller side road, don't ride up to the village. This small lane winds through some pretty forest and past wild grasslands, ending just beyond the village. Turn right and then head it up a few twists and turns before it levels out at the top of the hill. At the road's end, turn left back onto the 185 for the last km to the towns. If you stay on the 185 you will endure a softer but longer climb, both reach the same point at the top of a small hill.

19.4 Turn left staying on the 185. At the traffic light it feels like you are changing roads, but actually the 185 continues from here.

20.5 A long, soft climb starts as you head toward Sandimen. At the top on the hill the large suspension bridge can be seen in the distance.

23.4 Brow of the hill and the alt route rejoins here. Carry on straight, a few more turns uphill.

24.5 Top of climb, short descent toward the junction for Sandimen.

25.0 Head straight at the junction with highway T24. Stay to the right and carry on down the hill.

25.3 Head straight, do not turn right onto the first bridge. Follow the road further down to the second bridge, follow signs for Shuimen.

25.5 Turn right onto the smaller old bridge. Just right for stopping and gazing up at the towering mountains with the suspension bridge floating in view.

25.7 Straight after the bridge the road kicks up and enters the little village of Shuimen.

25.8 Lean left at the village Y junction. Here there are local shops selling traditional clothing and other handmade crafts, along with eateries. Take the left-hand road.

The little village is worth wandering around, especially to walk along the deep canal that runs right through the middle of the houses.

25.9 The mouth of the river that gives the village its name. Water gushes out from this hole in the mountainside at an incredible rate even during low water levels.

26.1 Head straight at the crossroads.

26.8 Head straight at the larger crossroads. Restaurant and large convenience store here.

28.1 Turn left back onto the 185 at the tight junction with a signal, following signs for the 185 and Liangshan Recreation Area (涼山遊憩區). There is a store here, the last one directly on the main route to Fangliao (枋寮).

28.8 Pass under beautiful foliage that hangs invitingly over the entrance of a short tunnel. Once on the other side soaring mountains again reach out in front, with moisture palpable in the air, if it isn't raining already.

29.6 Entrance to the Liangshan Recreation Area. After this point the road undulates for a few km up and over some low hills.

Liangshan waterfalls
A ticketed entrance to atmospheric, if short, hill trails and beautiful, viewing-only waterfalls. The main trail up the back to the high falls is fun but sadly, right before the wild streams high up into the jungle canopy the trail is closed, due to danger. But the walk is pretty if you haven't spent any time in the jungle yet. Outside the parking lot has a large grass area and well-maintained public restrooms, open all night.

38.6 Turn right onto the hidden bike path, at the start of an army base. Leave the main road just after the checkpoint booth at the corner of the large army base. If you miss the initial turning onto the path there is another a few meters down the road.

40.0 STOP! Turn diagonally keeping on the bike path, following on-the-ground km markers. At the end of the base wall the bike path crosses a road, taking a diagonal turn leaving the main road. Follow this path, keeping an eye on signs both on the ground and at junctions for the next few km's. It's almost impossible to describe this route, just follow the painted signs for the next 8km, heading mainly south but watching out for signposts that show turnings.

Wanjin Sugar Bicycle Network and Wanjin Basilica
This varied and chaotically wonderful bicycle network connects the Wanjin Basilica down through to Chaozhou (潮州) to the sugar factory in Nanzhou (南州), linking all of the county's highlights and farming areas. We will use this network over the next few km to take a laid-back path down the side of the 185. There are also wonderful routes that head west to the cities of Pingtung (屏東) and Chaozhou as well as the Wanjin Basilica (萬金) itself.

Here at this junction is a road that leads directly west to the village of Wanjin, which is famed for its Dominican church. Taiwan's oldest basilica is so out of place in this country, let alone in this small flat area of the rural farming south. Well worth checking out. Ride for 1km west, as you enter the town carry on through the lanes, turning left once you reach the center of this lively town. The simplest route back to the 185 is to return the way you came.

48.6　Cross over the main road, 185甲, onto the farming road. There is no road sign here but the end of the bikeway is marked by some bollards, mini traffic lights and on the right by an information board of the bikeway.

　　　Head directly across the road opposite the path's end. Technically part of the bikeway but unmarked. Follow this straight tree-lined track for 3km.

　　　At this junction of the 185甲 you can turn left off the bikeway and rejoin the main 185 road at the village of Laiyi. You will find convenience stores there.

<u>51.7</u>　Turn right back onto the 185. The track finishes at a small junction with the main highway. Turn right back onto the main 185 highway, heading west. The road widens here into a mess of a junction where the 185 turns south, don't follow it here, just head along the road until the village.

<u>52.5</u>　Turn left at the crossroads, leaving the highway. At a small crossroads turn left at the mural and lights, into the village where you will pass a few houses and some small shops.

<u>53.0</u>　Head straight, rejoin the 185 at the traffic lights at the end of the village.

54.5　After a bridge another series of bike paths shadows the main road. These cute, tree-lined paths are great for a bit of shade. Unfortunately, they un-ceremoniously stop and start at junctions and bridges, making them not really worth the effort.

　　　Stay on the 185 as it snakes its way south. The road is completely flat from here, passing alongside fruit farms and rice fields. The day is almost over as the air starts to change, a sea breeze starts to waft across our path and the blue sky gives the sense that the ocean is not too far away.

<u>68.8</u>　<u>STOP!</u> Turn right at km marker 68. Just before the end of 185 turn down a nondescript, unmarked side road that heads west through farmland.

Dongliu Ferry Terminal, Donggang
This little wharf is the jumping-off point for one of Taiwan's best island adventures, Xiaoliuqiu (小琉球). Situated midway along Kaohsiung's coastline. Donggang is an uncomplicated arrival and departure point. Traveling along highway T17 it can be reached easily from central Kaohsiung and is only a one-hour ride along the highway, west, from Fangliao. Just turn left onto the T17 after 1km along highway T1 west. See p140 for more details on the wonderful turtle-spotting island of Xiaoliuqiu.

If you miss the turning just carry on down the 185 until it reaches the T1, at the junction turn right for 2km until you reach the gas station at the main junction.

70.3 Turn left at the village crossroads. You will almost immediately spot the T1 junction just 200m away.

70.5 Head straight, crossing highway T1. At the end of the road, you come upon a busy junction on highway T1. Straight across at this junction is a gas station, we are heading for the green tin roof of the bicycle hostel. The painted cyclist mural on its side wall comes into view as you cross the main road.

70.7 The Iron Horse Hostel (鐵騎休息棧) is perfectly set up as a resting place for cyclists. We don't usually prescribe specific hotels but we will make an exception here. The owner is very kind and helpful in the quiet inclusive little space. The name is lovely, harking back to the colloquial term used for the steel steeds when first introduced to Taiwan.

From the junction of T1 and the entrance of the Iron Horse Hostel, head down Zhongshan Road (中山路), toward Fangliao, ignoring highway T1 for now.

71.5 After crossing the railway tracks our road bends to the left into the center of Fangliao.

72.0 Finish in central Fangliao! At the town's crossroads there are several stores, breakfast restaurants and the town's train station. Perfectly positioned at the crossroads with the southern peninsula, the southwest, as well as Donggang harbor. Just 20km away, Fangliao is a very well-positioned stopping point for most tours. There isn't much in the way of lodgings but there are guesthouses in the town and further along the coastal road in Fangshan (枋山). Stay at the Iron Horse Hostel if you can.

The oceanfront is just three blocks from this main crossroads down the street opposite the train station. There are some cute sculptures, viewpoints, a short walkway and a small park with public bathrooms along the front here. Sadly, no beach, instead watch the sunset over the waters as they lap against the sea defenses below.

Fangliao Train Station
This is the last stop before trains head across the mountains to the east coast. Should you wish to skip the southern coast, or if you took a train from Tainan (台南) or Kaohsiung (高雄) to skip some of the duller parts of the southwest, Fangliao station makes a good spot to start your ride again.

A bike-friendly train to Taitung (台東) passes through around 10am every day. Local trains allowing bicycles travel to Kaohsiung and the west throughout the day.

Clockwise Notes
South West

Fangliao through Pingtung, Kaohsiung and Tainan counties

Heading north up from Fangliao along the provincial road 185 is as much a breeze as it is in a southerly direction. Yes, technically more uphill than down, this flat road has very few sections that really feel like any kind of uphill. Finding the mini side bicycle route is difficult heading north; sticking to the main road is the best route if you don't want to spend time searching for the bicycle path's tricky entrance. The ride west along the T27 from Maolin toward Qishan is equally flat, and simple.

For the clockwise route head all the way to the center of Qishan and then head north along the T3 to Dapu and the Zengwen Reservoir. This is a more direct path than we recommend on our main route when heading south but in this direction the T3 is a comfortable route that requires minimal fuss. Finding the reservoir's dam road and riding up is not nearly as enjoyable in this direction.

For a completely different route north from Fangliao consider a trip to Xiaoliuqiu island via Donggang harbor and then a ride up to Kaohsiung city along highway T17. This highway also eventually takes a coastal route north into the heart of Tainan city, Taiwan's oldest and, we think, yes with a strong bias, its best city along the western coast. From Tainan you can take highway T20 to Yujing, Taiwan's mango capital, where you can rejoin the T3 and the last 20km north to Dapu village and the free campground by the waterside.

If you find yourself in Tainan and don't want a ride up through to Dapu and the reservoir road, consider taking a trip to Guanzhiling hot spring village and the beautiful coffee road that leads up to Chiayi county and our alternative western hill route. See p54 for more info.

A note on riding north along Taiwan's Cycle Route 1
If you ride up north from Tainan along the main CR1 be warned that large portions of the ride are unimaginably dull. While some of the smaller towns and villages you pass are lovely and the communities in Taiwan always offer a great experience the main route that runs up to Chiayi and beyond skips, avoids, and ignores the beauty on this side of the island. The western flat regions cannot match the east coast beauty or the natural greens and blues of the East Rift Valley. Industrialization, large swathes of agricultural land and overpopulated urban centers often leave riders uninspired. Our Dapu to Dapu alternative route offers a much more rich experience of Taiwan's western highlights as well as a richer sense of the island's beauty.

Outlying Islands

A t first glance Taiwan can seem to lack those tropical paradise enclaves so often associated with islands in South Asia. But look closely and there are sprinkles of that laid-back beach life everywhere—nowhere more so than on Taiwan's many outlying islands.

It would be a lie if I said we had visited all of the islands that are under Taiwanese control. There are many islands very far from Taiwan's main island. The Matsu Islands (馬祖列島), for example, are a ten-hour ferry journey away and Kinmen (金門) Island sits less than 10km from China's east coast, quite a journey from Taiwan, accessible only by air, or ferry via China first.

Luckily there are some incredible islands situated just off Taiwan's coastline that hit the right mark, that overwhelm the senses and are truly mind blowing.

The islands in this section offer the perfect combination of remote getaways, heartwarming local communities with unique Pacific island heritages as well as great beaches, marine wildlife and some of the best diving/snorkeling that Taiwan has to offer.

The idyllic turtle waters of Xiaoliuqui (小琉球) and the orchid beauty of Lanyu (蘭嶼) are accessible by regular ferries that depart from ports right on our main route's path. These bicycle-friendly journeys, with life-affirming, laid-back ease, help you to change the pace and explore with a relaxed Pacific island feel. With warm indigenous populations at the helm, tourist development of these islands has been kept to a minimum. Think less Phuket and more sleepy fishing village and quiet turquoise waters.

For this journey, we only deep dive (no pun intended) on these two island getaways. Taiwan has plenty of other outer islands close by worth considering. A good exploration is warranted on Penghu (澎湖), a wild archipelago, connected by ferry from Chaiyi (嘉義) and Tainan (台南) in the west. There is the volcanic rock of Turtle Island (Guishan Dao 龜山島), famed for its turtle-like shape, with day trips available from Yilan (宜蘭).

Then there is also the popular couples' getaway and diving site of Green Island (綠島), the big sister situated alongside Lanyu in the southeast. These two can be visited in tandem but visiting both can have a huge impact on your itinerary, especially if a typhoon rolls in. And for my money, Lanyu offers just that slightly more out-there adventure.

Both of the routes we highlight will add anywhere from two to four days to your itinerary. By all means stay longer, but a minimum of two days is needed when factoring in ferry journeys and route alterations.

By far the closest island to Taiwan's shoreline is Xiaoliuqiu, situated just off the southwest coast in Pingtung County. This popular little island is reached by ferry from Donggang (東港) pier, which is just 13km south of Chaozhou (潮州) train station and 20km west of Fangliao, our Day 9 destination. If you are in Kaohsiung follow T17 for 20km riding east of the downtown area.

Xiaoliuqiu

The ferry across to Xiaoliuqiu, also called Liuqiu, takes around 30 minutes and the ticket for a bicycle is a modest 50NTD. An adult ticket costs around 400NTD return. With a limited public service and two private companies running the short route, there is an abundance of ferries to the island and back every day. But be careful if you intend to make use of the day you arrive — note that there is often an early afternoon gap in services. Current times can be found at the useful island tourism website, *xiaoliuqiuguide.com*.

Did we mention the island is small? The loop road that runs around the entire coastline is just 12km starting and returning at the main port of Baisha (白沙) to the north. Apart from the loop road, there is one other main road that links through the center of the island, running southwest from Baisha down to the southern tip. Several minor roads link across the island, all paved.

The island is not flat; the undulating coast road is a joy to ride, just watch out for the initial steep climb up from the harbor when heading in an counter-clockwise direction.

Due to the island's position so close to one of the country's largest cities and with fantastic reputations for its snorkeling, diving, beaches and seafood restaurants, it gets overrun on holidays and hot summer weekends. Expect to have the island nearly to yourself midweek, the feeling of the place between these two times is incredible. We cannot advise this strongly enough: visit outside busy times, please. It is the difference between being on a near-private tropical paradise and in the middle of a claustrophobic festival. Just ask the local residents. Over recent years attempts have been made to control the number of visitors during high demand, with boat trips reserved for locals and those with prebooked accommodation.

Xiaoliuqiu's real draw is its giant sea turtle population. Shallow reef edges, an abundance of yummy sea grass and protection from big ocean currents have made this a haven for hawksbill and greenback turtles. With attempts to maintain the environment and a long-standing ban on hunting the hard shells, seeing these stunning creatures is a year-round assuredness. You can spot

them easily from the beaches to the northwest and with fantastic snorkeling opportunities to swim alongside these wondrous creatures. The nesting beaches are often out of bounds and you must follow all rules when interacting with this ecosystem, as touching or coming too close to sea turtles can have a huge impact on their well-being. The coastal reef that surrounds the island has suffered years of erosion, environmental damage and exploitation and as a result is in the early stages of renewal, as a protected area; touching or taking any coral is an absolute no-no. Take memories, nothing else.

We recommend camping on this island; there are so many lovely spots overlooking the ocean, but without any official camping areas left be sure to respect the spot you find, pack away early and take out any trash. The old campground of Samaji is still maintained despite no official operation and its bathrooms are no longer 24hr. The area's well-kept lawn sits on the oceanfront with a wide panoramic vista of the Taiwan Strait and is well worth a nighttime visit no matter where you stay on the island. At night, the lights of Kaohsiung can be seen in the distance while stars still shine above your head. The site is in the northwest just along from one of the best beaches for turtle spotting.

For a more secluded sunbathing spot, travel down the western shore looking for any small coves that have golden sand beaches and no development. The sunset point on the southern tip of the island is lovely at the end of hot day as the red sunset stretches out across turquoise waters.

There are two main towns, with shops and restaurants, that host the majority of the local population. Baishawei (白沙尾) to the north surrounds the small fishing port and is the entrance point for ferries. The larger town of Liuqiu sits in the center of the island, with roads running north, southeast and west connecting to the loop road. Both of these hubs are little more than small villages with a few seafood restaurants, tea shops and locally owned clothing stores, such pretty environments to wander around. In the evening is when they come alive as locals and tourists mingle down the quiet streets in search of some food.

The island has diving centers as well as equipment hire spots, although purchasing a cheap snorkeling set is also possible from small beach stores by the port. Travel around this quiet little place and you will quickly fall into the slower pace of life. Grab your mask and snorkel and roll those wheels around — you will soon learn the chill life. Swimming among the sea turtles is as life-affirming as it gets, and the fresh ocean air that drifts across certainly sweeps away the dust and dirt from days on the road. We cannot recommend Liuqiu enough, one of Taiwan's true highlights.

Lanyu

Much more of an adventure than the other islands close to Taiwan, Lanyu, or Orchid Island, is a true island paradise. A fun and proud local population lives on the edges of the world. This windswept idyll is a distinct footprint in the vastness of the great Pacific Ocean.

The Tao (also called Yami) people settled on this island long before the Chinese came to Taiwan, and they can trace their history back further than almost all other indigenous groups on the surrounding islands. Larger than Xiaoliuqiu and with a very distinctive look, Lanyu doesn't disappoint. Even as you approach from the edges of the horizon, great green peaks lift out of the waters covered in jungle vegetation whilst crystal blue waters surround the island, filled with marine life and underwater coral worlds. Great waves crash up against the volcanic rock that protects the island's inhabitants and allows for villages to exist so close to the ocean. This stunning island would not look out of place in Hawaii or Polynesia. It needs to be seen to be believed.

Two hours by ferry from either Kenting (墾丁) or Taitung (台東), the twin islands of Lanyu and Green Island are at the mercy of the weather and before tropical storms or typhoons the ferry services are shut off, leaving the island adrift. There are worse things than spending a few extra days on an island such as this during a storm. But just make sure to consider this when planning your schedule.

With a coastal loop road spanning some 38km it takes a little while to ride around the island, but the road is relatively flat and simple with some incredible sections of ocean-hugging bliss. Due to the mountain range covering the entire island the east and west shores are split, with the island's little villages situated on either side; the north and south capes are more wild and rugged due to their exposure to the elements.

Despite having just one loop road and one central mountain-crossing road, there is plenty to explore on the island. Gold sand beaches, hidden caves, snorkeling spots, diving, hill hikes, clifftop lighthouses and sunset points. But on top of all this there is the local community, with its traditional underground houses and unique food, language and traditions to interact with and learn from. You can easily spend four or five days here without running out of joy.

Two ferry companies run daily services between Taitung's Fugang (富岡) port in the east and Houbihu (後壁湖) port in Kenting that provide stops at Lanyu and Green Island. This route is perfect for anyone wishing to skip the ride from Kenting to Taitung and instead ferry across to the islands and then head to the next destination after.

From either port the route to Lanyu takes around two hours in fair weather. Schedules, booking companies and information at bluebus.com.tw.

Tickets need to be reserved in advance during high season and national holidays but other times you should be able to pick your tickets up on the day. Bicycles are inexpensive to take on the ferries and you just need to pay a fixed cash amount directly to the boat master...this is a set price that is nonnegotiable. The boat's luggage manager, who will be situated at the onramp as the ferry is loaded, will direct you for loading onto the ferry; follow any instructions as best you can.

Seeing the beauty of Lanyu by bike is at its best during a bright sunny morning, which is not that uncommon out over the Pacific Ocean. Although storms are possible at any point during the year, the island usually has some warning before larger weather fronts arrive. High winds as well as cold winter weather are something to consider before taking a trip; the best months to arrive are similar to Taiwan's main island, March and April or after 10/10 festival in October/November, but if there isn't a typhoon a visit in the summer will give you a relief from the oppressive heat of the main island as winds help to keep the temperature lower out here.

Unlike Xiaoliuqiu, Lanyu's remote location means it is a much quieter affair. Without day-trippers, it does not suffer the same overwhelming crush of people. However, with limited daily ferries servicing the island as well as a maximum capacity of people allowed, planning during peak seasons is a must. The reward for this little extra planning: an unforgettable remote trip that is unique as a bicycle touring ride in Taiwan. The views from atop the lighthouse grounds in the center of the island's mountain are incredible and truly awe inspiring. Just be aware it is an extremely tough climb to get up, with the last km having plenty of grades over 20 percent. The main connecting road that crosses over is steep but relatively short and not too taxing to ride up, outside of the heat of the day.

While on Lanyu consider staying at a family homestay on the eastern side of the island, in the villages of Yeyin (野銀) and Dongqing (東清). Yeyin is a perfectly laid-back place with some quaint homestays that are happy to accommodate cyclists. People can discreetly camp wild on the island, the southern end of the island near to Dragon Head Rock is a good quiet area. This island is sacred to its inhabitants, with many grounds being sites of community importance or private farming area, so tread lightly. There are a couple of paid campgrounds such as Jimmy Explorer campsite to the southwest of the island. Book your accommodation in advance during the typical high seasons.

There is so much to say about this island but best to leave it up to the imagination. Just get out there, experience this unique environment for yourself, oh and don't forget to try the taro ice cream (芋頭冰淇淋)!!

Táiwan Tail

Golden sand beaches alongside
  bucket and-spade villages
    all along this southern peninsula.
Remote island adventures are just
  a ferry ride away and cliff edge views
to leave your jaw hanging around every corner.

Climb through hillside jungle, glide around hidden ocean roads and camp by the island's best surf, sunbathing, and palm tree spots.

Here at the bottom of it all,

welcome to Taiwan's southern tip.

Taiwan Tail

aiwan's tropical southern tip is a wonderful peninsula of beach culture, pristine oceans, national parks and relaxation. As soon as we head along the southern highway we are greeted with the crystal waters of the Taiwan Strait. The enticingly close island of Xiaoliuqiu can be seen on the horizon as we roll down into Kenting.

Our ride takes us all the way to the southernmost point. On the way you can stop off at waterside cocktail bars and restaurants, or perhaps you prefer secluded hidden beaches instead; whatever your vibe is, it can be found down here. Ease up on the pedals, we are halfway through our journey so why not take a day or two off? Rest up by the beach, sit on a café balcony, swing in a hammock by the river in a serene campground or perhaps stand on a clifftop looking at the world of ocean stretching out before us.

Half of this peninsula is Taiwan's busiest tourist spot. But, as you will read, the population here is not one for overdevelopment; instead it is a fairly calm way of life for those that like to keep their communities subtle and understated. The east coast of the peninsula is wild and untamed. The national park here might not have the draw of those in the northern mountains, but the eastern shores offer a sense of calm, especially by the quiet surf village of Gongkou.

Riders often opt to skip this section of the country as the hill crossing over to the east coast sits at the northern end of the peninsula. But unless your time is that tight we really recommend taking the day, you won't be disappointed.

Finally, we start to head up Taiwan's famous east coast. We leave the peninsula along stunning coastline, past hot springs and up switchback hillsides. Stopping for lunch at wonderfully local restaurants, we then ride through grasslands to beautiful hilltop views before one of the best descents in the country.

The east coast stretches out before us as we glide around the traffic-free road. It is a delight, as are all of the adventures had in the warm tropical south.

Fangliao to Kenting

Sitting at the bottom of Pingtung County (屏東) is the beautiful peninsula of Kenting (墾丁), ringed by the stunning coastline of both the Taiwan Strait to the west and the Pacific Ocean to the east. The ocean rarely leaves our sights as we coast around the turquoise shores.

Boasting national parks, white sand beaches, clear warm waters, clifftop views and cute seaside towns, this really is Taiwan's holiday hotspot. As we finally start our coastal route, we quickly head for the southern tip, begin our journey north, and start to feel the laid-back life found up and down the eastern coast. The atmosphere from here all the way to the northeast is markedly different from the misty mountains of the interior.

This day is a breeze—and chances are you will also experience one or two strong ones along the way. High winds often rumble across the western coastline here, typically heading in a southern direction you could be lucky and have it at your back. Heading north can be another story altogether.

There are several route options across the hills that separate the two coasts, but don't think you can find a way that avoids the climb. There is no complete coastal route on the east side of the peninsula. All routes lead to one single point at the top of a hill pass, but trust us when we say it's a worthwhile adventure even for those who avoid climbing, this is a special treat for the senses. If you don't plan on exploring Kenting and want to skip the peninsula then head for road 199 as the best route over. This rural and quiet crossing starts at the town of Checheng (車城) in the west and climbs softly, avoiding the bulk of the traffic, and wind, that head over the main T9 highway.

Riding down from Fangliao (枋寮) and across the mountain in a day is totally possible, just leave yourself plenty of time and hit the crossing before the heat of the day rises too high. But adding one more day to explore the southern beaches is well worth it. Taiwan's southern tip, its beaches and surrounding region deserve exploration, it is a stunning region and you might just love it.

As we leave Fangliao we find ourselves, for the first time, on a coastal road, with near-constant views of the shimmering blue Taiwan Strait. Despite little to speak of for the first stretch beyond the occasional rest stop and roadside coffee pull-ins, it certainly is not a dull ride. The highway is wide with plenty of space for cyclists in a dedicated lane. The hills become more arid, traffic flows, and buildings line the road, but it is a pleasant ride south with the ocean just on your shoulder. Highway T1 that starts all the way up in Taipei finally ends as we enter the peninsula, and the coastal highway of the T26 is our main road for the day.

First up we pass through the town of Checheng and the chance to cross over the hills here along the provincial road 199. Instead we keep heading south, but soon turn off the highway.

Like everywhere in the world, Kenting's main beaches get overrun on a hot summer's weekend and during national holidays. It is Taiwan's true tourist location, but don't imagine overdevelopment and huge resorts. The island has largely resisted this and as a result much of the coastline is still wild and untamed. Even the town of Kenting more closely resembles a cute bucket-and-spade seaside village rather than any kind of party city.

After passing the town we go in search of Taiwan's southern tip. This is a worthwhile visit, where the two waters connect and Taiwan opens up into the big blue beyond. A real edge-of-the-world vibe lingers. The point offers a view into the endless Pacific, as well as handy stargazing at night. Leaving the southern tip requires a short climb up to the hilltops overlooking the dramatic east coast. There are sweet cafés along this climb, as well as an easy-to-spot military satellite base.

Our day ends as we ride across the plateau on top of the cliffs. Stunning views along the coastline at several off-road lookouts are worth stopping at before we finally drop quickly onto the east coast as we head to the surf village of Gangkou (港口), where our day ends.

Arriving at this surfing village you instantly feel the good vibes. This little junction village comes complete with a long, golden sand beach, some great local eateries and, just around the corner, a unique and hidden campsite, nestled by a river among the dragon fruit farms. You can spend an evening here chatting to the affable owners or take a drink by the quiet waters as the sound of crashing waves echoes around.

If you have time take an extra day off from the route here, spend a day riding around the peninsula, visiting the beaches, take in some surf or just ride around the many coastal roads in the area. It is the highlight of Taiwan's beach culture, cafés dot the roadside and there are plenty of quiet hidden beaches all over the peninsula. So, pack your sunscreen, a towel, perhaps a good book, and find a spot to unwind.

DAY 10
Fangliao to Kenting

75KM 🚲 6Hr ⛰

to T17 T1 185

T1

Fangliao

T1

T9

T26

Checheng T199

200
Hengchun

T26

Gangkou

200.4

Shady
Tree

South Bay

Houbihu
Port

Kenting

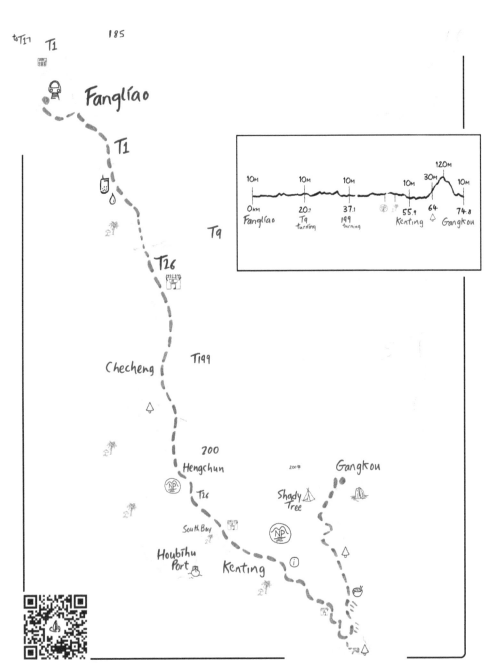

Inset elevation profile:

| 10M | 10M | 10M | | 10M | 30M | 120M | 10M |

0KM   20.7   37.1   55.9   64   74.8
Fangliao   T9   199   Kenting   Gangkou
           turning   turning

DAY 10

75KM 🚲 6Hr ⛰️

0.00 Start in Fangliao at the main crossroads! Head east on the main street, the road eventually passes fish farms until you hit the T1 again.

2.90 Turn right onto the T1 at the road's end. Watch for dashing traffic as you merge and start your journey south.

9.90 Large rest stop with several stores. Worth a break as it is our first beach on the journey. The restaurant inside serves ice creams and smoothies with beachside seating.

    The road from here flows along the Taiwan Strait coastline. Perhaps not as spectacular as the eastern coastline, but the atmosphere down here feels so alien from the first half of this tour. The cool mountain air is long behind us as the hot southern air quickly heats up the day.

    This road always puts a wide smile on my face, nothing beats rolling toward sun, sea and fresh adventures.

20.4 In the distance, as if a mirage, the road ascends high into the sky, at a seemingly impossible gradient. Don't worry, this overpass heading onto the T9 can be avoided.

    If you are planning on skipping the southern ride and taking highway T9 up to Shouka (壽卡) Pass then you can climb and turn here, but there is another turning a little later that eases you up and avoids both the climb and the strong headwinds that rumble down the hillside.

20.7 Head straight, keep to the right in the scooter lane. As you approach the rising overpass the road splits into myriad lanes. Ignore all signs as they are for cars, instead just keep to the furthest right-hand lane and follow the signs for scooters/bicycles as we slip under the main road as it lifts up into the sky. We pass coolly under the raised road.

21.4 Merge onto the T26. The small slip road rejoins the highway heading south. The T1 has finished, welcome to the T26.

22.7 Head straight, staying on highway T26.

    If you are taking the T9 up to the pass then here is your turning, following signs. It is a pretty ride but this narrow single lane is hectic with traffic as it's the main route for crossing the island. Expect little space as cars and trucks pass closely. Until you reach the car-only tunnel near to the peak of the climb you will have large vehicles on your shoulder. After reaching the tunnel turn right, staying on the now T9戊. This final section of the climb is beautiful, quiet and devoid of traffic.

    The quieter and rural road 199 further south is a more enjoyable ride up to the east coast.

    Find convenience stores and other shops here to escape the heat of the day.

35.0 Checheng (車城) coastal road. Turning on the right for a sweeping coastal road that follows the shoreline for a few km's around the back of the town. This area is quiet and used mainly by people looking for a spot to set up their fishing rods. There are lots of side roads that pull through a small line of trees and onto the beach beyond. This road eventually loops back around to Checheng.

36.9 Central Checheng. Restaurants, stores, etc. Here is the first turning for route 199.

37.1 Turning for the 199, a perfect road that passes up and over to the Shouka hilltop pass, joining the T9 for its descent to the east coast.

    If you don't plan on heading down to Kenting (墾丁) then we recommend taking this route. This road passes through quiet indigenous villages, gorgeously lush grasslands, an impressive dam and historical hillside tribes, including the famous town of Mudan (牡丹).

    The road climbs comfortably until you reach the large dam. From there you have a stiff 3km climb before it evens out again just before the old village. It climbs simply from here on out until you reach the junction at Shouka Pass, 40km along the road.

39.1 A right-hand turn that takes you onto a coastal road running around the edge of Kenting National Park (墾丁國家公園).

44.4 Lean right and stay on the T26. The left turn here at the entrance to the town of Hengchun takes you onto the 200. If you don't want to go to the southern point or beaches today but plan to take a rest day to explore instead, turn here onto the 200. It leads you directly to the town of Gangkou (港口) and the campground at Shady Tree.

50.0 If you are looking for Houbi port (後壁湖碼頭) for ferries to Lanyu (蘭嶼) and Green Island then turn right here. See our side trip info to Lanyu for more details on the ferry, p144.

51.5 Houbi Beach (後壁海灘), the first golden sand beach in Kenting. Probably the best beach for a swim and a relaxing day with plenty of restaurants and cafés nearby. Public bathrooms here.

55.9 Kenting town. The police station, information center and public bathrooms are situated along the main street. A perfect place to leave the bikes and explore. Kenting Beach is down a side road, turn right just as you enter the town.

56.5 Kenting National Park entrance and visitor center. The road widens for the next few km and with substantially less traffic.

63.4 Small village with convenience store. Turn here to visit the lighthouse; don't be confused, the lighthouse is not the southern tip. That is a little further up the road.

The one climb of the day starts here, beginning with two long, sharp switchbacks. The turning for the island's southern tip is just around a couple of bends. Make sure you stop here.

Back on the main road carry on up the climb. The road straightens here and loses its steepness. After 3km you reach the top. Look out for cows that may be wandering as you pass a small village, army radar bases and observatory.

Taiwan's Southernmost Point (台灣最南點)
After you head around the second switchback you can spot the sign for Taiwan's Southernmost Point, turn right here and wander down as the steep road heads to the short trailhead.

As you descend you pass some abandoned buildings, keep left. Eventually you reach a wooden barrier blocking motor vehicles from entering down a cute brick-cobbled walkway that passes through a grove. Follow this path for 500m until it opens out to show the sail-inspired sculpture at the southern tip viewing platform. This is a great rest stop that is super quiet at nighttime with unspoiled vista views of the starlit sky and vast, endless ocean.

66.8   Rest stop with great views up the east coast cliff line. Worth stretching the legs here. From this spot the road descends to our destination.
67.4   Another, and perhaps better, view of the coast heading north. Our first real feeling of being on the east coast.
         The winding road bends down fast to a beach and fishing village. Ride the last few small bumps to the village of Gangkou.
74.8   Finish at the surf junction of Gangkou! This village has small eateries, a famous surfing beach as well as a couple of guesthouses. We are going to tell you about a little hidden gem: a campground nestled just out of town in among the local fruit farms.

Shady Tree Campground
This open and inviting campground comes with lots of character as well as a large grass lawn to pitch your tent. The friendly owner knows how to have a good time and is a fountain of knowledge of the area, surfing and alternative riding options. Sit back and enjoy the evening atmosphere at the outdoor kitchen/bar by the riverside as monkeys play in the trees and the lights from nearby farms flicker in the warm air. If you are not camping they also offer simple, but comfortable, camping huts for an outdoor experience.

At the junction in Gangkou the T26 ends; turn left following the 200 甲 west. After 1km a small store is on your right. Look for surfboard signs on your left for Shady Tree Campground. Turn left here. Follow the weaving farm lane for 500m. At the T junction turn left down the sandy bank and cross the river along the concrete platform. Climb up the other side and immediately find yourself at the campground. Notice the fairy lights hanging in the trees and over the entrance to the communal bar and kitchen. They welcome drop-ins but you can message them in advance at facebook.com/rgcamping.

Kenting to Dawu

Well, well, either way, counter- or clockwise, high mountains or flat lands, novice or experienced, racer or laid-back adventurer, you have arrived at this point. There is one inevitability with cycling around Taiwan, one road, one point, where all will meet: welcome to Shouka (壽卡) Pass.

All cyclists must pass across this hilltop rest stop along the old T9 highway, the only road that allows cyclists to connect across the south of the island. This rest stop, managed by a local indigenous authority, usually serves as the half-way point for travelers trying to complete their Huándǎo.

Crossing over from the west we are presented with multiple route alternatives up to the pass, over varied levels of beauty, difficulty and distance. There is highway 199, a quiet back road full of indigenous villages, wild grass and minimal traffic. The main highway of the T9 from the top of Kenting (墾丁) offers the simplest route for those looking to cross as fast as possible from Kaohsiung (高雄). A small, stunning section of highway T26 offers a really incredible ride along a hidden piece of coastline. Then there are the tricky but rewarding hidden roads that pass up the middle of the peninsula through forest and bamboo.

Any route you choose to take to arrive at Shouka will be a rewarding one, but, for us, nothing beats the wild beauty of the eastern route along a hidden piece of highway.

Perhaps the best little bit of hidden coastal road on the whole island, a cut-off section of highway T26 is a stunning, ocean-hugging road, complete with sand dunes, roadside waterfalls and cute public hot springs. A stiff switchback climb, through jungle hills, then takes us away from the ocean, finding its way up to a junction with the 199 and the beautiful grasslands before finally reaching the pass.

Sadly there is no continual coastal road all around the peninsula. The T26 is cut adrift by cliffs and wild bays so riders coming from either direction only have one option, up to the pass. For rides coming from the east coast the T9戊 is a beautiful but tiring uphill slog. Once again, the counterclockwise rider gets to enjoy it as one of the best descents in the country. As we race downhill along sweeping bends you can enjoy some fabulous views of the rolling hills and ocean below, to finally land on the east coast highway.

The descent to the east coast is perhaps the most comfortable and fun descent outside of the central mountains. The wide, sweeping road has plenty of long, broad corners that allow for a zippy safe ride; you can let the pedals rest and roll down. It's a quiet and a beautiful end to the day. Most traffic now runs through a tunnel network that speeds across the island. This leaves this old but smooth highway to cyclists and the occasional tourist car. At the bottom you are instantly thrown out onto the east coast highway road and it is beautiful, if busy, from the off.

After ten days of riding, you have finally hit the famed east coast highway, a stretch of two coastal roads that runs unbroken from the northern edge of Kenting all the way up to the northern city of Yilan (宜蘭) some 350km away. If you want, you can race up the T9 to Taipei (台北). But with so much more on offer on this side of the country, you will certainly want to take it slow and soak in all that the east has to offer.

Today's journey ends at the first town we reach, Dawu (大武), just 5km along the coastal road. Chances are the sun is dipping and legs are starting to feel weary. Dawu, part roadside rest stop, part fishing village, is split into two sections, the first of which has a few places to eat and get supplies as well as small family-run guesthouses. Roads behind the convenience store lead to a pretty little village that is a lovely stroll at dawn. The train station and more stores are at the second section a couple more km down the highway.

You might consider pushing further along the coast to the other towns that sit alongside the oceanfront. There are stops every few km's or so, and depending on your start time and fitness levels you could end the day as far along this coast as Taimali (太麻里).

Jinlun (金崙), some 20km further north than Dawu, is possibly the best alternative stop with hot springs, a cute fishing village and plenty of small private guesthouses. See p180.

For now, choose your route out of the southern point, enjoy the hidden coastal road, soak in those jungle-lined climbs, and bask in that glorious descent down to the east coast as we get ready for the second half of our adventure around Taiwan.

With so much more to experience, ever-changing landscapes, communities and adventures the second half of our Huándǎo, you won't tire of this island's journey as it starts to pull on your heartstrings and drag you deep into its east coast soul.

DAY 11
Kenting to Dawu
75KM 6Hr

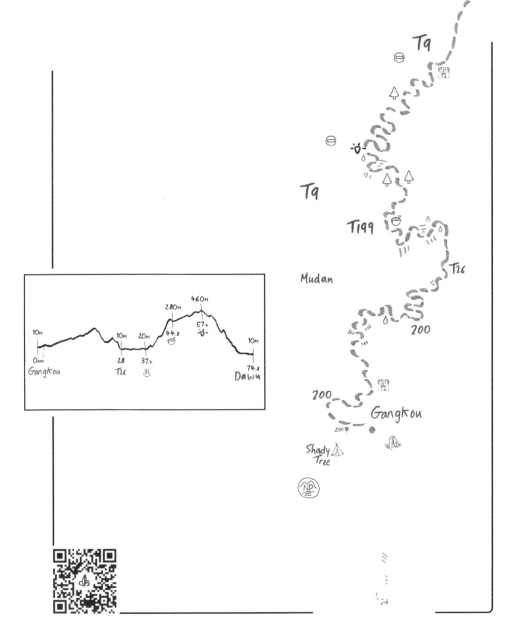

Dawu

T9

Tq

T199

Mudan

T26

200

200

Gangkou

200

Shady Tree

NP

Elevation profile

460M

280M

57.4

44.8

10M   10M   20M   10M

0KM   28   37.4   74.8

Gangkou   T26   Dawu

DAY 11
75KM /⋀⋀\ 6Hr △/仚

0.00 Start at the Gangkou junction! Head west along the 200甲 with the ocean and Gangkou (港口) at your back.

1.00 Turning for Shady Tree Campground on the left, look out for the cute surfboard signs.

2.00 The road bends right, keep on the 200甲.

3.87 Turn right onto the 200 at the T Junction. Turning left will take you back to the west coast and the town of Hengchun (恆春).

7.00 Small village with stores; stock up here because this is the last real store before the climb to the top. Make sure you have enough water.

7.20 Lean left as the road bends left and then right through the cute village of Manzhou (滿洲).
      Last chance for any meaningful stores on the day's ride.

9.00 The climb starts here, gradually at first and becoming tougher later.

18.2 Lean right, staying on road 200 as we enter a small village with a tiny store, keep to the right staying on the main road. Here we start a descent down to the coast.
      Here is the junction for the narrow mountain farm road 屏172. This route weaves its way up, and then down, the region's hills to the dam of Mudan on road 199. It's a lovely, remote if tiring climb.

28.1 End of road 200 at Gangzi (港仔). Just before the bottom of the descent, the road forces us up over a small hill before morphing into highway T26 at the village of Gangzi. No shops here, but the sand dunes are accessible from the parking lot. Public toilets and a dune buggy rental company, along with good ocean views.

The road follows the coastline for some km. There are no stores along this portion of the highway but there is a public bathroom here and again just before it turns inland to the hills.

29.9 Stunningly quiet coastal road begins.

30.0 Waterfall a short walk from the roadside at this corner.

32.0 Start of military-controlled area. Army buildings, bases and training area. Largely quiet but sometimes the road can be closed during training and war game sessions, carried out a few times a year. Still, beautiful views of oceans and the east coast cliffs off in the distance.

36.0 Rest area with open public toilets and a water source at the entrance to a hiking trail.

<u>36.3</u> Turn left onto the 199甲 at the T junction at the end of the T26. This road leads us up through the hills, to the 199 and eventually Shouka Pass.

37.4 Xu Hai Hot Spring (旭海). A cute little hot springs run by local authorities, a great place for a dip before the climb.

37.7 Start of the sharp switchback climb.

43.4 Top of the climb; the road levels out at grasslands.

<u>44.8</u> Turn right onto the 199 at the Y junction. There is bicycle parking at the junction. Turning left here will take you down the 199 and back to the west coast.

After turning right, you immediately see two wonderful local restaurants. Both can provide food, drinks and a great rest stop for cyclists. The left-hand stop is run by a local family who love to talk to cyclists about riding (their son and father ride bikes). The other restaurant is run by a kindly *āyí* who giggles her way along her day and will happily make food for a weary traveler.

This is the last place for provisions until the descent finishes on the east coast.

Now, heading north, we pass across the grasslands, a beautiful rural area of the country. The road remains narrow and quiet for some time before climbing up with wide vista views of the Pacific Ocean, have fun!

<u>57.5</u> Turn right onto the T9戊 at Shouka Pass. The end of road 199 and the peak of the climb. Here is the famous bicycle rest stop. Everyone completing a full circle of Taiwan has to pass here at the merge of highway 199 and the T9戊. The rest stop acts as a focal point and has drinking water, toilets, free access to bike tools and myriad places to park up.

Once on the T9戊, ensure which way you are pointing as both sides of the pass descend quickly. Turn right at the junction and head east and down to the coast and the town of Daren. This ride is sweeping, fun and safe. With a wide bicycle trail, almost all the way down the corners are fast and the straights faster. It's a great ride, with minimal cars, making this road the perfect tonic for all the day's climbing.

62.4 Halfway down the descent, this small temple rest stop has great views of the highway, hills and ocean below.

68.5 The bottom of the descent has you racing toward traffic lights.

69.1 At the lights lean right onto the T9. At the traffic lights turn right, following the flow of traffic. After the lights, follow the highway as it bends left, heading north, and starts to creep along the coastline. Finally, you are heading north proper now and we stay in this direction for some time so hope for fair winds.

74.8 Finish in the village of Dawu (大武)! Split into two sections across the next few km, Dawu has stores and restaurants as well as a couple of large rest stops right on the ocean's edge with 24hr public bathrooms. There are basic hotels and guesthouses also. Alas, no official campgrounds near the ocean road. If you still have energy, consider riding a further 20km to the cute fishing village of Jinlun (金崙), which features guesthouses and hot springs as well as being a great breakfast village.

Tomorrow's route has better options for sleeping. Between Dawu and Taimali (太麻里) there are a few towns with hotels and rest stops along the way. But if you have tired legs or are arriving late then stay here in Dawu. Either way, the east coast ride to Taitung (台東) is fairly painless and arresting.

Clockwise Notes
Taiwan Tail

Dawu, Taitung to Fangliao, Pingtung via Kenting

When riding clockwise from the east coast of Taitung to the southern peninsula of Kenting and Pingtung there is only one route to go, and that's up. Highway T9 races off into a car-only tunnel system leaving us cyclists to tackle the beautiful, if tiring, climb up to the pass at Shouka along the old highway, now named T9戊. This 400m climb might be the biggest of the whole trip for some riders, but don't worry the smooth wide road has a comfortable grade and you will reach the top in no time.

From the pass make sure you descend down the correct trail for your destination. If you are not heading to Kenting but instead want to travel directly to Fangliao, Kaohsiung and beyond then stay on the main road of the T9戊. However, be warned, if you plan to head to Kenting and the beaches in the south make sure you turn left at the pass onto the stunning 199 road. This winding road through jungle grassland and village will take you further south and a lot closer to those beaches.

If you intend on completing as much of the coastal route as possible, make sure you take the left turn and the junction with the small restaurants, leaving the 199 and onto the 199甲. This fast descent will take you all the way down to the coast and a hidden portion of highway T26. Well worth the ride out after.

Either route down you will eventually reach the southern point, for Fangliao, Pingtung and Taiwan's western cities; simply head north along the peninsula's western highway T26 until it reaches the top and merges onto highway T1. The ride from the bottom of Kenting to Fangliao is a simple, easy ride for a morning as long as the winds are not directly in your face, which they might well be.

Fangliao's train station has great connections further north to all of the big cities. Also note the harbor village of Donggang is nearby for the short ferry trip over to the stunning turtle-inhabited island of Xiaoliuqiu. See page138 for more details on Taiwan's outlying islands.

South East

Surf the concrete wave along Taiwan's pristine east coast. Laid-back vibes and eye-popping scenery await.

With plenty of oceanside exploration and endless adventures to have along this fantastic green and blue tapestry. Try to take it all in and your senses might overload.

South East

How to describe a feeling in the air? It's really hard to pin it down; maybe it's the warm breeze coming off the ocean, perhaps it's the surfboards strapped to cars that pass by, or it's the laughter and noise coming from locally owned cafés that dot this idyllic route. Perhaps it's the feeling that there is nowhere else to be, that here is where life is and in this moment, just for a brief time, we can forget the things that keep us from living it.

The first section up to the east coast city of Taitung (台東) has us climbing and dipping along the coastal road. It can be tiring if the wind is against us, but the views of the ocean from each high section will take your breath away. Luckily this undulating road flattens out as we head into Taitung, and once we reach the mind-blowing mountain views on the other side you will be freewheeling around golden sand beaches.

A broad smile will stretch across your face as you wake up in the surf village of Dulan (都蘭) and our guess is that it will stay fixed there throughout our trip north along Taiwan's famous east coast highway. Everything slows down around here, there is a sense of ease that is not felt around other parts of Taiwan's main island.

From Dulan the coastal road is an undulating wave that never feels tiring. Every corner brings out fresh views, stunning atmosphere and side adventures that will take you and your bike through paradise.

When asked which route to take up the east coast, the East Rift Valley or stay on the coastal highway we always recommend sticking with the ocean route, and Day 13's ride is the reason. Skipping this portion of the coast would be such a shame. There is just too much to enjoy. If you want to combine the two routes consider turning to the valley road shortly after this ride along highway T11甲, p221. Equally if you really don't want to miss the southern section of the valley ride then start our alternative route before heading over the mountains to the east coast road along highway T23, p206.

Unlike the southern portion of the east coast, this central section is calmer and quieter, and it feels smaller, in the best way imaginable. Most traffic went inland and here everyone is on holiday time. The locals that populate the small towns and villages are not in it for the rat race. Out here is where Taiwan feels most like a Pacific island, cut off from the fast-paced world. Here is where Taiwan really unwinds.

Dawu to Dulan

Our first taste of Taiwan's east coast highway is a real roller-coaster. The section of the highway that runs from Dawu (大武) north, until the edges of Taitung (台東) is a hectic waterside highway complete with dramatic views and breathtaking descents. Like a string binding all together the sweeping road dips and weaves into each town or village before rising up again along sheer cliff coastline. Winding our way toward the city of Taitung, and beyond.

Once we reach the outskirts of Taitung we say goodbye to the T9 and join our main coastal road, the T11. From here we head flat and fast through Taitung's beach park. This city is sprawling but has kept a quaint coastal feel.

The impressive train station is situated far out the back of the town by the mountains. While it loses any real sense of a center, Taitung's grid structure makes it easy to navigate. If you are heading through the city to the East Rift Valley (E.R.V.) then follow our alt route, see p200. You can take the T9 all the way but it really is no fun as it shoots straight and quick to Hualien (花蓮), and where's the adventure in that?

The beach park of Taitung acts as a good lunch break. Connect with the ocean in this quiet little spot with bathrooms, food stalls and stores. Taitung residents sing its praises for its food culture and access to the mountain regions. It can be a good place to spend the night if you are going to hike in the region, or if you plan on taking a ferry from the city's port to reach the outlying islands. Keep in mind that the port at Fugang (富岡碼頭) is some 5km north from the city.

As we leave we are presented with a jaw-dropping rest stop offering some of the best views that the entire east coast has to offer. Magnificent, lush green peaks strut out from the ocean into the sky, covered by cloud, like the crest of a forested wave. Well worth a break to marvel at the landscape ahead, whatever the weather.

The ocean road from Taitung to Hualien is very different from the earlier wild, sweeping cliffs. The road calms down considerably. There is a reason this next stretch of road often gets called Taiwan's travel highlight and is by far its most popular cycling touring area.

The last few km of this day have us glide around a vast bay. We ride past relaxing sandy beaches and beachfront cafés, a taste of the next two days' adventures before we reach the last sight of the day, the mind-bending sight of Water Running Upwards, a cute little attraction that is worth the five minutes off the highway.

Finally, we arrive at the near perfect sleepy surf town of Dulan (都蘭). Probably your first real chance to rest up and relax at a beach location that, year-round, offers something to enjoy. The black sand beach is more for surfing than swimming but it still has its charm and can be good for sunbathing and night-time wandering. The village has an eclectic mix of arts, crafts, unique guest-houses, and restaurants serving up flavors from all over the world as well as a cultural heart in its repurposed sugar factory, with nighttime performance from incredible local musicians that can make lifetime memories.

All along the east coast many police stations are part of the cycling rest stop network and several used to have campsites; sadly this network has fallen into disrepair. Dulan's station, the best of these free sites, sadly has closed down. Despite this change of heart police stations, at the very least, will help you to find somewhere to camp nearby. It is so warming to experience Taiwanese hospitality in full flow along the east coast.

Dulan has plenty of cycle-friendly backpacker hostels and guesthouses. If the police station remains unavailable there is a large grassy area overlooking the main beach of Dulan, just head down the lane beside the post office and roll down the quiet beach road.

This laid-back beach community sets the tone for our east coast adventure and the next few days have a distinctively happy, sunny, meandering vibe. In the evening head down to the sugar factory or nearby bars and enjoy live music from local musicians or grab a drink and chat to other travelers. There are not many places in Taiwan where travelers congregate, but Taiwanese and foreigners alike are drawn to Dulan and its laid-back vibes. It might just be hard to get back on the road again.

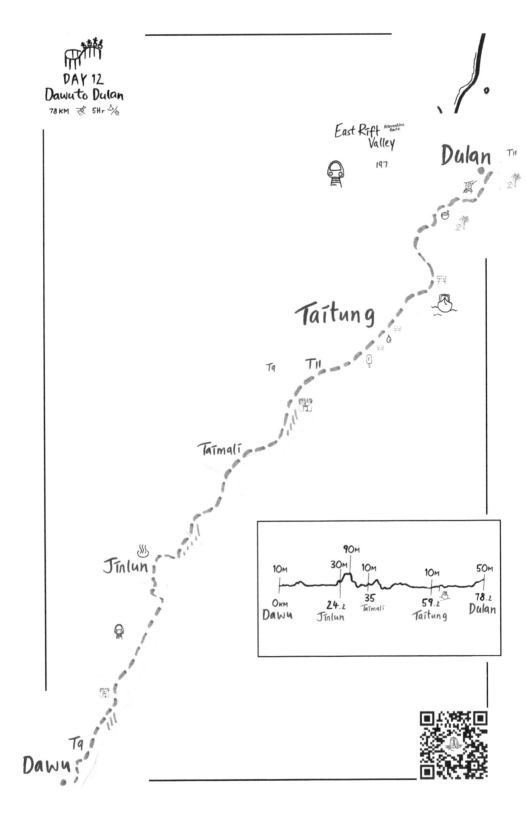

DAY 12
Dawu to Dulan
78 KM 5Hr

East Rift Valley *Alternative Route*
197

Dulan
T11

Taitung

T9   T11

Taimali

Jinlun

Dawu

T9

Elevation profile:

10M
90M
30M   10M   10M   50M

0 KM   24.2   35   59.2   78.2
Dawu   Jinlun Taimali Taitung Dulan

DAY 12

78KM 5Hr

0.00 Start at the edge of Dawu (大武), head north along the T11! There is a good chance you didn't stay here the night but it's where we pick up our journey for this day's ride.

3.26 Dawu rainbow overpass, traditional sculptures and ocean park.

3.60 Small rest stop with food stall, 24hr public toilet, covered pagodas over-looking the ocean.

5.70 A large rest stop with ocean views and bathrooms. Start of a climb as the road hangs to the cliffside, recently lifted higher after multiple landslides requiring a rebuild of the road. Climbing for 2km but a fun descent with good shoulder and amazing ocean views.

14.7 Store and turning to Longxi (龍溪), a small town with hotels and a train station.

15.1 Lean right onto and across the long, flat bridge.

21.1 Pass by another train station clinging to the hillside above. The road lanes split here as we pass a section of open-sided tunnels and sweeping views.

22.9 Turn left onto Jinlun Road after a short descent. Look out for the traffic lights. We are going to leave the highway here and enter the town of Jin-lun (金崙).

　　The climb on the highway here looks steep, but running through the small fishing village is a better little ride and only adds a little time. Park yourself in the waiting box to the right and cross the road on the green light. Go careful, speeding cars can miss the lights here.

23.3 Lean right, following the road as it bends toward the town. Cross the flat bridge.

24.0 Enter Jinlun. The town has stores and hot springs and is a very cute fishing village well worth a short walk or food stop. You can even spend the night and find those hot waters to relax in.

24.2 Head straight when ready to leave the town, uphill at the crossroads.

The town's focal point at the indigenous village hall. Turn left here for hot springs and turn right to see the small old fishing village with great breakfast stalls.

The road winds up above the town, rejoining the highway at the top of its ludicrous raised overpass.

24.9 Turn left onto the T9. At the end of the road, wait for the traffic lights, merging north once more.

A 3km climb starts here, but once again beautiful views with shoulder and rest stops along the way.

27.5 The top of the climb, marked by a nice rest stop with views and seating. The descent is fun and fast in dry weather, but large trucks use this road and at times the shoulder randomly disappears.

32.7 The town of Taimali (太麻里) sprawls from here. With shops all along the highway road no need to leave it. The town has a train station should you need.

Right after this town the T9 has one last climb for the day, it can feel rough in the heat, with minimal shade. But once again stunning views and tantalizing Taitung (台東) can be seen in the distance.

39.0 The top of the climb. This descent is fast and straight, enjoy!

44.7 Turn/lean right onto the T11. The road splits here and highway 9 runs off to the left. We say goodbye to it and join the real coastal road.

Even if you plan on heading to Taitung train station or the East Rift Valley, do not follow T9 here. You can find the train station or the E.R.V. from Taitung beach park easily enough.

From here the traffic becomes significantly lighter and the road truly flattens. The long straight road runs to Taitung's coast park and the edge of town after some 12km of flat, windy riding.

58.5 You are now on the edge of Taitung city, by the coastal park. Any right-hand turn from here will lead you to the green grass by the ocean.

Taitung seashore park. Plonk yourself down on the shaded grass or overlooking the stony beach. Take a rest. Here are a few basic eateries, ice cream stalls and 24hr public bathrooms. We are going to use the park's bicycle path to navigate around the town. There is also a small supermarket, two blocks north of the park.

If you are going to stay in Taitung for the night, enter one of the leafy northbound streets that lead into the heart of the town. With no real center to speak of, it can get a little confusing in the city's grid system. If you are looking for the train station, keep on our route for now as the bike path leads all the way there.

60.2 Stay on the T11, heading north at the Mahengheng Boulevard junction. At the lights is the start of a wide six-lane boulevard with signs for Taitung train station and the E.R.V. If you are heading to the train station then look to the bicycle lane (last lane on the right) and follow it up for a further 8km all the way to the beautifully large train station positioned on the edge of town.

62.7 At the end of the bridge stay on the highway, following floor markings for the bicycle lane that cuts in the middle of the strange junction.

65.1 Fugang (富岡). Small seaside town, home to Taitung's small port.

This ferry port services routes to Lanyu (蘭嶼), Green Island (綠島) and Houbi port (後壁湖碼頭) in Kenting. See our *Outlying Islands* for details p138. There are a couple of hotels in this town if you need to stay the night before an early ferry ride the next day. The turning point for the port is at the traffic lights, just before the road climbs up a hill.

66.2 Large rest stop with paid camping, tourist shops and public toilets. But unless desperate, wait a further 1km for a much more spectacular rest stop.

67.4 A huge grassy rest stop filled with ecological sculptures, boy oh boy, does this place have some amazing views of the east coast mountain range and the curve of the bay ahead. Even on a bad-weather day this is a dramatic spot to take in the atmosphere and soak up the journey ahead. You are now about to enter the tarmac surf of the east coast. And it is a delight. Has public bathrooms.

71.3 A pretty beach, cafés and some good rest points if you need.

75.0 After climbing out of the long sweeping bay we arrive at the Water Running Upwards attraction. Well worth a stop, right on the roadside and just outside of Dulan (都蘭), this naturally occurring optical illusion looks like it is running uphill. As always with Taiwan's roadside attractions, temper expectations.

77.6 The town of Dulan, first its sugar factory on your left. From here and for the next 2km is a row of hostels and cute eateries and restaurants. A very chill vibe in this unassuming beach town right along the ocean highway.

78.2 Finish in central Dulan! The sugar factory is situated at the southern end of the small village on the highway. After which you quickly come across the short strip of stores, restaurants and hostels. As mentioned before, you can either stay down by the main beachfront or at the many wonderful hostels here, most are very bicycle friendly, Dulan Travel Bug is a personal favorite.

Dulan to Shitiping

What a day. From start to finish, the tarmac rolls, skipping up, down and around bays as we really fly along the coast here. It is such a bright, friendly and appealing part of the country. In part by accident and in part by design this is Taiwan's most bicycle-friendly stretch, bringing joy to every type of tourer. Your bicycle will seem to take pleasure here, the wheels just turn ever so slightly quicker, free hub indeed.

We always bristle with excitement when we know we are about to ride this happy area of the country, full of mini adventures along the way. Laid-back surf towns, hidden bike paths through palm-lined coast, rocky outpost adventures, clear beaches, fishing towns, atmospheric cave networks, mystical mountain roads, panoramic ocean views and jungle-strewn mountains, to name just a few. The views are stunning; brightly lit colors illuminate your way.

Hopefully you have had a nice long rest in Dulan (都蘭). Take a day, swim in the ocean, eat some good food, take a walk and enjoy this hub of arts, surfing, and laid-back life. After leaving Dulan the road tantalizingly keeps the ocean in and out of view. Make sure you take a stop at the unassuming ocean-view café at the hilltop rest stop of Jinsun (金崙遊憩區).

Soon you will arrive in the next surfing town of Donghe (東河), a rival to Dulan for laid-back vibes and beach. The old bridge over a beautiful gorge river is worth it to interact with the monkeys who own this place. There is also the mountain road T23 that heads to the E.R.V., a beautiful option on a fair-weather day.

Next up, ride through the third surfing town of Douli (都歷), here take a sneaky detour off the road and find the beach for gorgeous views and another cheeky dip.

Shortly after Douli you will find the Baonon Bikeway, a sweet little stretch of ocean road spun as a bicycle path, avoiding the highway and cars. Riding uninterrupted along the ocean, if only briefly, is a lovely feeling.

If you enjoyed that, then the hidden bike path that leads from the town of Chenggong (成功) to the island of Sanxiantai (三仙台) truly isn't one to miss. Leading from the town, it eventually runs down a hill through palm trees. Arriving at the ocean a small blue bay greets you as the road becomes a winding flat path. You are taken through a thick forest of trees and bush that lines the water's edge.

This wild piece of coast is great and to top it off, all of a sudden you end up, as if by magic, at the entrance to the eight-arch bridge that leads to Sanxiantai, a small rocky island well worth an exploration. Make your way to its clifftop lighthouse for spectacular views and an excellent adventure high. The beach at the foot of the bridge is usually calm and great for a lunchtime swim.

Take a break in Changbin (長濱) and ride up King Kong Boulevard to visit the beautiful Zhongyong bicycle trail through rice fields; it easily competes with, if not surpasses, the rice fields found in the E.R.V. Add in the jaw-dropping cliffs that rise up into cloud, and you really will feel like you are lost on Skull Island itself.

Our last stretch of road has a few more unique attractions: the Baxiandong caves (八仙洞遊客中心) followed by the Tropic of Cancer line (北回歸線界標) and then the ocean village of Jingpu (靜浦).

At the end of the day we arrive at Shitiping (石梯坪), a rocky ocean park that sticks out at the edge of the land. This protected marine park has incredible rock formations to explore and some astounding views of the coast. There are two campgrounds here as well as a couple of hotels. But despite the tourists it's a very quiet rest for the night. Both campgrounds are set away from traffic and people. The government-run campground in the site of Shitiping has incredible open huts under which to pitch your tent and offers a very unique location for a night's camp. Unfortunately getting a pitch during any kind of national holiday or summer season is out of the question. The privately run campground just next door is well looked after and has incredible ocean views right from your porch.

If you are looking for a free spot for the night then you can head north along the highway after Shitiping. There are a few beautiful rest stops that overlook the cliffs and ocean. 3.5km from the natural recreation park is the wonderful astrological rest stop of Shimen Banshaojiao (石門班哨), an open-air amphitheater, the perfect ocean stargazing experience, and on a clear night it does not disappoint.

It's a great end to a wonderful day. Taiwan's east coast has served up its best and it doesn't disappoint. I sit here as I write, brimming with memories and joyous anticipation of your time to come riding along the highway wave.

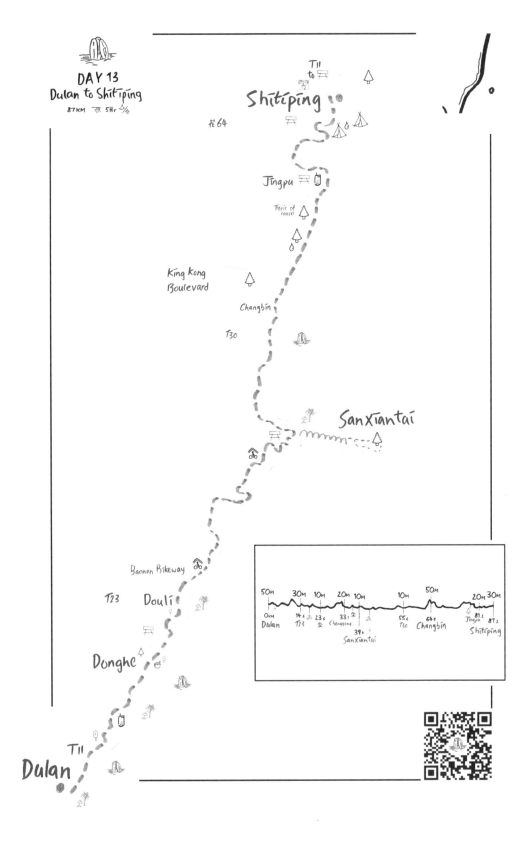

DAY 13
Dulan to Shitiping
87KM 5Hr

Shitiping
T11 to

ti 64

Jingpu

Tropic of cancer

King Kong Boulevard

Changbin

T30

Sanxiantai

Baonen Bikeway

T23   Douli

Donghe

T11
Dulan

Elevation profile:

50M — 30M — 10M — 20M — 10M — 10M — 50M — 20M — 30M

0KM Dulan | 14.6 T23 | 23.6 | 33.7 Chenggong | 39.7 Sanxiantai | 55.6 T30 | 64.9 Changbin | 81.2 Jingpu | 87.2 Shitiping

DAY 13

87KM 𝕉 *5Hr* ⌂/⛺

0.00 Start from central Dulan (都蘭), heading north along the T11! The road out of Dulan is smooth and blissfully undulating for the entire day's coastline ride. The tarmac weaves and winds around the many bays and mountain bases. The rises and dips keep the wheels rolling, allowing you to stretch your feet and relax. You are on beach time now, don't rush.

7.00 Longchang (隆昌) has a small police station, a couple of homestays and cafés.

9.70 Atop a short hill sits Jinsun rest area (金樽遊憩區). A great place to take your first break for the day, big open outdoor space with great ice coffees and panoramic views of the ocean and the bays below. The public toilets at the far end are also good.

12.4 Turning for Jinlin harbor (金樽漁港) on your left. The small fishing village has a huge parking lot rest area right on the seafront, where RVs and vans like to spend a night. 24hr public toilets.

12.9 Lean right, staying on the T11. A turning for Donghe (東河) is on your left, head down this side road if you want to skip the stores and head straight for the old bridge. The highway links with the main town a little further down the road and both routes eventually cross the small gorge, arriving at the same point.

13.8 Surf stores, convenience stores, ice cream and eateries at little Donghe. Also watch out for the famous bāozi (包子) store. Super popular for its yummy steamed buns.

14.6 After leaving the town, cross a short bridge and notice the old bridge at the mouth of a gorge. Turn left just after the bridge to view. This area has been taken over by a troop of Formosan rock macaques. Great to watch, please don't feed them.

This is also the turning for the T23, an option for riding through to the East Rift Valley (E.R.V.).

T23 to the East Rift Valley
The T23 is a stunning road to take but leaving the ocean route way too early, you can consider starting at Taitung (台東) and riding up the E.R.V. until you reach the T23, then ride across the hills, arriving here and starting your adventure further north, p206.

Midway up the T23 you are hit by jungle vista views of the surrounding region, its mountains and indigenous communities with their farms and homes spread over the area.

The ride from the east coast to the pass is an uphill ride, but with no difficult grades it is as easy as a 30km climb can be. Once at the pass it is a very pretty descent into the valley, with long sweeping corners providing panoramic views of the mountain ranges across the valley floor.

The 東23 side road connects Taitung with the T23. Running parallel to the coast road, it traces a route though the mountain range that splits the ocean from the valley. This quiet little area is great to explore with some stunning scenery. Just be warned that there are some climbs in there. From Taitung the road starts along the 197 just by highway T11. It can also be accessed from Taitung train station, see our alternative E.R.V. route for more details.

21.0 Douli (都歷), another small surfing village.

23.6 Turn right onto the Baonon Bikeway. The entrance for the Baonon Bikeway (八嗡嗡單車道) is marked at the junction with a cute sign. Turn here and leave the T11 to ride the old coastal highway for a few km.

The road is quiet and beautiful, running alongside the lapping waters. With cute stenciled cyclists highlighting the way. The only beach is a small one almost at the beginning of the route opposite the luxury hotel.

28.0 Before the road ends it climbs sharply, leaving the bay.

28.5 End of the climb, a small rest stop.

28.6 Turn right onto the T11 once more. See if you can spot the giant waterfall on the side of the mountain off in the opposite distance.

31.2 Small climb just before the town of Chenggong (成功).

32.5 Turn right onto Gomgmin Road (公民路) leaving the T11 follow old bikeway signs, turn just after the traffic lights. The highway it bends left. The single-lane road is directly straight in front of us.

The small lane races downhill past homes before bending and curving left, throwing us into central Chenggong.

33.3 Head straight onto Zhonghua Road (中華路). At the junction keep heading straight, taking the largest road.

Now we are working our way through the main street in Chenggong passing stores and restaurants. Head straight crossing every junction.

<u>33.7</u> Head straight across the large crossroads.

<u>34.0</u> Turn right onto Taiping Road (太平路) at the very end of Zhonghua Road, at the T junction.

<u>34.1</u> Turn left onto Zhongshan E. Road (中山東路) leaving the town and passing the parking lot that hosts the local market.

<u>34.2</u> Lean left staying on Zhongshan E. Road. The road widens here at this junction. You will have a park on your right and a bike trail will form alongside the road. Follow signs for Bike Tour 45 toward Sanxiantai (三仙台).

<u>37.1</u> Turn right down the lane. As the bike path hits a crossroad on the brow of a hill, it is painted green on the floor. Turn right here, following a brown bikeway signpost and leaving the main bike path route. The new road is a single lane that runs downhill toward the ocean. A large vista of fields, ocean, palm trees and mountains opens up as you start to head down the hill.

At the bottom of the descent the road ends and becomes a bike path proper. It bends left through and past palm trees and the crisp blue ocean. Follow the road as it bends left and right, becoming smaller until it narrows further to a single bike lane. Watch out for bollards designed to halt cars.

This bike path is flat and fun as it rolls secretly through the shrubs, trees and forest that line this section of coast. Expect butterflies, the constant sound of nearby turquoise waves, and bright green bush with a stunning blue sky overhead. Soon enough it comes to an end, arriving at a mini path junction.

<u>38.9</u> Turn right at this small junction of lanes, follow the path to the bridge. Watch out for people fishing and their rods.

39.4 Sanxiantai beach and bridge.

This island is a treat and well worth exploring. Even if there is a large crowd, few venture as far as the lighthouse perched at the top of the island's hill on a cliff. Take a walk and go see. When you have finished with the island and the bridge and perhaps taken a dip on the stone beach, there are plenty of stores, ice creams and bathrooms at the parking lot as well as an information center with drinking water and a bicycle repair station, when open.

The path from the beach leads back up to the parking lot, this is where we will be heading off from.

<u>39.9</u> Head straight out of the parking lot keeping the famous bridge behind you and the ocean bay on your right. Use the bike path to bypass the gated entrance and then head up the hill.

<u>40.2</u> Turn right at the small Y junction at the top of a short brow, turn right, heading downhill into the fishing town.

41.0 Pass by Pisirian (比西里岸) fishing village.

41.5 Community field with a large grass lawn and public bathrooms at the northern edge of the village.

42.3 Merge right onto the T11. Rejoin the highway once again heading north. The T11 rides fast for the next while, with little to stop at but a few ocean viewpoints.

55.6 Junction with the T30 that connects to the E.R.V.

T30 tunnel to the East Rift Valley
This road climbs halfway up a mountainside before diving into the heart of it through a new, deep tunnel. It's a great challenge and worth it as the views from the platforms at both sides of the tunnel are great. You can ride through to view the E.R.V. and then return. Only if you have the legs for it mind.

64.4 Turn left onto Changbin main street (長濱路). Leave the T11 and ride through Changbin, our last town for the day. Convenience stores here at the traffic lights and at the other end of town. This town has the last stores of the day so stock up on supplies.

72.2 Baxiandong cave network (八仙洞) on your left. An important archeological site and cave network. Hear the ocean cascading (and echoing) out from inside the cave walls. Bathrooms, water and information center here.

80.7 Tropic of Cancer monument. Crossing over the Tropic of Cancer line here. It is marked by a large white tower (北回歸線標碑) great for sunset times.

81.2 Turn right into Jingpu, leaving the T11. Just before the entrance of Jingpu (靜浦) the T11 bends left, we head down the sleepy side road and into the coastal village, which has a lot of character and charm.

Follow the town road as it bends at the river and heads away from the ocean. Lots of cute little green areas here to sit and relax by the mouth of the river. The local indigenous population are great and love to crack a smile your way. There is a lovely artist-owned café with good coffee just as you enter the village on the left.

83.2 Turn right, rejoining the T11 at the bridge. The information center here is huge. The police station has a grassy parking lot in front and the officers are very helpful. Cross the bridge.

83.5 Turning on your left for 花64, another route through to the E.R.V. This one is more rugged with an uneven road surface, a small farming village at the end of a stiff climb, as the road traces along a deep river gorge.

If you want to combine the two routes of the coastal and the valley then a good option is stopping the night in Shitiping (石梯坪) and crossing over on the T11甲 from Fengbin (豐濱) the next morning. This route to Hualien offers a fun, remote section of the East Rift Valley, pick up the route here p210.

85.3 Pass through the village of Gangkou (港口). Some stores and food stalls here.

King Kong Boulevard–Changbin Cycling Route 1

After traveling down Changbin main street for 300m make sure you turn left at the traffic light junction. Head up a small lane following signs for King Kong Boulevard. As the road heads uphill toward the looming mountain wall you will be flanked either side by bright green rice shelves. Carry on up the hill until you reach the village at the base of the mountain. Turn right following signs until you reach the Zhongyong bicycle trail. This almost dead-straight road has the illusion of running down the hill falling off into the ocean. Well worth a photo or two, or twenty. When finished, follow this road downhill toward the ocean. After a few corners you find yourself back on the T11 just north of Changbin. From here turn left, head north, and carry on our trip once more.

86.3 Private campground just before the recreation park. Well maintained, friendly owner and great views right on the water's edge. A little pricey.

87.1 A couple of seafood restaurants and a large local store on the bend.

<u>87.2</u> Finish at Shitiping Scenic Recreation Park! Entrance to Shitiping (石梯坪 遊憩風景區). Ignore the toll booths, bicycles go free. Our day is done, tomorrow we will pick up from here for our last day on T11 as we head to Hualien.

See Day 14, p221 for rest stops further along the T11 that offer some stunning views and potential free camping options. For guesthouses you might need to stop earlier near Jingpu or ride farther to Fengbin (豐濱).

Clockwise Notes
South East

Shitiping, Hualien to Dawu, Taitung

The clockwise route heading south along the coastline from Shitiping in Hualien County to Dawu at the bottom of Taitung County could not be simpler. Following the stunning highway T11 as it glides and rolls ever further down the island is a joy and is one of the most, if not the most, popular routes in Taiwan.

From Shitiping follow the coastal road south, make sure to make a brief stop in the cute village of Fengbin. You cannot miss the giant monument crossing the Tropic of Cancer line, officially entering into Taiwan's tropical south.

One km north of Changbin is a turning right onto the quiet country lane that will take you up to King Kong Boulevard and the stunning rice fields that cover the area below some incredible mountains. The popular spot is a great opportunity for spectacular photos and is often clogged with people snapping away in the middle of the road. If you miss the junction just head into tiny Changbin itself and take a right at the small central crossroads following signs.

The coastal road is a breeze to ride after Changbin with just a couple of uphill pushes around the end of each dramatic bay. After another 35km of riding follow signs for Sanxiantai, the stunning rocky island connected by the cute eight-arch bridge. Once finished there find the wonderfully hidden bike route away from the bridge sneaking you south. To find the path just look for the fishing rods and scooters parked up by the rocks and keep to the pedestrian path heading south before finally turning into the mangrove, eventually the path ends at some palm trees by a pretty little bay. The road turns uphill from here, at the brow of the hill turn left and ride downhill and flat to Chenggong.

From here simply follow the highway all the way along to Dulan, and then through to Taitung itself. If you are heading for the outlying islands of Lanyu or green Island then you will find the ferry port at Fugang situated 5km before the city itself just after the long sweeping bay.

If you are in need of Taitung's train station then after you cross the long, windy flat bridge just north of the city turn right up the wide boulevard and keep on this road, following signs for the station some km inland from the main downtown area.

Consider a rest in Dulan or Taitung before heading further south as shortly after the city we reach highway T9 and the constant rise and fall of the coast road as it heads south to Dawu. This can be a tiring section of the route especially if the wind is against you. It really is pot luck with that one.

Shitiping Scenic Recreation Park
Travel down past the entrance at the highway. At first you will pass a couple of hotels before you lean south, the ocean will now be on your left. There are several entrances to the rocky outpost with bathrooms available. This short walk to the cliff edge is well worth it, as you can view some stunning coastline from here and watching the waves crash below is always mesmerizing.

Further down the road from the entrance is the campground. There is usually a camp manager wandering around with his money ready, should there be a space available. At the end of the road is a small roundabout and a police station, with public bathrooms.

East Rift Valley

Alternative Route

Valley

Bookended by the east coast cities of Taitung and Hualien

The inland East Rift Valley
offers an abundance of beauty.
A quaint alternative route
    up and down Taiwan's east.

Alternative Route

East Rift Valley

E qually as engrossing as the east coast road, the East Rift Valley (E.R.V.) is a sprawling landscape-rich valley that offers an alternative route between the coastal cities of Taitung (台東) and Hualien (花蓮).

Dramatic views of cascading clouds, mountain peaks and vast, lush farmland. From here you can access some of Taiwan's most loved hiking trails up into the central mountain ranges.

There are hot springs, waterfalls, as well as farm paths crisscrossing paddy fields, colorful flower meadows and temple complexes. Indigenous villages dot the ridgelines, all connected by quiet tree-lined boulevards. Converted rail lines offer cycle-only viewpoints of the landscape and connect quieter back roads that happily skip and avoid the major highway trundling up and down the valley.

Navigating the valley route seems an obvious endeavor. The main CR1 plots a route that follows the T9 as it snakes its way up through the valley. But this largely skips and skims the highlights of the region as it rolls along the increasingly busy highway. Not ideal for laid-back exploration.

We propose an alternative option that takes us away from the large flow of traffic, riding local roads through to the highlights of the region, which provide stunning scenery and a quieter journey that hits a few lesser-known areas along the way.

Sticking to the eastern edges of the valley, along the connecting highways of the 197 and 193, our route is not exactly flat, but, with no long climbs to speak of over the course of the route, we still have a very laid-back journey through the E.R.V., and its farming heartlands.

You can race up the valley in a day or two, or take your time and spend multiple days exploring the many side hikes and villages that cut into the mountain ranges on both sides. How you break up this route will be determined by what activities you plan to do along the way.

From Taitung, a good break point for a two-day ride might be the hot spring area around Ruisui. Alternatively, if you plan a hiking trip to Jiaming Lake (嘉明湖) or the Walami Trail (瓦拉米), then a break around Chishang (池上) or Yuli (玉里) would be beneficial.

Starting from either Taitung train station or the Taitung beach park we find our way toward, and up, route 197. This sweeping hill road climbs and dips

around the edges of the city and then across the open geo landscape. Much like Tainan's Moon World in the western flats, the unique gray cliffs that jut out of the ground around here are unique to this island and you feel a world away from the lush green and shimmering blues of the coast. This start to the trip is tough on the legs as the road undulates up and down for some time.

After rising and falling along a higher section of road, passing through quiet indigenous villages, we finally fall into the valley proper where everything flattens out. From here you can stop off and experience a famous photo op of the Brown's Boulevard crossroad: a crisscross of smooth tarmac in the middle of huge, bright green rice farms. This area in spring and throughout the summer seasons is a beautiful patchwork of greens and yellows, with water trickling all around the flooded paddy fields.

On the edges of Chishang we also pass by Dapo Pond, a beautiful park with great reflections of the surrounding mountains on clear days. For the next 20km we ride along the T9 on a pretty and quiet section of the highway as we search for a bicycle-only trail. If you feel the urge for some uphill grinding consider a short but grueling ride up the eastern slopes to visit the stunning tea plantation hillside of Liushishi (六十石), which offers quite astounding views of the valley floor and its mountain walls. Not to mention great tea to be had up there.

Next, we reach what is one of the highlights of the E.R.V. cycle trip, the cycle path along the converted railway line from Old Dongli train station to the town of Yuli. This rail route starts at the cute old train station complete with traditional café and historical photography exhibit. The main platform is still intact, but sadly the symmetrical roof that once hung over the station collapsed after an earthquake in 2022. From here the route follows a flat line around the valley floor with some great views of the mountains. As you reach the outskirts of Yuli the route runs along a beautifully raised train bridge that winds and bends over rivers.

Yuli is the gateway to the second hiking option of the Walami Trail, a popular mountain trail that connects up into the high mountains through a path first conceived of by the occupying Japanese rulers who were determined to tame and farm the inner mountain's forests. From here you can choose between a beautiful day hike and an overnight return adventure spending a night in one of Taiwan's delightfully rustic camping huts. For the most adventurous of you, the Walami Trail is also the start of an epic seven-day trail that takes you all the way up to Taiwan's highest peak, via its back routes. No permits are needed for a day hike up here, but once you cross onto the trail proper and head for an overnight sleep at the mountain hut of Walami then permissions as well as reserved beds are required. Information here ysnp.gov.tw/en.

After leaving Yuli we find ourselves on the beautiful side road of the 193. This old highway hugs the eastern flank of the valley and is a great quiet ride around the northern section of the E.R.V. It leads us first to the town of Ruisui (瑞穗). Situated at the narrower point of the valley, this town and its neighboring village of Hongye (紅葉) are where you will find the region's hot springs and spa hotels.

One of the most famous and developed areas of natural hot springs. Like a lot of hot springs in Taiwan, don't expect wild streams, rather a mix of private hotels and spas that offer passes to their pools.

After we leave Ruisui we now follow a quiet hillside through the jungle farms of the undulating 193 as we head closer and closer to Hualien. From here we pass alongside cute villages, streams, old private farming that differs from the larger farms of the valley floor. Expect to see farmers still tending their crops by hand and small paddy fields mixed among bamboo, betel nut and wild forests. Monkeys play in the trees, and along this route some of Taiwan's rare birds and butterflies hang close by.

As we near the end of the 193 the road has a few climbs in shaded quiet, but the last section eases down to the coast and the edges of Hualien where we connect with the Hualien Coastal Bikeway, a truly beautiful end of ride that leads into the heart of the city via its wonderful beach boulevard.

There is so much more we have not covered in our E.R.V. adventure, such as Liyu Lake (鯉魚) on the northern edge of the valley. This area is beautiful with a fun lakeside path, and great mountain views. A worthwhile trip if you happened to skip Sun Moon Lake (日月潭) or fancy a relaxing afternoon ride. All the major towns along the route have great information centers that can provide a lot more details on highlights and adventures that can be had. So, take your time and explore the region.

So, ride the coastal route or the East Rift Valley?
Despite all that we have said and the beauty of the valley, for our tour we have still chosen the coastal route and kept the E.R.V. as an alternative route. With the absence of dramatic views and wonderful beachside adventures the E.R.V. cannot match the pleasures of the coastal road.

During autumn and winter the lush greens of the paddy fields in the E.R.V. are replaced with brown soil and gray skies. This should not put you off, rather to mention that the real highlights of this area should be seen during spring and the summer harvests.

But it is a great option to explore some hikes and see some beautiful agriculture. This flat portion of the country allows for a really happy and simple ride without any fuss. The air is clear and the life is quiet here. Take a break, soak those tired feet and gawp at the high-looming mountains.

Those of you who want to mix the two together may consider switching from coast to valley shortly after Shiping (石梯坪). At the coastal village of Fengbin (豐濱) turn up the hill crossing highway T11甲. This lovely road is the softest climb of all the E.R.V. crossings. It also happens to be one of the prettiest, supplying some of the best views as you descend into the valley. Once over the hills you can join straight onto the 193 for the most northern sections of the E.R.V. route. You might have missed some of the famous rice fields lower down, but this region's fields offer matching views with a quieter feel.

Taitung to Dapo Pond

0.00 Start, from the main boulevard junction of the T11 in Taitung! Head north from the eastern edges of Taitung (台東) along Mahengheng Boulevard (馬亨亨大道). Follow signs for the train station. See p180 for the route.

From any location in Taitung you can follow this route through the valley, just ride to the train station and follow from there.

4.25 Head straight. At the crossroads, cross at the lights staying on the bike path. The road bends northeast from here.

5.85 Taitung train station. Keep straight, heading north at the junction with Xinxing Road (新興路), here is the main junction one block down from Taitung train station. This station has great connections across to the west coast, Hualien and the north.

If you are joining here from the train station, exit the station entrance, cross around the taxi/car pull-in and head down the avenue that runs opposite the station front, turning left on Xinxing Road.

6.17 Turn right onto Beian Road (北安路). A side road into residential houses. Follow this side road through several small junctions as it travels down a suburban street.

6.50 Lean left at the end of the road; it really narrows and bends sharply down a small lane.

7.00 Lean right after passing houses. The regular road seems to end. Head right down the slope, toward the stream below.
Cross the small water canal.

7.10 Turn left, taking the second turning on slightly higher ground.

7.45 Turn right through the vegetable farm. Just before the underpass cross through the farm lane.

7.50 Turn left onto the 東45. Here turn left onto the road facing the red-and-white telephone tower.

7.80 Cross the river along the flat bridge.

8.45 At the end of the bridge the road bends left, northbound. Pass the sign for E.R.V. recreation park.

11.7 The road starts to climb here as it nears its end.

14.2 Turn left onto the 197 at the end of the 東45. The road heads uphill here.

22.8 Junction with road 東23 at the small village. This side road cuts through the coastal mountains and joins with the T23 and Donghe (東河) after

45km. It is a truly stunning route but the initial and then second climb up at the beginning are tough. If you want a more remote challenge head this way.

23.9 Bottom of the descent. You have two choices here: stay on the 197 as it climbs for 8km or, alternatively, turn left here, cross the river to Luye (鹿野) and a flat ride along the north of the river. The 197 here is a tough, tiring climb. If your aim for the day is to minimize strain then don't ride this portion of the road. On the other hand, the road up is lovely, quiet and with some great views from on high. The descent is short but fun.

Avoiding the climb along the 197
From the town of Luye head north along highway T9 until the right turning for the 東29, following signs for Ruiyuan (瑞源). After passing through the town the road runs alongside rail tracks, after further km turn right onto Bao Hua Road. Follow signs for Baohuashan (寶華山), crossing the rail tracks and then the river. Once you arrive across the river follow a steep set of switchback road up above the small village to reach the main 197 again. Turn left back onto the 197, rejoining after its largest climb.

33.1 Top of the climb.
43.6 The road joins from Baohua village. From here the 197 undulates up and down, for the next 20km until it reaches the village of Wan'an (萬安).
60.5 Village of Wan'an, from here the 197 is flat on the valley floor. Follow the road as it first bends right and then left through the village.

Paradise Road and Brown's Boulevard
At the corner turn in Wan'an a small left lane will take you to the edges of the paddy fields that are strewn across the valley floor. Here is the start of the famous Paradise Road and Brown's Boulevard. These roads crisscross through the middle of the rice fields and offer great panoramic views of the farming area, the mountains and, no doubt, the rolling clouds that linger above them. The two roads cross in the middle and so you can navigate down one, turning back up the other to keep you on the 197. Plenty of people on rented electric bicycles adds to the atmosphere.

61.2 Entrance to Paradise Road on your left. Head down the straight road through the fields. Watch out for the electric buggies being driven by tourists enjoying the day.
61.3 Public bathrooms beside the church, plenty of buggy rental stores here.
61.4 Turn left at the small lane looking for a cycle path that runs parallel to highway 197. If you can't find the path just stay on the quiet road, north.
Lean right onto the bicycle path, heading north toward Dapo Pond (大坡池).
62.9 Finish at the entrance for Dapo Pond! There is a bike path that circulates around the entire pond. The exit at the opposite side of the pond leads to the large town of Chishang (池上) and the T9.

Dapo Pond to Ruisui

62.9 Start at Dapo Pond, any exit, head north! From the pond or from Chishang town we need to find the T9 and head north along the highway. Leaving Taitung County behind, we are now officially in Hualien (花蓮).

64.4 Turn north onto the T9. The 197 ends here as you join the T9. Follow the road as it weaves its way north.

69.2 Junction with the T23.

T23 mountain crossing
This road heads up and over to Donghe (東河) arriving at the monkey bridge and the stunning east coast highway, p187. It is the longest of the many roads that connect the E.R.V. with the east coast. It is a beautiful, vista-filled journey. From the valley, there is a soft 15km climb up to the pass before a lovely, long 30km descent to the coast. If you have had enough experience of the E.R.V. this crossing takes you to the near beginning of the east coast route, meaning you will still see most of the main route's highlights.

82.5 After some straight road the lanes split and widen just before the town of Dongli.

83.5 STOP! Dongli train station. Hidden to your left is a real gem, the old train station has been transformed into a bicycle station and the start of the Yufu bicycle trail (玉富自行車道).

Yufu bicycle trail
The Dongli to Yuli bicycle route is a fantastic bikeway that winds around the valley along an old railway line. Passing fields, forest and old stations, with a long wooden platform that lifts you away from the highway, and gifting great views. You can join the bikeway at the Dongli old train station. Enter through the main doors of the station or around the side. Lots of places here to sit and relax. The views of the surrounding mountains from the old platform are wonderful.

The bike path finishes just after a long train bridge after our turning onto the side highway 193. You can ride into Yuli from here but at the end

Walami hiking trail

Originally a through path conceived of by the occupying Japanese rulers, who were determined to tame and farm Taiwan's inner mountain's forests and communities. The Walami Trail is a beautiful day hike that starts in the valley's hills and winds up high in the mountains. The trip can be extended into an overnight return adventure with a night in one of Taiwan's delightfully rustic camping huts. The route is popular and the trail well trodden. Pass through forest across suspension bridges and up into the mountains. The trail stretches around a mountainside, giving incredible views of the hidden depths to Taiwan's spiky peaks.

For the most adventurous of you, the Walami Trail is also the start of an epic seven-day trail that takes you all the way up to Taiwan's highest peak, via its back routes, and into the heart of the fantastic Yushan National Park (玉山國家公園).

No permits are needed for a day hike up here, but once you cross onto the trail proper and head for an overnight sleep at the mountain hut then permissions as well as reserved beds are required. ysnp.gov.tw

of the raised bridge turn left and off the path, the road will lead down and loop back under the bike bridge. Turn left again and follow the lane toward the slope up to the main T9 highway. Head back along the T9 on the bridge with the bike path bridge now on your right, turning left onto the 193 shortly after.

86.7 Antong (安通) cycling station. If you are not too interested in the next 3km of bike path then leave the path here. Pass through the station and then turn left, north, back onto the T9.

87.6 Turning on right for T30 mountain crossing to the east coast highway. This crossing is quite direct and leads you to the center of the east coast route. The views of the valley from the top of the pass are great, as is the long tunnel that cuts through the heart of the mountain. The winding route down to the coast from there is fast and you will be at the ocean highway in no time.

Antong natural hot spring
A rarity in Taiwan, natural hot spring waters right by the roadside. Just 2km up the T30 from the valley is the hot spring of Antong village. The river that runs by the roadside has hot spring waters and there is a free access point behind the small resort. The pools are shallow and only really suitable for dipping your feet, but the hot waters are great for giving them a good soak and rest.

If you want a full dip you will need to pay for one of the two resorts there. The main resort on the other side of the highway has an extensive collection of outdoor pools at different temperatures; with a respectable day fee this is not a bad way to spend an afternoon.

90.6 Turn right onto the 193 on a long sweeping corner. There is one convenience store here. If you took the bike trail cross over the river along the bike bridge then head back along the highway. The 193 weaves and runs flat through farms and small villages. Enjoy the quiet ride for 20km.

Head to the town of Yuli. For stores, tea shops, a train station and a helpful information center where you can find maps and details on the surrounding area and the nearby Walami Trail (瓦拉米).

114 Finish at the town of Ruisui (瑞穗)! Cross the river heading toward the town. There are several turnings right to bypass it if you don't need provisions, but the rest of the 193 has very little in the way of stores. It is worth stopping for at least a break here.

This town is similar in size and scale to Chishang and Yuli before, but as the name suggests (Ruisui, literally meaning "hot water"), this little spot is the center of the E.R.V.'s hot spring culture. There are plenty of options for hot springs at the back of the town, just follow the road that leads directly up the hill from behind the train station. Most hot springs are also resorts or hotels, but most offer day passes for their facilities. Many of the valley's hot springs are tucked far into the hillsides and can be expensive affairs. Ruisui offers easy access to a nice hot soak.

DAY 3

Ruisui to Hualien

<u>114</u> Start, at the town of Ruisui! Turn north, out of Ruisui on the 193, follow signs for Cimei (奇美). The quiet highway turns north through the town two blocks east of Ruisui train station.

From here until we reach the end of our ERV route there are very few chances for food or supplies. The small villages we pass through have minimal stores that are unreliable. For water stop off at police stations you pass as they are always open and available.

<u>115</u> Head straight, cross the river one more time.

<u>116</u> Turn left, staying on the 193.

花64 mountain crossing
Turn right here for the 花64 that heads back across to the coast and arriving at Shitiping (石梯坪). This is a beautiful mountain road passing up, over and down following an oceanbound river as the road weaves through indigenous towns. This is possibly the toughest of the east coast mountain crossings, and it takes a long time to navigate. The end point is the beautiful coastal sight of Shitiping, p218.

<u>136</u> Turn right at the T junction in a small village, staying on the 193. As the road ends, first turn right then turn left, following signs.

T11甲 mountain crossing
The T11甲 is the last mountain crossing to the east coast before we hit the city of Hualien. This is perhaps the best crossing; the climb is easy and short and the views lovely. Crossing from the east coast to the valley at this point is a good option for those not wanting to miss too much of the coastal route while wanting to experience the valley and its pretty northern farming area. Crossing from the valley to the coast here makes little sense as most of the coastal road's highlights have been passed and the coast's one long climb is still to come.

144 The 193 runs along beautiful rice fields and farms here, but after some km's it dips and climbs as it leaves the main valley floor area and passes through a wild part of the hillsides. It's a really beautiful part of the ride. If you have combined days two and three together then this section might prove to be a little tiring.

147 Lean left at the junction at the village of Shanxing, stay on the 193.

148 Turn right, at the junction, keep on the 193 at this interesting bridge and viewpoint. Cross the bridge if you want to find the T9 at Fenglin.

169 Turn left then right through the last village of Yumei. Here you can get snacks form a local store and top up your water at the friendly police station.

179 Turn left, onto the T11 at the end of the 193. Crossing the river we leave the valley behind us. now on the T11 highway that came from the coast. Finish, turn onto Hualien Coastal Bikeway! After crossing the bridge turn right onto the Hualien Coastal Bikeway. Look for the small wooden entrance onto the forested boardwalk, here we rejoin our main route toward the end of Day 14, p224.

Hualien & Taroko

The height of our coastal adventure ends
up narrow gorges, roads chiseled into
cliff walls, campgrounds wedged in beauty as
suspension bridges sway. We ride deep into
the mountain where rapids gush below and
hikers ramble overhead.

Giant green knuckles loom large and
stretch up the entire coastline as the
Pacific Ocean laps at these island-sized
toes. Stunning cliff-hugging road offers
epic views of the scene along
Taiwan's newest cycle paradise.

Hualien & Taroko

The gorge that runs through Taroko National Park is a wondrous sight of nature's scale, size and beauty, while the ride up and down the road that weaves, cuts and climbs its way through this narrow space is something truly unbelievable; it has to be seen. This is a place to remember and an adventure that is best served up on two wheels, lucky us then.

As we leave the coast and take the long bike trail into the coastal city of Hualien, the peaks that launch up into the sky just become even more colossal. The mountains on the coast of Hualien stretch up thousands of meters into cloud and don't stop there. The scale is magnificent and it shows the enormity of the adventure just around the corner.

Spend a night or two in this quirky city with one of the best night markets on the island. Hualien also has, like a lot of the east coast, a vibrant arts scene, it feels lived in and loved by its residents. As we wander the streets here you are never far away from a view of those impressive mountains. Leaving the city, we face them head-on, as the land narrows leaving not much room for anything else.

Next up on our never-ending list of adventures is perhaps the best of the lot. Certainly one that every tourer should undertake. Welcome to the frankly stupendous Taroko Gorge. Taiwan's premier natural wonder.

A day spent riding up this magnificent gorge might just be the most perfect freewheeling adventure out there. With so much to stop at and see, and with limited space for parking, riding up on bicycle allows you a freedom other road users only dream of. Add in the option of staying at Taiwan's best free campground and spending a night up in between the cliff walls might just make this the highlight of your trip.

Goosebumps are never far away as you stretch out on grass and stare up at the hills rising around you, the sound of the gushing rivers below and the freshest air you have ever breathed. Riding the gorge road back down to the coast is epic, mind bending and joyous. Enjoy.

The last day from Hualien up to the northern city of Yilan is a new, wondrous coastal adventure, wild, largely car free and with world-beating views. Forget what you have heard, this last stretch of the east coast is magnificent, unparalleled and breathtaking. Trust us when we say that this reborn highway is fast becoming Taiwan's favorite stretch of ocean touring.

Shitiping to Hualien

Once we leave Shitiping (石梯坪) we head for the northern end of the T11, and the east coast city of Hualien (花蓮), gliding along the last piece of gentle coastal road. As we set off we're squeezed between sheer green hills and jaw-dropping ocean. This narrower road is a stunning start to the day, with 15km of gliding, dipping and weaving around bays and cliffs to the first village of the day, Fengbin (豐濱). This fishing village has a couple of stores to take a break from the sun, or the rain. This also marks the last chance to cross over onto the E.R.V. before we reach the end of the coast road and the city of Hualien.

The east coast road carries on ebbing and flowing with the waves before throwing us one last surprise. At the gorgeous bay of Jiqi (磯崎) the road climbs away from the coastline; after a few switchbacks we pass a beautiful cliff-hanging viewpoint and free campground before riding up and over a series of small passes. When we hurtle back down to the ocean blue again through a series of stunning tunnels the wind is really at our back. Make sure to stop at the small café at the top of the first ascent; it is a cute affair with locally grown coffee beans and a host who is very friendly to cyclists.

Once back on the oceanfront, it is a fast, flat race to the end of the coast road and the fringes of Hualien city. As we run out of road we drift away from the ocean and point toward the city. Here we cross the wide river mouth and end our day leisurely following the Hualien coastal bike path: a beautiful meander through mangroves, along river, beach and bustling promenades that eventually ends just as the city's famous night market switches on its lights and sound, ready for the evening of games, music, drinks and of course, delicious food. This is the ultimate bike path entrance to a city. You will really feel you have earned a short city break here in the shadows of the mountains.

We end the day's route in the center of the city by the train station. This area is rife with hostels but it is also the best path out of the city the following day. Hualien is a cool city nestled at the base of some glorious green peaks.

If you don't want to sleep in the city and have the energy to push on through to the other side, just carry on the coast bike path as it skirts beautifully around the fringes, taking us toward the town of Chongde (崇德) at the mouth of Taroko Gorge (太魯閣). Equally people have happily spent the night camping by the Qixingtan (七星潭) beach park in Hualien or on the beautiful coastline to the east of the city.

The next day takes us to the famous, unique and unbelievable gorge road inside Taroko National Park (太魯閣國家公園) and a free campground in one of Taiwan's most beautiful settings. So enjoy the city in the shadow of mountains and clouds, rest up and dream of the gorge adventure ahead.

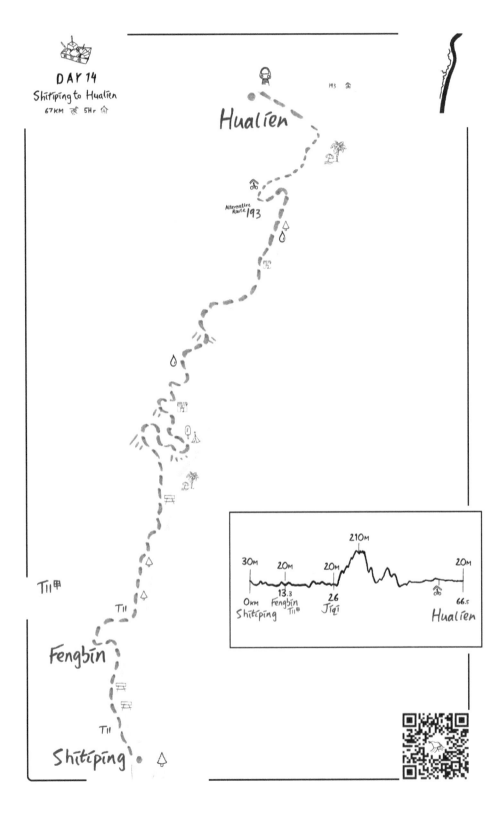

DAY 14

Shitiping to Hualien

67KM 5Hr

Hualien

193

Alternative
Route 193

T11甲

T11

Fengbin

T11

Shitiping

Elevation profile:

30M — 0KM Shitiping

20M — 13.3 Fengbin T11甲

20M — 26 Jíqi

210M

20M — 66.5 Hualien

DAY 14

67KM 🚴 5Hr 🏠

0.00 Start by heading north from Shitiping (石梯坪) recreational park! The T11 is narrow and without a shoulder until we reach Fengbin (豐濱).

3.50 Shimen Banshaojiao (石門班哨角) rest stop. Incredibly beautiful and well-designed open-air ocean and star amphitheater. Built for you to sit, forget the road behind you and just look out at the vastness of everything, beautiful.

3.80 Shimen rest stop, with toilets. Head down the steps to the ocean rock archway, used as a location for Martin Scorsese's *Silence*, filmed entirely in Taiwan.

5.14 Pull-in with an elevated platform with views of the ocean and coastline, stunning on a sunny morning.

13.3 Fengbin. Shops and breakfast cafés galore in this small town.

13.5 Lean right, crossing a short bridge.

13.8 Turn right keeping on the T11 after crossing a bridge. The road splits, lean right to keep on the coastal highway.

Left and uphill will take you onto T11甲 toward the E.R.V. This is our prefered route over to the valley if you are combining the two. This is the last chance to do so before we reach Hualien (花蓮).

18.5 A rest stop with some public art and photographs of the area. With a café and fruit stall sellers.

22.6 Old road that used to be able to stretch through all around the cliff. Now a tourist walkway with ticketed entrance.

22.7 Tunnel well lit with cyclist warning light system.

26.0 Jiqi (磯崎) beach rest stop. Toilets, campground (often closed) and views of the bay from an open pagoda to the south.

There is a simple clifftop walk here, if you have the energy to climb up the set of steps just beside the small parking lot and jetty, with great views—but where doesn't have great views around here?

28.1 Start of today's climb. A few undulations before a sharp climb around a few switchback corners.

32.0 Rest stop on the corner of the last switchback. Amazing views of Jiqi bay from up high as well as a café that sells coffee and ice cream.

With public bathrooms and a secret hidden official free campground. This is not the top of the climb, take a short break here but save your big rest for when you finish the climb.

33.5 First false peak but a sense of satisfaction as the harder part of the climb is finished. A short tunnel marks the end of the climb, leaving the coast shortly for a beautiful inland ride.

33.9 On your right shortly after the tunnel is an amazing rest stop. Public toilets behind a local store with a very friendly owner who grows and roasts his own coffee beans, which results in a great cup. He is very warm toward cyclists and will happily chat with you. Otherwise, take a seat outside and admire the views.

34.4 A short ride and finally you have reached the peak of the climb. Now the real fun begins. Stunning views as the road smoothly bends and twists around hillsides.

39 The road plateaus at the town of Shuilian (水璉), which has a gas station and a couple of small shops.

40.3 As you leave the flat straight, the road climbs for one last time, a short 1km climb is a bit tiring but after this the day is nothing but flat.

41.3 Top of the last climb.

41.9 The start of a long tunnel section and descent. There is plenty of space inside for bicycles and a bicycle warning system to notify cars you are in there. Well lit, this tunnel is straight and heads downhill so you can ride fast through. It's exhilarating, especially when it opens up occasionally to give glimpses of the coast and green cliffs to the right.

44.4 End of the tunnel and the road bends down to the coast.

Now is the last stretch of the coastal T11. A 10km length of straight fast road with a few dotted seafood restaurants and resorts. A long rest stop with bathrooms and a path about halfway along. Time for one last break and view of the ocean.

56.8 Lean left, away from the ocean. The road curves away from the ocean, almost completing a 180° turn; you are momentarily heading south again.

57.3 At the bottom of the short hill, as you face southward, the East Rift Valley is in front of you. A long flat bridge crosses the wide riverbed.

57.6 Turn right across the bridge. Hop onto the curb crossing over the stony river; stay on the bike path that is a slippery white stone for some reason.

Our alternative route along the East Rift Valley joins us here from the side road 193.

58.1 As you leave the bridge make sure you are in the bike path, after a few meters you can see the wooded gateway onto the Hualien Coastal Bikeway.

<u>58.2</u> Turn right onto the Hualien Coastal Bikeway at the narrow entrance through the wooden gate. A beautiful end to the day and a very relaxing entrance to the city. If you worry that the main road would be a faster entrance to Hualien then think again; it is clogged with traffic and a continual blockade of traffic lights.

If you need supplies you will find a convenience store next to the gas station just ahead, just double back for the bike trail.

59.8 After a couple of km on the bike path you come to a parking lot, keep to the right and follow the path where it is closest to the water's edge. Re-enter some more woodland before coming to a park.

<u>60.6</u> Turn right, onto the beach path at a blue information sign. Here the path arrives at a beach. It feels like you are heading straight onto the sands. At the info board turn right and follow the path, once again, that is the closest to the shore. All of a sudden, the path slopes up off the sand and pulls you onto a raised platform that trundles along a promenade raised up above the beach.

<u>62.9</u> Stay on the beach promenade crossing the wooden bridge and then turn right to carry on the beach path, once again keeping you on the shoreline. People-watch with glee as you travel along the (concrete) boardwalk as we enter the city.

63.7 Here the bicycle path finishes and heads down away from the beach. All of a sudden you are upon the brightest blue you have ever seen. You can be forgiven to think you have arrived in the middle of an Olympic triathlon event.

64.0 At the end of the blue path, you are underneath an overpass. Instead of turning right back to the beach, here we leave the bikeway.

<u>64.0</u> Turn right onto the 193 at these tricky traffic lights, using the waiting box. When the lights go green head forward as the road bends slightly to the right. You will see the large night market area on your left.

Riding through Hualien

If you want to skip around Hualien city and head further up the east coast toward Taroko (太魯閣) then head up the ramp to your right and stay on the ocean bike path. Follow the bike trail and signs as they lead you along and around the city's harbor area, eventually bringing you out at Qixingtan to the north of the city and highway 193, which is now a quiet coast road. You can rejoin our main route here on Day 15, p231.

<u>64.2</u> Turn left onto Zhongshan Road (中山路); almost immediately at the next set of lights turn left onto the long wide road, pulling up alongside the entrance to the large night market.

You are on Zhongshan, or central mountain, Road. Sure enough, at the most northern point of this road you can see some giant mountains reaching up into the sky. You can use this road as a focal point as you navigate the city's grid pattern.

Hualien night market

Here you are now outside the entrance to the night market, a great, sprawling, never-ending place to taste, drink and play with all of east Taiwan's delights at nighttime. Possibly the best night market outside Taipei.

<u>66.5</u> Finish beside Hualien train station! After traveling north up Zhongshan Road, crossing many blocks of the city's main shopping area, you reach the corner of a small park, and the junction with Guolian 1st Road (國聯一路). The road ahead ducks underneath the main rail line. Turning right here takes you to Hualien train station.

This is where we leave today's journey. This area has lots of hostels. If you want to carry on farther out of town, keep heading straight underneath the railway line, and follow our route for Day 15.

Hualien to Taroko

Dramatic high peaks loom over the coastal city of Hualien (花蓮). If you wake up on a brisk morning look out your window, wander down Zhong-shan Road (中山路), or perhaps you slept by the breezy coast and you peek out of your tent to see soaring high peaks rising out from the ocean along the bay ahead. The misty mountains offer the sense of adventure that is just around the corner. The narrow entrance up into the mountains at Taroko Gorge (太魯閣) is waiting for us, there's anticipation in the air.

Taroko National Park (太魯閣國家公園) is possibly Taiwan's most famous natural attraction. Dramatic peaks and beautiful hiking areas that straddle a unique gorge, which winds up between steep cliffs. The single, narrow road up, highway T8, starts all the way down at the river's mouth, tracing alongside the water no matter how narrow the space gets. It winds, climbs and crawls along cliff edge, through tunnels cut into the rock, and over bridges that crisscross the gushing waters below. Finally, it all gets too much and it pushes out and onto the other side, somehow stretching even steeper up, away from the river, disappearing into Taiwan's high mountains above.

The meandering journey up through the gorge is a great example of a bicycle's being a perfect vehicle for exploring, eclipsing experiences from the windows of larger vehicles. With plenty of sights along the way, having the freedom to stop and take in the atmosphere is very welcomed. The feeling as you wind your bike up or down this narrow gorge is exhilarating. It is a worthwhile day's ride. But if you simply don't want to stay up here, either a round-trip from Hualien is doable with an early start, or you can stay by the coast at the mouth of the gorge at Chongde (崇德) and head up for the day from there.

If you are riding from Hualien all the way to Yilan (宜蘭) in one day, adding this as a side trip would probably be too much, but you can always include the

226

first section up to the Changchun (長春) shrine and then zip back down the old mountain road. This only adds a couple of km to your day and will still give you a sense of the area.

The journey to the campground nestled up in the gorge beside the raging but elusive river is not a long one, around 40km from Hualien train station, but with a few steep sections and a lot of sightseeing to do along the way this is a day to savor. Make sure you arrive to pitch your tent in the early afternoon, this gives you plenty of time to explore a little farther up the road and to find dinner and provisions from the small shops on offer.

Leaving Hualien is straightforward and all main roads can be avoided. Keep following Zhongshan Road directly toward the mountains; this will feel odd as it is the wrong direction for the northern area we are heading to. But after reaching the stadium to the north of the city we take a sharp turn and race along toward the coast, where we cross the busy T9 highway and find the 193, which has now become a quiet side road. Heading north finally we roll through old atmospheric graveyards, past photogenic beaches and quiet tree-lined rural farms before crossing the T9 again, avoiding this busy road and taking one last beautiful back road with incredible views of lush mountains and crystal blue rivers at the indigenous village of Sanzhan (三棧) before a fun route through Xiulin (秀林) up to the edges of Taroko National Park.

When you reach the small village of Taroko you will not think much of its shabby shops and wide, developed boulevard. This is simply to provide facilities for the holiday cars and tourist buses that come through here all year long.

But at the farthest point of the town, the road suddenly narrows and ends at the beautiful old gate entrance where the gorge road comes into view. This is a great spot to grab a photo and take a break before the ride up really begins.

The adventure starts almost immediately as you pass through a tunnel network to reach Changchun shrine, a picturesque temple hanging over a gushing waterfall, etched into the side of the cliff. Further up from here the gorge narrows, leaving only space for our winding road and the fallen rocks below. Even on bad-weather days this area is stunning, and you should take your time as we pass one beautiful turn after another, with plenty of reasons to stop at most.

Arriving at the entrance to the Swallow Grotto Trail, leaving the main road behind you can take your bike through, walk or ride through the rock-etched tunnels that peer over the waters below and breathtaking cliffs above. An implausible path chiseled out of sheer rock face, this area is not one to ride through in a hurry. This is one of the best vantage points along the ride but we are hardly done yet.

Follow the cliff road as it weaves higher and higher up into the mountain, revel in the sights and sounds of the gushing river and the unscalable heights of the mountain cliffs. Take a break from riding and walk along the Tunnel of Nine Turns, a thoroughly pleasant cliff walk with historical information and, dare I say it, even more views.

Shortly after, we arrive at our camping area in Lushui (綠水). There are two campgrounds; my money is on the free campground with few facilities but picnic tables, clean bathrooms and riverside views, all hidden away from the main road. Meet other cyclists and hikers who are pitching for the evening. If you don't camp then there is one expensive hotel in the village above, but otherwise there are plenty of guesthouses in Chongde at the bottom of the mountain by the coast.

After you have set up camp, take your much lighter ride and head a couple of km up the road to the monastery village of Tianxiang (天祥). There you will find a convenience store and other eateries as well as an information center. Be aware that once the sun sets a lot of these stores close.

Farther up is the tail end of the gorge and some great short walks through tunnels and cliff sides. Then T8's true climbing starts as it sharply heads up to the top of Taiwan's high mountains. See p238 for more information on the famous climb up to Taiwan's highest road pass. After a night's rest at the campsite you might feel like tackling this route.

For now, head back to camp and enjoy your night listening to the gorge sing as you stretch out under the starry sky. It's safe to say, this day is full of wonder and joy. We bristle just at the thought of it, jealous of your adventure ahead. If you are new to riding and worry about any climbs, rest assured Taroko is a must; with easy grades and simple uphill sections, it leaves plenty of energy to be left speechless as you stretch your neck up and gawp at the nature of it all. Splendid.

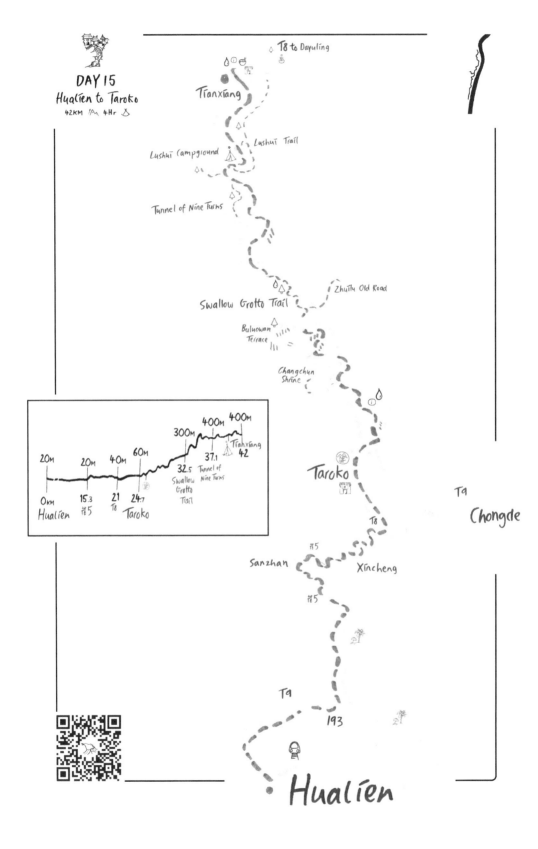

DAY 15
Hualien to Taroko
42KM 🚴 4Hr ⛺

T8 to Dayuling

Tianxiang

Lushui Trail

Lushui Campground

Tunnel of Nine Turns

Zhuilu Old Road

Swallow Grotto Trail

Buluowan
Terrace

Changchun
Shrine

Taroko

T9
Chongde

T8

Sanzhan
#5

Xincheng

#5

T9

193

Hualien

Elevation profile
20M
20M
40M
60M
300M
400M 400M

Tianxiang
42

37.1
Tunnel of
Nine Turns

32.5
Swallow
Grotto
Trail

0KM
Hualien
15.3
#5
21
T8
24.7
Taroko

DAY 15

42KM 1/^ 4Hr 人

0.00 Start on Zhongshan Road in central Hualien! We start our day at the junction of Zhongshan Road (中山路) and Station Road. Facing north, the road dips under the rail tracks.

1.00 Head straight, carry on north through the intersections, pass the hospital on your left.

2.10 As you leave the city behind pass the baseball stadium on your left.

2.60 Cross the river, our turning is shortly after the bridge ends.

3.00 Turn right onto the 花T9. Notice the signposts for cycle routes that seem to lead in every direction. Largely ignore them, turn right onto highway 花T9, heading east.

3.50 Initially quite straight, the road passes a large army base on your left.

5.80 Lean right, keeping on the road as it bends to the right.

6.40 Cross the rail tracks.

6.80 Head straight, crossing the T9 at this main crossroads. Some stores are here if needed. Ignore the main highway here.

7.60 Pass alongside another larger army base.

8.46 Turn left onto the 193; at the end of the road you arrive at the quiet and beautiful 193. Those of you that took our E.R.V. route will recognize this, now tail end, of a rural road. It is a lovely quiet ride that offers access to great beaches and views as well as avoiding an ugly part of the main highway.

A right-hand turn here will take you quickly to the Qixingtan Beach Park (七星廣場), where people park up for the night, with an occasional night market and views across the beach and ocean beyond.

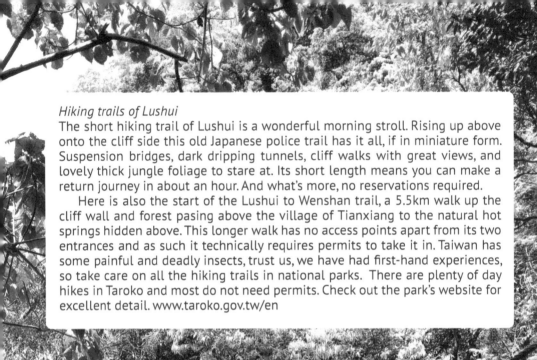

Hiking trails of Lushui

The short hiking trail of Lushui is a wonderful morning stroll. Rising up above onto the cliff side this old Japanese police trail has it all, if in miniature form. Suspension bridges, dark dripping tunnels, cliff walks with great views, and lovely thick jungle foliage to stare at. Its short length means you can make a return journey in about an hour. And what's more, no reservations required.

Here is also the start of the Lushui to Wenshan trail, a 5.5km walk up the cliff wall and forest pasing above the village of Tianxiang to the natural hot springs hidden above. This longer walk has no access points apart from its two entrances and as such it technically requires permits to take it in. Taiwan has some painful and deadly insects, trust us, we have had first-hand experiences, so take care on all the hiking trails in national parks. There are plenty of day hikes in Taroko and most do not need permits. Check out the park's website for excellent detail. www.taroko.gov.tw/en

9.40 The road winds through a cemetery. It's considered unlucky to disturb the ground in graveyards so best not linger here too long.

13.0 At the little seaside village of Jiawen (加灣) there is a beach entrance with an often calm, flat bay, perfect for a dip and jaw-dropping views of the mountains of Taroko (太魯閣) looming ahead.

14.5 The road leaves the coastline, narrowing and weaving through trees and long grass as we travel with mountains rising all around.

15.2 Head straight, cross over the junction with the T9. The 193 ends at a junction with highway T9. Wait for the lights and cross onto the small local lane opposite.

Head straight, across the busy road on the traffic lights. Now we are following a stunning old bike route over the railway track along narrow roads, past indigenous villages and sneaking us to the edges of Taroko without having the hassle of the traffic-heavy highway. You can ride along the T9, it's just nowhere near as enjoyable.

15.3 Turn right onto the quiet 花5 road. At the lane's end, turn immediately right onto the overpass and head up and over the railway tracks. Great views from on top of the mountains and railway lines.

16.1 Lean right, crossing the bridge. The road bends away from the village over a bridge and turns away.

Entrance to the village of Sanzhan (三棧), a beautiful village at the edge of a very swimmable river and impressive mountain backdrop. Worth a little break if you want to explore its narrow streets or swim in the cool river water with the locals.

16.9 Turn left, stay on the 花5. Now we are facing back toward the ocean. Look out on your left and just before the community park, turn left, down what seems to be a smaller side road but is actually the same 花5 route. If you reach the train tracks before turning then you have gone too far.

18.8 Lean right at the junction where the road splits at the village of Xiulin (秀林). Follow it right as it curves around the government buildings and cute cartoonish murals.

19.1 Lean left then right, staying on the main road heading northeast through the town as the road gently climbs. Some local shops and cafés here.

20.5 Turn left down the hill, toward the concrete mill at the road's end.

On a clear day there are great views here. The contrast between the brutalism of the industrial architecture and the natural green of the national park that threatens to consume it is ponderous. The road switches down a short descent before reaching the entrance of the factory.

The history of the cement factories of Taiwan and how they impacted the many indigenous communities is a sorry story. The lingering destruction of the natural landscape and communities can be felt further up the coast as there are many quarries and factories that line the edges of the national park.

21.0 Turn left in front of the factory entrance and train crossing. Cross the rail tracks with the factory entrance on your left.

21.4 Turn left, onto the T8 heading north toward Taroko. The T8 starts here.

The narrow T8 Central Cross-Island Highway snakes all the way up and through the national park gorge, and eventually above and beyond to the high mountain passes.

For the highway north and the seaside town of Chongde (崇德), turn right here and then cross the main bridge on the T9. Beachside campsites, homestays and a perfectly positioned train station are just over the bridge.

23.7 The town of Taroko, here you can find convenience stores and small tourist restaurants. Take a break here if you need to eat or stock up on water. The next real store is at the end of our Taroko ride, up above the road in the village of Tianxing (天祥).

24.4 Taroko old gate. Hanging across the road in front of the cliff archway is the old gate that marks the start of the adventure.

24.7 Turn right across the bridge. The road behind the gate is just for descending vehicles. Cross the bridge and take in the wide mouth of the gorge; if you are underwhelmed at this point, remain calm. This mountain road is just getting started.

24.8 Turn left, up the hill at the end of the bridge. This steep little push is the toughest bit of road and not an indication of how the rest of the gorge road will be.

Turning right here will lead you back down to the T9, the north, and Chongde, see p244. We will head this way on our Day 16 descent.

25.0 Head straight at the junction. Lean left as the road curves around the corner. The Taroko museum, with information and toilets, is just to the right.

25.1 The first tunnel of our climb, a nice and bright comfortable tunnel.

25.5 The tunnel opens up at a bridge that crosses in front of another gorge.

A hiking trail to the right and a parking lot area to the left. Enter another well-lit tunnel, after the bridge, often full of cars and coaches parked on the opposite side.

27.0 Junction with the old gorge road and Changchun shrine. Finally, we have reached the original gorge road and the cliff walls start to get close from here. Head straight up the T8 gorge road.

Here on your left you can spot the Changchun shrine on the cliff face across the river. This impressive shrine arches over an ever-flowing waterfall. It is well worth taking some time to walk the short trail up to the shrine or just marvel at it from the riverside viewpoint. You can do this when you leave the gorge if you don't want to stop on the way up, but if you have clear weather take the opportunity. We will head back this way for the descent.

From here the road is narrow, with a cliff wall on one side and cliff edge on the other. Don't worry, there is plenty of room and a guardrail all along the gorge route. There are rockfalls along this road, especially after a heavy rainfall, so often traffic is controlled for repair work. Go careful all along the Taroko route.

30.5 After some beautiful riding, scenery, bridges, and a tunnel you turn some sharp corners and arrive at the mouth of a dam. Here there is a pagoda rest stop. On a good-weather day the color of the water is an unbeliev-able hue.

31.0 Free helmet rental not needed, really, just keep your bike helmet on.

31.4 Left turning to the Buluowan plateau (布洛灣).

The suspension bridge and plateau views up there are great, the switchback road heading up is the steepest road in this part of the gorge, just saying. No through road up there so you will be returning the way you came, but up on top you might just be happy for the spectacular sus-pension bridge that hangs over the gorge. Also has bathrooms, informa-tion center and pretty grounds.

32.5 STOP! Turn right onto Swallow Grotto Trail. On your right is the entrance to the Swallow Grotto cliff trail. Head this way, take your bike and ride or walk, up to you. Meander and marvel at the amazing cliff walls, thunder-ing river below and the narrow atmospheric archway road that winds up, offering mind-blowing views. This is often the highlight of many people's trip.

Note the ticket booth for hikers. This is also the starting location of the incredible Zhuili Old Road trail (錐麓古道), a stunning day hike fa-mous for its narrow cliff walk without barriers. Advanced bookings needed for this one; foreign nationals have a quota but need to apply far in advance, it fills up every day so you can forget it without a reservation. Apply here: npm.cpami.gov.tw/en/apply_1.aspx.

33.1 A lovely rest stop just before a bridge crossing with views, as well as bathrooms and simple meals and snacks.

33.9 The end of the grotto trail, careful of merging with traffic if the lights are off. The road impressively skirts in and out of open-walled tunnels as it traces the river closely. Stunning.

37.1 Tunnel of Nine Turns. At the end of another new tunnel network is a new bus and car pull-in at the entrance of the Tunnel of Nine Turns. This re-built part of the old gorge road has been converted into a lovely trail that runs along a cliff edge overlooking the rapids below. With lots of infor-mation on the road's construction and the area's history. Well worth the break off the bike for the short return walk. Bathrooms here.

39.2 Foot suspension bridge with great view at the starting point of another stunning hiking trail. Entrance off the roadside up a few steps.

39.4 Heliu campground. The national park campground has raised platforms, bathrooms and parking. Reservations in advance must be made and there is a nightly fee for reserving a space. Not the end of the Lushui hiking trail here.

40.0 Lushui (綠水), information center and entrance to hiking trail. Public bath-rooms under the small, disused museum.

40.1 Lushui free campground. Steps down next to the parking lot for the free campground in a cute grassy area just above the gushing river. Potable water taps, picnic benches and a few raised platforms.

No reservations needed and no specific pitches but with only a few picnic tables, arrive earlier during busy times to snag a spot next to one. With only one hotel on the gorge road, this is the best location for a night's sleep, and boy what a lovely little spot it is. One of Taiwan's best free campgrounds. It is a basic affair with potable water taps and shade from trees; picnic tables and 24hr bathrooms are back up the steps behind the small museum. And did we mention the great mountain views, sounds of the gushing gorge river below and bright night sky with no light pollution, bliss.

41.2 Bridge with amazing views of cliffside temples and high-walled mountains. You are now entering the village.

42.0 Finish at Tianxiang village! Small food stalls, convenience store, information center, bus depot and public toilets in this little mountain rest stop. Perfect to grab supplies for the afternoon and evening. After getting everything you need, ride back down to the campground and enjoy your atmospheric night away from everything. Hope for clear skies and an amazing sunrise as beams of light shine down through the trees and cast light on the sheer cliff faces above.

This small village marks the end of the Taroko Gorge. The highway of course travels up into the clouds and beyond but this is where the tourist buses turn and head back down to Hualien. After the information center there is one more famous trail and parking lot area before the mountain road starts to become ever more steep and winding up the mountainside. See p26 for more information on the rest of highway T8's climb.

Notes on Taiwan's most famous mountain highway and the infamous KOM route

From Taroko Gorge the T8 Central Cross-Island Highway travels up through some of Taiwan's highest mountain ranges. It is an epic ride, honored every year with the world famous KOM Sea to Summit road bike race. Not for the faint of heart, this 100km, 4000m climb pushes riders to their limit as they contend with steep grades, relentless climbing, the effects of altitude sickness and, to top it all off, a strict time limit with hourly cut-offs for the slowest riders. Brutal indeed. But don't worry; those who want to tackle the route at their own leisure need not face such physical stresses and can enjoy the views.

The highway starts traveling up steeply after Tianxiang village. Shortly after is the trailhead for Baiyang, a great short walk through tunnels and along cliffs hidden in the mountains. Here also marks the road's departure from the gorge as it rises high into the mountains. Next up is the entrance to the Wenshan trail that leads to a natural hot spring right inside the gorge. Apart from a couple of cliffside stores, expect them to be closed; the road is deserted as it hugs the cliff walls and rolls around the mountains. Some sections are soft to climb but almost every km has some steep turns and high gradients.

About halfway up the ride you will come first to the narrow tunnel shortly before the Bilu Giant Tree. The tree is over three thousand years old and the café alongside is a warm welcome from the now cold air that envelops you. After the giant tree the atmosphere changes, as the mountains open up and the road starts to ride cliff edges overlooking whole ranges and clouds now far off across the horizon. You are nearing 3000m above sea level and the air is cold. If there is cloud or rain, you will need layers. As you pass by the climb's second public bathroom rest stop then through a narrow dynamite tunnel, you enjoy a short descent before climbing again; after a soft 10km the highway finally reaches the junction at Dayuling.

From there the T8 heads north and downhill toward Lishan, while the T14甲 heads up for the last 10km to the top of Wuling (武嶺) Pass. For more information from here see Day 3, p26, km marker 28.3, for the last of the ride up to Wuling.

If you take this route up the mountains expect one special adventure. The 40km mountain road up is almost indescribable in its beauty, but what it has in awe you will have to match in strenuous effort to reach the top. Expect up to a six-hour journey from Tianxing to the junction, up to two hours more to make it to Wuling. There are a few rest stops along the way where you could pitch for the night, but very little in the way of services so make sure you pack food and water if you plan to do so.

As much as we adore the challenge of this climb it is in descending the T8 that you will find a truly incredible experience. It is the best downhill ride in Taiwan. See the notes on the Central Cross-Island Highway, p26, where we delight in the journey down from the mountains to the east coast.

Taroko to Dongshan

Only one word comes to mind when talking about this day—traveling along the ocean cliffs from Hualien to Yilan is nothing short of epic! Starting from the top of the Taroko Gorge we glide down through the quiet early morning air, following the narrow river as it cascades toward the ocean. Once there we head north and arrive at sheer cliffs that fall straight down into the ocean. Some of the world's most stunning coastal roads are here, and we get to ride them, alone, without traffic, until we reach the end of our eastern ride and prepare for our last days in the north.

In days gone by the wild and winding coastal roads between Taroko (太魯閣) and the northeast coastal city of Yilan (宜蘭) would have been described as tough, exhausting and stressful. Many cyclists and concerned Taiwanese would suggest skipping the route altogether and taking a train. But times have changed and the now renamed highway T9丁, previously the only available route between the two coastal highlights, has been transformed into one of Taiwan's premier bike routes, eclipsing even the coastal highway in Taitung (台東). Get lucky with the weather and it might just be the best ride of your trip.

Sweepingly smooth cliff edge roads raise you up to glorious views of crystal clear blue ocean, green lush mountains that fall into the horizon and long golden sand beaches. Jaw-dropping roads fall into tunnels, dipping, carving and burrowing their way through and around this unique landscape. Not to mention the vibrant fishing villages, miniature temple rest stops, oh and the jungle fringes of Taiwan's Taroko National Park.

Rivers escape the lush green and flow into the ocean, while bridges of all manner of sizes and styles carry the highway across, over and around a seemingly abundant, unending nature. This is an incredibly wild and unique part of the country—this route could even give Northern California a run for its money.

Officially on the Taiwan CR1 route, this northern portion of highway T9 splits the traffic in two. Everything on four (or more) wheels spins off into a series of tunnels zipping them quickly up and down the coast on the new T9.

The old road has been transformed into a sleepy, almost hassle-free, bicycle paradise. You will find yourself riding in the middle of the lane, stopping where and when you please as the cliff road weaves, dips and slides around an ever-eroding coastline. The Taiwanese are in near-constant exhaustion rebuilding and repairing the coastal and mountain roads and no doubt, not too far into the future this route will slide into the sea, so get on it while you can.

So that's the good; what's the downside? Well, first is the amount of climbing to do, across the 100km of this day there is a total of 2250m. That's a lot of climbing to get through, across three main climbs that each get bigger and longer throughout the day. Individually not a huge struggle, but it does make this one of the longest days on our route. You could consider splitting this up into two days or skip the last climb of the day and take a train across to Yilan. Personally, I prefer to end the day as dusk takes its hold. Tackling the final fun descent down into Su'ao (蘇澳) with the sun setting off over your shoulder, and evening mist creeping in, is a treat.

The introduction of the new road sections has dramatically lowered the traffic flow over the last few years. However, the largest downside to this day remains a tricky section of road and tunnels at the beginning of the ride as the highway travels out from Chongde (崇德). Heading north, the new tunnel network is 7km away, and this stretch of road holds all of Taiwan's traffic at once. With three tunnels to tackle, this section can be a bit of a tough start.

Despite this warning, the section of road is not difficult to manage. With a smart cycle warning system and slow-moving traffic, not to mention the excellent rest to be had at Qingshui (清水) Cliffs along the way, this section is perfectly fine to tackle. And once you roll out of the third tunnel, you reach the splitting of the highway and solace on the now quiet T9丁.

The first 20km of our day is a startlingly wonderful breeze. From the free campground in Lushui (綠水) high up along Taroko Gorge Road we race back down the mountain in no time, past all the previous day's sights and in front of the Changchun shrine, until we reach the ocean and rejoin the T9 north at Chongde. The road's directions are simple for the rest of that day as we follow the T9 and T9丁 north along the coastal cliffs.

This is a personal journey; approach it based upon your confidence and energy levels. For example, taking a train from Chongde lends itself to a calmer journey and a time saver for those who need. Consider skipping the final climb of the day at Nan'ao and taking a train into Dongshan (冬山) avoiding potentialy exhausting rides at the end. In cycle touring everyone has their own way but we also find pleasure in ever-changing plans, occasionally saving your breath and relaxing on a train with the world going by outside the window.

Riding the whole route is a great achievement and the unique feeling of descending down the ocean road as it hugs the cliff walls with no stress of vehicles is a joy. Having ridden this route both before the tunnels opened and since the change, we can confidently say this route is immensely more enjoyable and stress free. It is one of our favorite roads on the island. On a warm sunny day, it stands alone and is truly special, so, if you can, grab the chance and ride.

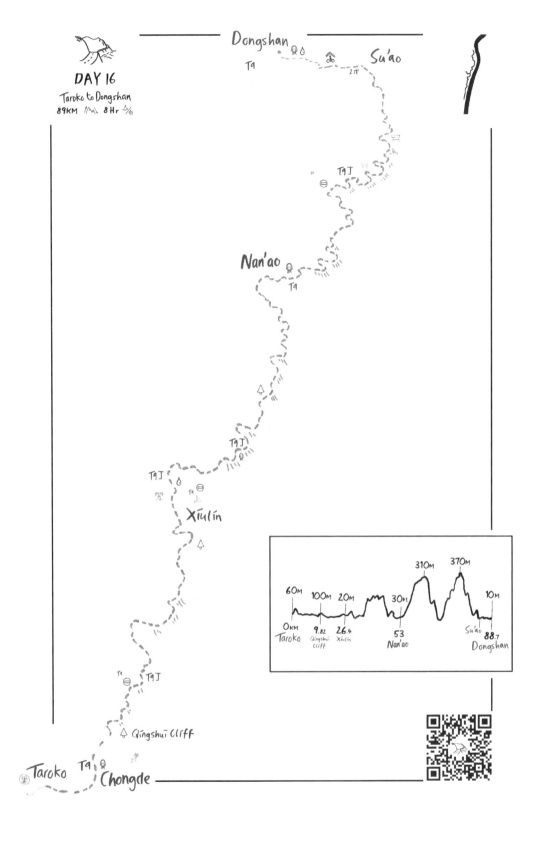

Dongshan

Su'ao

T9

2F

DAY 16
Taroko to Dongshan
89KM 8Hr

T9J

Nan'ao

T9

T9J

T9J

T9

Xiulín

Qīngshuï Cliff

Taroko   T9

Chongde

60M
0KM
Taroko

100M
9.82
Qīngshuï
Cliff

20M
26.4
Xiulín

30M
53
Nan'ao

310M

370M

10M
Su'ao

88.7
Dongshan

DAY 16
89KM /ᴧᴧ\ **8Hr** ᐟ⁄ᐣ

Notes on riding down the gorge road. Day 16 log starts at the Taroko gate, p244.

0.00 Starting in Tianxiang ride back down the 台8 Central Cross-Island High-way, the first stop is Lushui.

1.89 Lushui campground, information center, public bathrooms and trail head. If you slept here for the night then leave the campsite early, taking in any sites again along the way is a delight. No matter the time of year, it is quiet of traffic and audibly mesmerizing here in the mornings.

14.8 Turn right toward Changchun (長春) shrine just before entering a tunnel.. The shrine should now be directly in front of you.

15.1 Changchun shrine. Viewpoint opposite the cascading waterfall at the mouth of the temple. There are hidden public toilets at the viewpoint.
   To access the shrine cross the red bridge and follow the steps down to the right. A cave network etched into the side of the cliff wall leads to the shrine, where you can view the beautiful structure up close as the water flows all around you.

15.2 Cross the small red iron bridge shortly after you enter through a tunnel as the road bends left and away from the shrine.

15.4 Entrance to a network of trails on your right. Enjoy the downhill journey from here.

15.9 Turn right merging with the main highway, turning right back toward the old gate and the bottom of the gorge road.

17.1 Large parking lot and viewpoint below the road. Turn left here to find it.

17.5 Pass through one last archway, reaching the old gate once more. Take one last look back up toward Taroko (太魯閣).

<u>0.00</u> Start at the mouth of Taroko Gorge and the beautiful old gate! Turn across the bridge here heading north. Our day's ride north along the incredible costal highway starts here.

<u>0.15</u> Turn right, heading down the hill at the end of the bridge, following signs for Chongde (崇德). This side road heads down the hill quickly, reaching the ocean while avoiding the traffic.

<u>2.74</u> Turn left merging onto the T9, northbound. The traffic is busy but there is a shoulder as we head into Chongde.

3.25 The town of Chongde. As the highway rises onto the main drag of Chongde, a right turn here will take you into the sleepy farming village, with campsites by the ocean and some great views if you want to see the cliff highway before we head off.

5.00 Plenty of stores along the highway here, last chance for supplies for another 25km or so.

5.46 A small slip road for Chongde Train Station. With local trains throughout the day. Turn here if you are going anywhere north toward Yilan (宜蘭) or south for the short ride to Hualien. Tickets for the walk-on bicycle slots can be purchased at the counter without booking in advance. From here the road narrows with no shoulder for the next few km.

7.70 The first tunnel of the day, the road climbs steadily through the first two tunnels. This first section both bicycle and traffic are side by side in these intimidating tunnels, but don't worry, this is only for the first three tunnels that come in quick succession.

9.80 Stop at the Qingshui Cliffs. As you exit the third tunnel take a break on your right. A viewpoint of the cliffs along the old coast road, ride your bike along the way to see some incredible views.

10.7 Enter the last, long tunnel before the road splits.

<u>12.7</u> STOP! Be sure to take the right-hand lane joining the T9丁. Leave the new highway! As the road rises up to enter a long tunnel, leave the main highway here, taking the slip road down and to the right.

Do not enter the car-only tunnel, there are strict rules on this section of the T9 highway. Cyclists will be picked up by police and fined at least 10,000NTD.

<u>12.9</u> Turn right as the slip road sits underneath the T9丁, lean right and follow the old coastal highway as it narrowly hugs the cliff wall. There is no shoulder along this old road but as the traffic disappears, so do your worries. Enjoy the views and quiet cliff ride.

As the road descends bask in awe at the views ahead, the ocean hits the wide beaches and the mountains climb out of the ocean. The road dips and weaves through stone archways and there is barely a moment where the view ahead is not overwhelming. When in sunshine the flow of this road is unmatched in Taiwan.

<u>16.8</u> Merge right at the end of a descent. Here the T9丁 momentarily ends and rejoins the main highway just outside the village of Heren (和仁). The road has a wide shoulder from here and multiple lanes.

17.3　Cross the river mouth passing under a quarry conveyer belt. To your left, the edges of Taroko National Park and a large quarry complex.

17.6　Turn right onto the T9丁. At the crossroads at the end of the bridge, turn right traveling around the large fire station and leaving the T9 once more as it races off into another tunnel, their loss.

18.5　Enter a small tunnel.

23.2　Pass under the main highway before rejoining.

23.5　Turn left rejoining the main highway at this junction. Again wide with a shoulder.

26.4　Head straight, entering the town of Heping (和平) staying on the road into town, ignoring signs for the T9.

43.5　Stores and restaurants here at this dusty industrial town.

27.6　Turn left at the unmarked junction, as the road ends we rejoin the T9丁 toward Yilan.

28.0　Public restrooms and water can be found at the gas station here.

28.5　As you leave the town you are momentarily heading away from the ocean inland before the long flat bridge over the wide riverbed curves right.

29.3　Tunnel up ahead marks the end of Hualien County. Crossing into Yilan, the traffic is light here.

31.0　The road heads back toward the ocean after exiting the tunnel.

31.9　Keeping on the T9丁 passing under the T9 that is once again heading into the mountain. Our road is narrow and winding for some km's with great views in good weather.

32.5　Pass Hanben (漢本) rail station on your right, it is a good rest stop with ocean views from the platform.
　　　　From here the road climbs and winds around the cliffs. It is a stunning part of the day with some incredible views, and some very stiff climbing, especially if you are in the heat of the day.

37.6　At this long corner note the Buddhist shrine, behind there is a fast-rushing stream where waterfalls and jungle sounds can be heard all around.

39.5　Incredible views back down the road as it swings around the cliff corners. The ride is less steep after this next corner but still climbs for some glorious km's.

44.4　Top of the climb as the road bends away from the ocean. From here we slide down into the valley along a beautiful descent, with lovely sweeping corners.

48.3　The road flattens out as we reach a river. Watch out for quarry trucks.

49.4　Lean left across the river.

49.9　Turn right as the road heads under the main highway, now we are on a long straight stretch of smooth access road.

51.5　The T9丁 passes under the highway again here.

53.0　Cross the railway tracks, after which we immediately reach a store as we rejoin the T9 at the lights. From here the highway is a single-lane road that passes through the large town.

53.4　Enter Nan'ao (南澳), stores and a train station. In the wide flat valley is the last town with stores before our final two climbs of the day. Rest well here.

54.1 The road climbs out of Nan'ao from here. Unfortunately, we are climbing with the traffic as the two highways merge, but usually the traffic is respectful and slow to pass. The climb winds up through beautiful scenery and soon enough you reach the tunnel at the pass.

58.7 The highway hits the mountain as the mist descends upon our heads. Enter the tunnel here. It is a long but well-lit affair with two wide lanes giving plenty of space for you and traffic. Don't be afraid to take a little space.

60.2 Leave the tunnel and view the bay of Dong-ao (東澳) ahead as you descend.

64.1 Head straight at the junction, do not enter the main highway here as it turns left into the tunnels. Carry on into the small town.

64.7 Lean right at the traffic lights. As soon as you turn the road climbs. The road leaves the town from there. After this point the quiet T9丁 has one last long, sweeping climb up and around a cliff edge. It's a very beautiful ride and quiet from traffic. But it is long at over 7km before you reach the true top. The initial 3km climb will burn tired legs.

67.6 Rest stop at the shrine with views back down to the stunning bay.

70.1 Viewpoint at the top of the climb! Enjoy the vista, sunset and pulsating descent.

76.0 Viewpoint on the descent that overlooks the bustling port town of Nanfang-ao (南方澳).

78.9 Near the bottom is a slip road to the right, turn here if you want to visit the bustling little fishing port. The beach has yellow sand and the town has some great local food options. It really comes alive at night, well worth a look if you have time.

79.6 Turn left at the road's end, turn into Su'ao (蘇澳). As we pass through the town's main street you can find a train station, restaurants, stores and hotels.

81.4 Head straight across the highway at the edge of town. The T9丁 ends at this busy junction. Follow signs for the T9 and Dongshan (冬山) as several lanes cross each other.

From here we leave the ocean for the day; the rest of the ride along the T9 is dull and heavy with traffic. Make sure you catch the cycle path in a few km, which is poorly marked but is welcome relief from the now relentless traffic.

85.4 Turn off the T9, onto the bicycle path. A small bicycle lane on your right, this path takes you off the highway as you enter Dongshan. The path follows under the main train line and crosses through parks and across roads. Much more pleasant.

88.4 Pass in front of Dongshan train station. This large station front hosts the town's night market and has good facilities. Carry on in front of the station along the path. Bicycles are allowed to cycle here, just be aware it can get busy during evenings the market is on. Keep under the shadow of the railway tracks.

88.7 Finish at the bicycle junction in Dongshan Park! Shortly after you pass the station you reach the main park in Dongshan, where the bicycle paths lead off in all directions. Here is where we finish our ride for the day. Tomorrow we head into the island's north via Yilan's (宜蘭) coastal bikeway, our last ride along the east coast.

The region around Dongshan and southern Yilan has plenty of campgrounds, guesthouses and hotels for the night. If you want to free camp, follow the easy 13km along the bike path toward the coast where the coastal bikeway has rest stops.

The excellent Green Park homestay in Luodong (羅東) is a great option for the night. This charming homestay is well run by fellow cycle tourers who love to swap and share stories with other travelers. Right beside the wonderful Loudong park and river bikeway, there is easy access along the riverside to the coast in the morning.

Clockwise Notes
Hualien & Taroko

Dongshan, Yilan to Shitiping, Hualien

The ride from Dongshan in Yilan over the coastal mountains to the mouth of, and cycle up to, Taroko Gorge is a big ask for anyone to complete in a day. Despite our love for this coast road and its new-found position as a quiet cycle highway taking a train, at least for the first section to Nan'ao, can make for a more rewarding day.

The first climb up highway T9 from Su'ao is the longest and highest of the day, followed up by the car-heavy climb and descent to Nan'ao. Climbing out of Nan'ao valley is a much calmer affair and the ride down from there is superb. It is a simple enough riding day, with just one highway for the coastal route, just be aware you cannot stumble into the car-only highway T9, just like heading in a northerly direction you need to make sure you don't follow the flow of cars and trucks into the new tunnel networks. The fines are hefty.

For the path up to Taroko you can follow our main route, p231, as it is a return leg that starts and ends from the same coastal point. After passing through Chongde you can turn right up the slip road entering Taroko from the northern bank of the river.

The ride into Hualien from Taroko is simple enough especially if you take the quiet 193 along the coast. You can stay on this small road all around the outside of the city if you don't want to spend any time there. From Hualien you can ride simply enough to the coastal highway T11 or stay on the 193 as it becomes the beautiful and quiet back road south through the East Rift Valley. To reach either of these two routes simply head to the beach in Hualien and follow the bike path south until its end at the wide river mouth south of the city.

The coastal ride from Hualien to Shitiping is largely flat and rolling, often with the wind at your back. The climb up and down to Jiqi takes some time and comes in two sections. The first a simple enough straight climb that travels through some wide comfortable tunnels. It is the second climb that takes your energy, especially in the heat of the day as the road is fully exposed to the elements with little shade heading south. Luckily once you reach the top the final descent and 30km to Shitiping is simple and fast.

North
East

Singing bike tunnels, giant sand castles, tea houses plucked from the movies and looming giraffes.

Villages run by cats, rock-formed swimming pools and active volcanoes.

Whitewash lighthouses perched at the edge of the world and sweeping coastal roads that all lead to Taipei's jade jewel.

The end to our tour is magic realism in action.

North East

T ired, maybe, ready for a rest, for sure, but wow do the last two days serve up just the perfect ending to an adventure. Packaging up everything that has made Taiwan so great and sprinkling it across the next two days of glorious, triumphant bicycle touring.

Quirky cultural affects and temple song drifting on a breeze, you bet ya. Delicious food streets with even more to try, um, yes. Hidden sleepy villages and back roads skipping around busy highways, of course. And a hill climb to knock your socks off, well, it wouldn't be Taiwan without one. Are there stupendous open views from up high? Naturally. Do we get to ride along sweeping ocean road and swim in crystal clear waters? Yes and yes. There's even another edge of the world to peer out from, too.

Tunnels through mountains and lights dotting the nighttime hillside, naturally. Local farms beside surf villages, *dui a*. Convenience stores, bubble tea shops, night markets and hot springs, duh. What about bicycle paths through parks and along riverbanks? Well, we have to bookend it somehow.

Yilan's coastal bike path, another treat just for us bike people, leads us to the northeast coast along a stunning bay with great views of the well named turtle island. Through to the surfing villages of northern Yilan.

Eventually we arrive at another piece of bike infrastructure, the wonderful and never-dull bike tunnel to the north. This wondrous old train tunnel transports us from east coast oceanfront through mountain and out the other side to sand castle competitions, sweet rural villages draped in mist and one last jungle climb to Taiwan's most famous, justifiably so, hill town.

After a night of eating and drinking along the cobble streets of the old mining village we are ready for our last day of the tour.

We start off much like the day before; leaving the heights of the hill town we roll through cat villages, hidden bike routes in old tunnels, past the port city of Keelung and some of the most swimmable locations on the island.

From there we ride the sweeping northern coast. The last stretch of riding is flat past whitewashed lighthouses to photograph, crisp clear waters to swim in and more old towns to explore.

We end our trip just perfectly along the riverbanks of Taipei. Once we arrive in Taiwan's capital you can spend a few days relaxing and remembering the adventure had along the roads above the clouds.

Dongshan to Jiufen

The route from Yilan Coastal Bikeway (宜蘭北濱自行車專用道) to the hill town of Jiufen (九份) marks the end to our east coast ride and the start of the final loop toward Taipei (台北). A day of special experiences both on and off the bike, quite unlike anything else we have experienced so far on our journey.

Get ready for turtles the size of islands rising out of the ocean, cool surf culture, magical musical tunnels, giant sand castles and atmospheric climbs to tropical mountaintops, all before descending to one of the country's most mythical hillside towns, complete with loving tea houses and stupendous views of the world below.

The coastal path that sweeps around Yilan's bay completely sidesteps this huge urban and farming sprawl. Traveling along this well-maintained bike path is a great early morning ride through what feels like a wild unburdened area. Once we leave the bikeway, we pass along Taiwan's northern surf towns that, during high season, offer up some of those California vibes. Full of wetsuits dripping in the sun, sand-covered boards leaning against car doors and laid-back, chilled-out Taiwanese. There certainly is a different vibe along this northern wave.

Next up is one of Taiwan's best pieces of bicycle infrastructure. An old train tunnel, stretching over 2km, has been turned into a magical bicycle path. From the southern point, you leave the breezy hot ocean highway; emerging on the other side, you are transported into northern Taiwan with its low mountains, lush green vegetation and electric skies.

The resulting feeling is transformational as you freewheel through the cool tunnel, listening to the music that is being pumped through the speakers and joyous screams from riders echoing off the old red-bricked walls.

Passing into New Taipei (新台北) and the north coast town of Fulong (福隆). If you are an aficionado of the international giant sand castle competition circuit then this unassuming town will be known to you already. The long, wide yellow sand beach is home to Taiwan's international sand castle competition. Truly an oddity but worth a visit with year-round displays.

Up to this point in the day the route has been easy, super relaxing and flat. But now to get up and over northern Taiwan's hills we need to climb. This is of course not even comparable to the high mountains in the center of the country, or the climb down south when crossing from Kenting (墾丁) to the east coast. But after five days of fairly relaxed riding this feels like a difficult climb. There are other options here and if you really want to keep it flat, you can ignore the mystical Jiufen (九份) altogether. But the top of today's climb and the descent into the little hill town serves up, quite possibly, one of the most memorable rides on the trip. The views and the feelings of emerging up onto a low mountain that overlooks the ocean and the mysterious village are truly unique in Taiwan.

A fanciful tale about Jiufen floats over this hillside village like the mist that settles in on a chilly evening. It is said that one of Japan's most famous movies was inspired by the narrow lanes and tea house found here. This infamous and, sadly, tall tale is still widely believed by many in Taiwan. People throng here from all over the country during the weekend and festivals, bear that in mind.

As the penultimate day of the journey, it really sums up the ride in Taiwan. It is glorious, full of surprises, there is a price to pay but well worth the effort.

At the end of the quiet and sweaty ride, the road heads over a pass above Jiufen. Buyanting (不厭亭) is one of Taiwan's most famous hill passes, a marker that all cyclists in Taiwan want to reach. Its photogenic road glides around the hillside and provides the perfect feeling of achievement. Equally, once you pass over the top of the hill you are rewarded with incredible views of the hillside below and the deep blue ocean stretching off into the distance. The descent is not a disappointment, apart from being over all too soon. At the end of it all you drop into Taiwan's most mysterious and well visited hillside villages.

Jiufen is an old mining town with small lanes and alleyways, crooked brick houses all stacked up on each other as moss grows out from the cracks and cats prowl the lanes. Tea houses, restaurants and food stalls tumble over themselves along the old street. Venture a little farther to find unique guesthouses wedged into the hillside artist studios, crumbling relics and tunnels. The views are glorious, the feeling of an old lost way still lingers. Spend a night in one of the small stone homes sipping on tea and really get spirited away.

All this leads us to our last day. Riding down from here through the backstreets past the cat village of Houtong (猴硐) we head to Taiwan's far north. Diving around the northern coastline we chase the sun to the island's most northerly point before heading to the end, toward Taipei and a final sunset on Taipei's riverbank bicycle hub. The ride along the river toward the city as it starts to glow in the golden hour is an incredible journey's end. These last two days really do serve up the best of traveling through this unique place: old yet modern, small yet rich, sleepy yet chaotic and on built yet natural land.

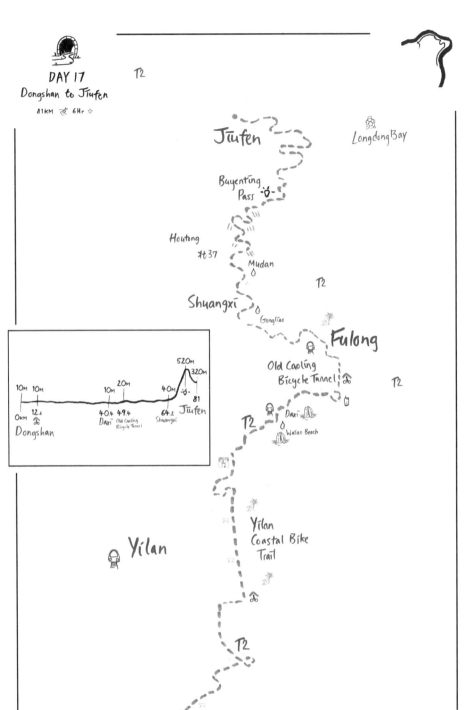

DAY 17
Dongshan to Jiufen
81KM 🚴 6Hr ☁

T2

Jiufen

Longdong Bay

Bayenting
Pass ☀

Houtong
北37

Mudan 💧

Shuangxi

Gongliao 💧

T2

Fulong

Old Caoling
Bicycle Tunnel

T2

Daxi

Wailiao Beach

T2

Yilan
Coastal Bike
Trail

Yilan

T2

Dongshan

Elevation profile:
10M 10M   20M
        10M   40M
                                  520M
                                  320M
0KM 12.6   40.4 49.4   64.2   81
     Daxi Old Caoling Shuangxi Jiufen
Dongshan   Bicycle Tunnel

DAY 17

81KM 🚵 6Hr 🏠

0.00 Start at Dongshan (冬山) Park crossroads, turn right at the bicycle junction, heading under the railway tracks. Follow the bike path as it runs along the river, which will be on your left. Follow this path alongside the river for a while heading toward the ocean.

7.88 Turn left onto the T2 by passing first under the highway before heading up the ramp and crossing the river.

10.0 Cross the river mouth at the edge of the ocean, along the flat bridge. This is the last bridge before you hit the ocean, so if you miss it, you will soon realize.

12.0 Turn right off the highway onto a beach lane at an unmarked set of traffic lights, beside a house. This is the first turning after the bridge and this road will take you up and onto a sandy trail and the start of the Yilan Coastal Bikeway (宜蘭北濱自行專用道).

12.6 Yilan Coastal Bikeway! Turn left heading north along the bike path. You can find plenty of rest stops and beach pull-ins along this secluded 15km bikeway. There are only two bathrooms: one in the middle and another at the northern end, by the start of the km markers.

   Exit at 12km or 8km markers for direct routes to Yilan city center and train station. Watch out at the occasional beach access point.

25.0 End of the bikeway there is a new raised seawall. Take the road that runs below it.

25.5 Turn left up the dirty side lane as the road reaches its end. This will bring you onto the T2.

25.7 Turn right onto the T2, immediately crossing a river over a bridge.

26.7 Turn right into Dakeng (大坑), after crossing the bridge, the road heads toward the town. This quieter road avoids the highway for a while.

29.1 Turn right back onto the T2 at this main junction and ride on the highway as we enter surfing towns. There is a useful convenience store here.

30.8 Enter the surf village of Wai-a (外澳). During the surf season see people in wetsuits carrying long boards crossing the street.

    This lively town is worth a break to see the beach and catch some vibes. Ride the coastal road for some km here. After the seaside town of Gengfang (梗枋) there is a large rest stop with ocean views and cliff walks.

39.2 The town of Daxi (大溪) starts here with local stores; water at the police station.

    An alternative road to the northern hills rises steeply up from behind Daxi. It is a beautiful route to the town of Shuangxi (雙溪) but it is arduous and the climbing takes its toll on a hot day. The plateau on top of the range is beautiful and passes through an incredibly unseen farming area. Imagine the shire, but in Taiwan.

44.4 The village of Dali with train station.

48.0 Pass Shicheng train station (石城) on your right. Keep aware. The small turning for the bike tunnel is coming up.

49.1 STOP! Turn right leaving the highway onto a small lane in search of the bicycle tunnel. At the brow of a short climb look out for a brown sign in Chinese for the bikeway and a small turning next to a mini rest stop with a black stone table. We leave the highway here. If you missing this turning there is a second turning just a few meters later on your right.

    The narrow road immediately heads downhill. Spot the old railway markings on the ground. Follow the cute, well-made path that heads underground through a pedestrian tunnel.

49.3 Arrive at the entrance to the bikeway tunnel. Here there are viewpoints, public toilets and old buildings converted into stores and little eateries. Say goodbye to the main east coast route, we leave it here for good.

49.4 Enter the bicycle tunnel. It is a long, straight glide, feel the breeze and listen out for happy day riders and the soft music pumped though. The tunnel is such a fun little ride. No rush here.

    If you have arrived too late in the day and the gates are closed (17:30) then stay on the T2 around the coast. While pretty, it is not unlike the rest of the coast and skipping it for this tunnel is for sure the better choice.

51.5 Exit the tunnel. See the train line adjacent with regular trains passing through. Here we have some more bike rental stores and snack stands.

51.9 Turn left, crossing the train line after the train display. The road is well maintained with lots of cyclists here as you head toward Fulong (福隆).

53.7 Lean right outside Fulong station, down the small hill to the junction where we find the T2 highway once again. A hubbub of tourist restaurants and bike rental stores are here. There are a few places to buy snacks, and the police station has free water.

    Fulong is a good lunchtime rest. Famous for the bike tunnel and the international sand castle competition held on its long golden beach. The beach, during sand castle season, has an entrance fee. After leaving Fulong our ride starts to become harder as we pass into the hills.

53.8 Turn left onto the T2 at the bottom of the station road. You will find public toilets, information center and beach entrance at the large parking lot on your right shortly after the turning.

55.1 Turn left onto the T2丙 at the gas station, leaving the main T2 highway.

T2 to Longdong
If you don't want to travel to Jiufen (九份) via Shungxi then this alternative has one of Taiwan's best snorkeling spots and is a beautiful coastal route. The fishing village of Longdong is famous for its diving centers and its rocky snorkeling spot. The remarkable waters here are a great way to spend an afternoon. The village has a hostel or two. Note that the coastal route is not flat and the climb up to Jiufen from the north is also an arduous affair.

59.1 Turning to Gongliao (貢寮), a small village with a train station.

64.2 STOP! Turn right just before the tunnel onto the 102 into Shuangxi. After the road bends to the left you pass alongside the river and a red bridge at the village of Shuangxi. Follow the signs to the town.

To Taipei
If you are heading into Taipei city and cutting out the northeast then keep on the T2丙 and follow it until you reach highway T5. From there head west into central Taipei. Note it is not a flat ride and still a further 50km from this point. And of course, our tour ends in the city's center.

64.5 Lean right on the 102 into Shuangxi, crossing a river. Shortly after you turn into the village you will pass the temple, restaurants, stores and police station.

64.8 Turn left before the river, just after the police station, staying on the 102, the road passes out of the town, beside the atmospheric river.

65.0 The 102 heads north with the river on your right, the road is lush and quiet.

<u>68.0</u> Start of the climb at the small village of Mudan (牡丹), keep straight on the 102. After this town the road really starts to climb. It is 7km from here to the top. Take your time and make sure you have water.

68.7 Turning left for an alternative road straight to Houtong (猴硐) the cat village.

<u>75.0</u> Top of climb, phew! What a ride right? Tough for sure! Now you have made it to the pull-in, viewpoint and rest stop of Buyanting (不厭亭), a badge of honor for cyclists who reach it thanks to its stiff climb and iconic views of the road you just came up.

From the viewing platform just above the road you can see panoramic views of the climb you just completed, the road ahead, surrounding hills and ocean as well as cities in the distance. Incredible, take it all in.

75.2 A small kick along with a few tiring uphill corners for the next km and a half. Now the ocean really comes into view as the road plateaus. The views of Jiufen (糾紛) and the ocean are arresting.

77.0 Rest stop with incredible views of the surrounding landscapes and the ocean beyond.

<u>80.6</u> Head straight over the brow. From here the road curves left and down into the town. One of the many incredible roads out of Jiufen. If you have an extra day and the lungs, well worth a trip back down and up!

Junction on the right with 北34, which leads down to the gold mine museum, a beautiful sulphur waterfall (view only) and the ocean.

<u>81.0</u> Finish at the Jiufen old street entrance! Information board, public bathrooms, stores and tea shops at this sharp switchback. Jiufen old street starts here on your left; this is the main point at the center of the hillside's sprawling mass of stacked houses and narrow lanes. The last day of our journey starts from this point, but you can pick up the journey anywhere along the lower road or the 102 heading west.

The main old street cannot be comfortably navigated by bike when people are around. But the lower street that runs parallel is wider and has few, if any, people wandering. Your homestay, hotel or campground will be somewhere in the stacks, good luck.

Jiufen to Dadaocheng Wharf Taipei

Oh what a last day. Another great reason for the counterclockwise route is that it gives the perfect end to a trip in Taiwan, finishing in the country's north and its capital while at the same time offering up some truly unique and original experiences. We hit cute villages, serene landscapes and one last ocean drive, and we end the day on a truly inspiring bicycle path that takes us right to the heart of Taipei (台北). All without losing sight of green grass or blue waters. As the sun casts an orange glow over the emerald skyscraper of Taipei 101 and the foothills of this unique landscape, you can revel in the journey finished. You have made it to the end, here you are.

Leaving Jiufen (九份) in the early morning is like eating your favorite cake: you take the last bite, overwhelmed with satisfaction just as the sense of loss starts to consume you. If only you could hold that feeling forever. How to bottle it? How to keep that pure, wide-eyed joy? Can't there just be one more time around, one more corner?

This road leads us to another kitsch locale. Hidden in the valley of Houtong (猴硐) is the famed, if for some, underwhelming, cat village. But even if you don't love our feline friends, this idyllic old village is worth the visit. Houtong is a rabble of old stone streets and homes cobbled together on a hillside, now overrun with moss and dripping heavy with dew.

In the narrow lanes above the train station a population of cats controls the streets; an area devoid of cars, scooters and dogs has helped to keep the space well and truly safe for the little fur balls. But don't worry, these docile felines are a pleasure to hang out with in the mornings, they lounge and wait for tourists who happily stroke and feed them throughout the day. It is a funny little place where the old people who make up the scant human population barely seem to notice the people fawning over the four-legged layabouts. And this stop is more than just cats. The old mining town a little further up the river is also worth a stroll with its mine museum, hike trails and stunning river that explodes in color and sounds as it rumbles over boulders and stone.

Once you have filled your Hello Kitty boots we finally leave any hills and mountains for the last time. Another stunning and well-built bikeway bends around and down through hills via river paths, wildflowers and train tunnels. This section of the journey is wild and quiet. Great to be done just as the sun is making its mark on the day.

Hitting the city of Keelung (基隆) brings you back to reality; you start to get the sense we are entering a heavily populated metropolis. Luckily just as this feeling arrives we quickly skip away from the cities and embark on our last coastal road.

The arching northern tip of Taiwan rotates around the central mountains of Yangmingshan National Park (陽明山國家公園). This coastal highway is flat and beautiful, offering up lots of lovely beaches and Taiwan's most northern point, marked by a classic whitewash lighthouse.

Now we're racing south, toward the capital, but just as we start to feel over-whelmed by the idea of hours stuck in traffic we meet the city's well-main-tained and secluded riverbank bikeway: the 30km stretch of bike path that leads us from the ocean mouth at Tamshui (淡水) all the way to the heart of the city. This route completely takes us away from the traffic and, instead, we ride through mangroves, along wide embankments, across cycle-friendly bridges, past baseball pitches, basketball courts, shrines and parks. This reclaimed green space is loved by all active members of the city and you will be joined by joggers, walkers, skaters and of course, cyclists.

As you finally arrive at our route's end point you can enjoy a drink as you watch the sunset across the waters of Pier 6. The fun Dadaocheng Wharf (大稻程) offers the perfect place to pull up, lean on the water's edge and watch the day's end. Full of Taipei residents out for an evening ride. This place is over-loaded with people and riders of all kinds and seeing hundreds of bikes parked up certainly adds to the dream of a cycling paradise.

From the gate at the wharf here you can easily head into the heart of down-town Taipei. This is where CR1 enters the river path and leads you all the way down the banks until you leave Taipei, heading south, and eventually find our starting point back in Sanxia (三峽) at the edge of the mountains once more.

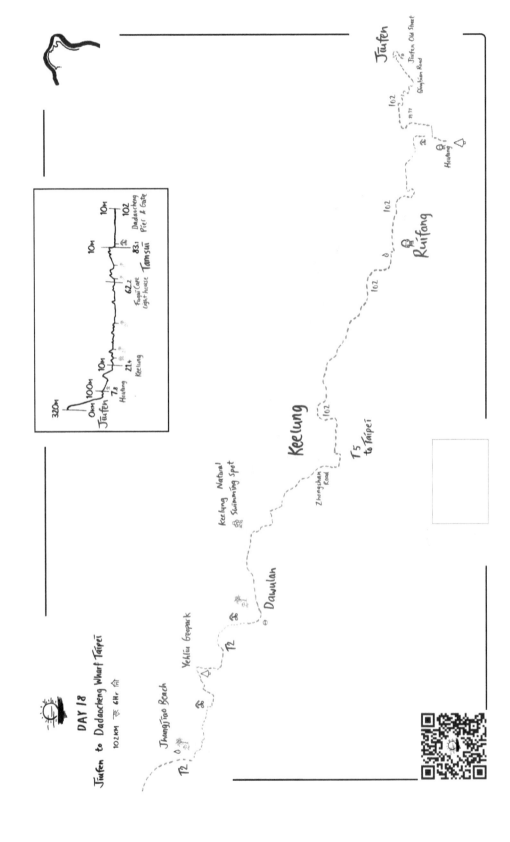

DAY 18

Jiufen to Dadaocheng Wharf Taipei

102KM 6Hr

Jiufen

Jiufen Old Street
Qingbian Road

162

H-37

Houtong

162

162

Ruifang

162

162

Keelung

162

T5 to Taipei

Zhongshan Road

Keelung Natural Swimming Spot

Dawulan

Yehliu Geopark

Zhangliao Beach

T2

T2

T2

Elevation profile:

320M

100M

0KM

Jiufen

7.8

Houtong

10M

21.4

Keelung

62.2

Fugui Cape Lighthouse

10M

83.1

Tamsui

10M

10M

102

Dadaocheng Pier & Gate

DAY 18

102KM 🚲 **6Hr** 🏠

0.00 Start from the entrance of the old street and information board. Head down the main road 102 as it twists downhill. Go slow, we turn again soon.

0.25 Turn left onto the temple forecourt immediately after the first switchback of the day. It looks like a dead end in front of a temple. But you will quickly notice it becomes a narrow lane. Here we start our mini tour though old Jiufen (九份).

0.32 The road passes a staircase before becoming a narrow lane squeezed between houses. The path remains flat for the rest of the ride through the village.

0.40 Lean left along the small lane. The road curves left at a viewing platform with benches. From here the lane meanders through an old part of town, take your time.

0.76 Jiufen's famed tea house sits on the hillside to your left up a few steps.

1.00 A small park with views of the ocean and green hills below.

1.10 The edge of the town, the slip road that goes up the hill back behind your left shoulder is the other end of the old street promenade.

1.25 The last viewpoint of the ocean and surrounding hills.

1.35 Lean left and enter the narrow tunnel. Just before the houses we ride through the beautiful old archway tunnel dripping with moss and puddles. This marks the start of the descent away from Jiufen. Watch your head!

1.50 This small lane weaves fast through a small-forested area. Go careful on sharp bends.

<u>2.36</u> Turn left onto the 102 at the bottom of the descending lane. Follow it downhill out of Jiufen and toward Houtong (猴硐). The road's sweeping corners offer open views of the ocean below.

<u>4.20</u> Turn left onto the 北37 as the road straightens you reach traffic lights, following signs for Houtong and the 北37.

Even if you don't intend on spending any time in Houtong, turn left here for the beautiful bike path. Unless you are in a rush of course, then carry on down the hill to the village of Ruifang (瑞芳).

<u>6.30</u> Keep right after you enter the outskirts of Houtong staying close to the river all the way.

7.00 A bridge that crosses the river and takes you to the brand-new information center. If you really don't want to see the village then cross this bridge, turning right at the information center. Follow the river back along the opposite shore. Rejoining our route at 11.7km.

<u>7.49</u> Turn right across the river along the red bridge.

<u>7.56</u> Turn left onto Houtong Road (猴硐路) at the end of the bridge.

<u>7.83</u> STOP! The entrance of the train station. A staircase leads up to the ticket office. And entrance to the village. This odd station is also the entrance to the cat village, which you can only reach by walking through a cat tunnel hanging above the station. Opposite the entrance to the train station is a side courtyard with local restaurants, small stores and a pretty museum, where in the morning hordes of cats can be found lazing about.

Houtong the cat village
Take a walk up the steps following the signs to the cute little cat village. If you want to avoid crowds it is best to visit here early in the morning, however the cat stores, cafés and postcard sellers usually open later. There are several narrow lanes to walk around with views over the train stations and the surrounding hills. It is a stunning location with some sweet Taiwanese touches, just don't expect too much and you will come away with a very pleasant experience.

Further up the main road you first come upon a beautiful rest stop by the river. From here you can admire the great views of the river and the surrounding hills.

The road carries on further into the sprawling old village. There are some cute alleys with amazing little old nooks and crannies along the way. The old mine and shower rooms, now a museum, mark the end of the path and the start of beautiful hiking trails that head up into the surrounding hills. Crossing the river here the road carries on south to the sweet village of Sandiaoling (三貂嶺), there is no through road to Taipei though.

<u>8.08</u> Turn around facing north, as we now head back the way we came. From the train station, keep the river on your right.

<u>8.30</u> Head straight once you reach the red arch bridge, staying on this side of the river, following the blue bicycle signs.

8.50 Head straight at the new information center. The road becomes a cycle path here and rolls between the railway tracks and the river. It's a great little ride as you are alongside rushing river and gushing trains.

9.50 The path travels through old tunnels, now repurposed. Enter a forested area. Very cute and otherworldly.

10.4 Turn left as the bike path passes under the railway tracks. Completing a 180 out on the other side, briefly heading south before passing through the final barriers as you reach the end of the path. Turn right here leaving the train tracks behind. Pass a few houses on a smooth road toward the town of Ruifang.

11.1 Play area and basketball courts.

11.2 Turn right crossing the bridge then head straight past houses as the road bends left, head for the overpass of the highway in front.

11.7 Turn left under the overpass and onto the 102. On the other side of the overpass join the northbound lane. Slightly disorientating you find train tracks again, now on your right side. Follow the 102 west as it skirts around Ruifang.

12.8 Turn right across train tracks immediately on your right, keeping on the 102. Straight after crossing the tracks the road rises and curves left. For trains to Taipei carry on straight here for the station.

12.9 Head straight keeping on the 102 as we come to a crossroads beside the police station. For a short while the 102 is a narrow village street before widening again as it leaves the town.

14.4 Head straight at the large junction with the T62, keep on the 102. This is one of a very few sections of heavy-traffic roads for the trip. We are not on it for long.

17.3 At the traffic light the road awkwardly splits, keep to the left following the larger flow of traffic.

17.6 Pass under the freeway. The road descends sharply as you race down toward Keelung (基隆).

19.1 Keep right. The road splits again, but carry on straight, slightly to the right as you enter the city.

19.5 Keelung canal should be on your left as the one-way traffic of four lanes heads dead straight for the port area.

21.4 Turn left and keep to the right. The road comes to an abrupt T junction at the port. Keep close to the port promenade. The road curves to the right as it goes around the port. Welcome to Keelung.

21.8 Turn right in front of the port onto Gangxi Street. Head around the side of the port past the bus stops. You have gone too far if you cross under the highway. The port terminal entrance should be on your right. It is easy to see as you pass taxis, unloading and loading passengers.

Swimming the northern coastline

Keelung natural swimming pool
is an amazing outdoor swimming spot as we hit the ocean road. With natural rock protection, outdoor showers and toilet block in the parking lot. It is a great place for a dip if you have time, or at least watch the locals enjoy their morning constitutional. Some of the beaches further along also provide plenty of chances for a dip, p274.

Dawulun (大武崙)
is a lovely, secluded little beach with shallow clear waters and soft white sand,. p274.

Wanli (萬里)
has a long, sweeping beach that is good for a dip at the southern end away from the resorts. Can sometimes collect a lot of ocean trash, p274.

Zhongjiao (中角)
beach rest stop is a long stretch of beach just before the highway heads to the northern point. It is a great place for sunbathing, swimming and taking a break. There is a restaurant, good public bathrooms with showers, lockers and plenty of space, p275.

Baishawan (白沙灣)
Just after the turning to the northern lighthouse is the bay of Baisha, just off the highway before a climb. This golden sand beach is long and wide, with swimming possible some days, p277.

Qianshuiwan (淺水灣) Seaside Park
The last beach on the tour, just as the highway starts to pick up traffic is this last rest stop. Bathrooms, stores, restaurants and a sand beach that is flooded by locals on the weekends, p277.

22.4 Turn right onto Zhongshan 1st Road. The parking lot becomes a boulevard and there is a left then a right to perform at the traffic lights. Leaving the passenger terminal behind. Follow this now-wide road for a while.

23.5 Head straight seeing the large fire station in front of you, stay on the main road passing convenience stores on either side of a crossroads.

24.5 The road passes under a high flyover of freeway 2己.

24.8 Turn right off at OK mart, follow bicycle sign painted on road just before the road climbs up a hill. Follow the bicycle floor markers down a side road, which immediately curves up past houses.

25.2 Turn left at the ocean mural. Follow the road until it hits the seawall, turn left and then right as the road heads downhill toward a small fishing port and parking lot.

25.8 The natural swimming pool is here as the road swings left onto the ocean drive. The coastal bike path starts here. You can keep on the raised path along the oceanfront toward the beach of Dawulun and our main road for the day, the coastal highway T2.

28.5 Head straight onto Dawulun Beach Road. DO NOT head up the hill. Ignore any signs for T2 here. Carry on onto the beach, passing some rest stop pagodas. This road might seem like a dead end but it's not and Taiwan has made another great little bike shortcut for us here.

This small bay is a safe and pretty swimming spot. There are a couple of small beach shops for snacks and drinks and public bathrooms next to the golden sand and clear waters.

29.4 Enter the bike path next to the restrooms. Carry on down to the road's end, you can see the T2 up above your head as it drops toward the ocean in front. At the end of the road there are some more public toilets and a helpful bike path that follows along rocks and shoreline, keeping you off the highway until the next bay. It is a lovely little route and you will thank your lucky stars you didn't have to climb up the highway before just to descend to the same spot.

After a little while you reach a rest stop at Lion Park, with parking lot and more public toilets. At the far end of the parking lot the cycle path picks up once again, rolling downhill seemingly toward the water below. Keeping you off the road, it really is a lovely ride right over the water.

31.9 Wanli has a long white sand beach with development. Just as the bike path ends you reach the southern tip of the beach. Here there are steps that lead down and offer easy access to the ocean without having to travel too far from your bikes.

33.6 After passing through the seaside town of resorts, hotels and restaurants, T2 enters into two tunnels and bicycles are not allowed. Instead, just before the tunnel entrance turn right, leaving T2 and onto the Shijiao Road (石角路). If the mood is right and the sun is shining the atmosphere along this coastline is unlike the rest of Taiwan. A really enjoyable, relaxed middle of the day.

35.7 Enter the town of Yehliu (野柳) and the entrance to the famous Queen's Head rock sightseeing spot. The road curves around the big parking lot and main entrance.

Yehliu Geopark: The Queen's Head Rock
If you want to see this little but cute rock formation on the edge of the ocean in the Yehliu Geopark (野柳地質公園), you will need to pay for a ticket and follow one of the government-controlled trails. The Queen's Head rock is the main attraction, along with crashing waves, ocean viewpoints and other interesting geo formations.

35.9 At the northern tip of the parking lot and main entrance, turn left away from the entrance. Follow the fishing harbor road for another 2.5km until you reach T2 again, merge and head north.

36.4 Turn right at the port onto Guanxi Road (港西路), follow signs for the T2.

38.4 Turn right back on the T2 for a short period.

39.9 Turn right off the highway into the parking lot on your right. Notice from the main road that between some shrubs is a bicycle route sign and a bike path leading into the unknown. Follow it, we will not describe this route until its end, just follow the signs all the way.

If done right this bike path cuts off 5km of highway and brings you out at the quiet surf beach at Zhongjiao.

46.0 Zhongjiao Beach rest stop, showers and toilets. Take a well-earned rest and use the facilities. Take a lovely cold shower or go sit on the beach and take a dip. These facilities are open 24hr at this very relaxed place. Take an extended break here if you have the days.

Look for the T2 once again. Turn right, heading north. The next 13km you ride right along the oceanfront, with dramatic views of the clouds that hover over Yangmingshan peaks behind you.

There are few stops along this pretty stretch as the road rides right along the water's edge. We are now heading to Taiwan's most northern point, where our ocean drive is almost over.

A left hand turn here will take you to the T2甲. This quiet road heads up to the heights of the center of Yangmingshan National Park (陽明山).

Riding with the locals – weekend trips up Yangmingshan
Road cycling is very popular here in Taipei and nowhere more so than on a weekend morning up the side of Yangmingshan National Park (陽明山國家公園).

Hundreds of eager solo riders and club rides climb and descend the narrow, steep, sweeping roads around here. It is an excellent way to explore the national park right on Taipei's doorstep and great for training your legs for the rest of the island's mountainous landscapes. You can expect to see plenty of lycra-clad riders training themselves for the Taiwan KOM race held every year in Taroko.

A great place to start is the National Palace Museum. From there ride north up the T2甲 which starts at the base of the mountain. From its highest point in the park turn left onto the 101甲 and ride down the mountain's western hills hunting out views of the steaming volcano crater of Datunshan before descending towards Tamsui and Beitou. Another area popular with cyclists coming down from the peaks.

DAY 18

Jiufen to Dadaocheng Wharf Taipei

102KM 🚴 6Hr 🏠

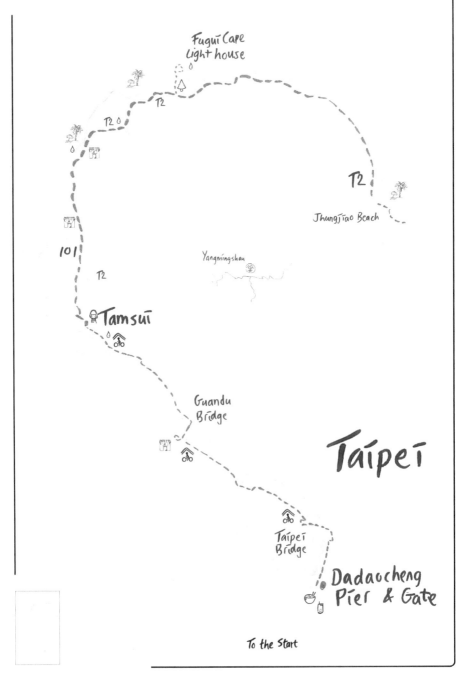

Fugui Cape
Light house

T2

T2

T2

T2

Jhungjiao Beach

101

T2

Yangmingshan

Tamsui

Guandu
Bridge

Taipei

Taipei
Bridge

Dadaocheng
Pier & Gate

To the Start

59.0 The village of Laomei (老梅). You can head in here to the most northerly point but best to follow the western approach. This small fishing village has some stores and a great little Vietnamese restaurant.

60.8 Turn right toward Fujicun and the lighthouse at Taiwan's most northerly cape. At the lights take the right-hand turn for the village of Fujicun (富基村).

61.2 As the road curves to the right take the left-hand slip road that leads down to the fish market. Pass along in front of it through the parking lot.

61.6 At the very end of the road, you come out at a couple of stores, head behind them. And look for the entrance of the lighthouse walk.

Fugui Cape Lighthouse: Taiwan island's most northerly point
Take your bikes and wander along the new path that leads to Taiwan's most northerly point. Along the path are bike rails to assist the steps. The whitewash walls of the lighthouse are a great place to get those bike pics. The path around the lighthouse circles back to a road down to the parking lot we started from as there are bathrooms at the lighthouse.

63.5 Turn right back onto the T2. Turn right, keeping the ocean where it has been all day on your right shoulder. Unfortunately leaving the northernmost point marks the end of a sleepy coastal bike day. From here the highway becomes markedly busier and more taxing as it heads south to waters and the twin cities of Taipei and New Taipei.

    Over the next 8km there is an alternative bikeway path that meanders through groves and beside beaches. But with the day getting away from us we choose to stay on the highway here and head south. The bike trails abruptly stop and start with no clear sense of direction.

65.2 Turning for Baishawan beach as the road climbs. This pretty beach is free to use with facilities.

68.0 Lean right, staying on the T2 at this large intersection,

72.4 After a couple of stubborn climbs and busy descents we arrive at the ocean again at the more developed Qianshuiwan beach park, a long grass area next to a long sandy beach. The public restrooms and rest stop are comfortable and there is a large convenience store just across the main road. From here there are restaurants and stores all along the highway until we reach our goal of New Taipei's excellent river bikeway.

79.4 STOP! Turn right off the T2 onto the 北T1. Just after another easy climb the road widens further and turns left down a hill; instead turn off here, leaving highway T2. Follow signs for 北T1 and Zhongshan Road (中山路). The road instantly becomes quieter and leafier. A much-needed break from the monotony of the traffic flow. This quiet road heads downhill toward the town of Tamsui (淡水).

80.1 The road enters a high-rise residential area. Now you really feel like you have arrived in a large city. Luckily here the traffic is slow and comfortable with a wide bicycle lane. Unfortunately, the traffic lights are relentless.

81.7 Following signs for the 101 and central Tamsui the road widens still further. As it splits keep to the right.

82.5 At the bottom of the hill the road ends and arrives in central Tamsui. Turn left onto T2乙 and follow the southbound traffic flow. We have almost finished with roads for the day.

83.1 STOP! Join cycle route 1-13 at the riverside park behind the large Tamsui train terminus. Here is our connection onto the Taipei bicycle river path network. If you have a wide brith or heavy setup, sorry about the barriers.

    Facing the river take the route left, heading south along the riverbank, following the bicycle route signs for the next few km as it bobs and weaves alongside the MRT line until it enters the mangrove.

    The historic town of Tamsui has a lovely riverside area to take a break as well as a famous old street. There are plenty of tea shops and snack vendors around. It is worth a wander; the further north along the old street you walk, the quieter and more pleasant it seems.

88.7 Cross the Guandu bridge, following the colorful ramps. After some riding on the bikeway, you find yourself approaching a large red arched bridge that highway T15 crosses. Luckily there are brightly painted bicycle ramps leading up to a bicycle path on either side of the bridge.

    At the bottom, there is a rest stop with public toilets at the circular bicycle intersection. This area is popular with cyclists of all ages out for weekend and evening rides. Turn south, heading along the bike path, now with the river on your left.

92.4 Pass under the bridge as the wide river swings away from us as we head underneath the 103 flyover. The bike path splits and crosses several paths here, but for our main route we want to be under the highway traveling directly underneath it.

Alternative bike route
You can head right here and along an incredible public green zone of bike paths, jogging lanes, basketball courts and wild grassland. Head this way if you are skipping central Taipei and want Taoyuan (桃園) or beyond, as after 10km it eventually brings you out at the main river, heading south along the western shore.

93.0 Turn left shortly after the bike rest, bathrooms and information boards under the flyover leading us out from under the bridge, following a bike path. The left-hand exit brings us up alongside another road and around a water lock station before we ride along a high-rise levy that looks east over the river, central Taipei and the Yangmingshan (陽明山) mountains in the distance.

96.5 Drop off a raised levy into the riverside bike trail. We now have just 6km of really enjoyable bicycle path that runs through and around a well-maintained and giant public space. This stretch of the riverfront has been kept for walkers, cyclists and basketball courts.

    We are nearing the end of our adventure and we ride gently toward Taipei central. The sun might be setting around you as the day grows long.

Taipei, Taiwan's jewel city

If you enjoy just one city break in Taiwan it really should be Taipei. Hard to miss really, this sprawling capital was split in two and now New Taipei City encircles the older center. Its mass of population bleeds into nearby Taoyuan, Keelung and the surrounding mountains. It is a fascinating urban playground.

Boasting Taiwan's largest night-market, wonderful museums and galleries. All of Taiwan's culture is available here as well as the best city hiking on the island. It can rival Hong Kong for surrounding peaks and places to explore. Hot springs, active volcanos and the world's former highest building, the gem that is Taipei 101. With great transport links and city wide bike paths you really should spend a day or three here. The bike rental system is the most used on the island and the roads are safe to ride on as well. So find a place to plonk your bags and go explore.

For an all in one bicycle shop in Taipei you can't go wrong with Taipei Bike Works (taipeibikeworks.com). MathewBike is another great store known for its rentals (mathewbike.com).

Take in the memories and feelings of Taiwan as a hazy cityscape can be seen in the distance. With Taipei 101 and the rolling misty mountains basking themselves in the evening dusk.

101 Turn onto Taipei Bridge, following signs for Dadaocheng Wharf.

At long last we have reached Taipei Bridge. This nondescript bridge takes us over the river and lands us at the sunset spot of Dadaocheng (大稻埕). The ramp to reach the raised bridge path starts a few hundred meters before the bridge itself so head up the ramp to your right; if you miss this ramp, ride under the bridge and then swing up the southern ramp. Either way up, the bike path runs along the southern side of the bridge.

101 Turn right down the ramp on the other end of the bridge, turn down the bike ramp with the river on your right now.

102 Turn left along the path. Heading south along the bike path, follow signs for Dadaocheng Wharf.

102 Finish at Dadaocheng Wharf, Pier 5 and City Gate! Arrive at the wharf. This is Taipei's sunset spot, on a clear day you can grab a drink from the hip food stands and watch the sunset across the river.

From the gate here you can ride into Taipei with its main stations, airport MRT, hostels and restaurant areas all close by.

Alternatively keep traveling down that trail, soften your step, lighten your grip as the world opens up in front of you.

Keep pedaling into the unknown.

Clockwise Notes
North East

From Dadaochang Wharf, Taipei to Dongshan, Yilan

Starting your route in Taipei you could consider a more gradual first day, riding east along highway T5 to Keelung, skipping the north coast road. From Keeling port join the T2 coastal road east for 12km along before turning right up road 35 to Juifen. This northwest climb is perhaps the least taxing of all the routes up to the hilltop village.

For the original route: Follow the Taipei river bike paths north following signs for Tamshui. From Tamshui old street head north up road 101 until you reach T2 north and follow the coastal road around the north coast.

When you arrive at Keelung port carry on around the port, keeping it on your left before turning right down road 102 east. Follow this road uphill to the edge of Ruifang. Cross the river at the town, then head east along the southern bank. This road heads to the same sports park noted on p271. From the road's end join the bike path that heads under the railway track, this will take you to Houtong cat village. From there you can rejoin the 102 east at the base of Jiufen, climbing up the winding road from there to the day's end.

The route from Juifen to Yilan starts on the 102 with a short but tough climb up the back of the village to Buyanting pass. But from there the road is a near constant descent to Fulong and the bicycle tunnel to Yilan. This makes the route a comfortable and fast ride.

Once you have descended from Buyanting just follow signs for Fulong. From the sand castle village find the train station and turn left in front of the entrance, this road travels to the bicycle tunnel. On the other side head south along highway T2 to Yilan. After the long, flat bridge take any left turn to find the coastal bike path. We really recommend riding farther to Dongshan or even through to Su'ao as the next day's ride to Taroko is a beast.

If you are thinking of riding from Jiufen to Fulong along the coastal road then take the descent down the back of the hill village on the 北34 heading northeast. This descent to the ocean is stunning, if sadly short lived. Do not expect the ocean road to be a flat, easy ride, there are some stubborn hill climbs along here and the traffic is heavy throughout. If you do take this route you really should take a break and have a dip at the great swimming spot of Longdong, a popular diving school and lovely snorkeling site.

Index

Index

Key

🚲	mainly flat route	T28	road name (see pxxx)
🚲	flat route with a hill	Kaohsiung	location name
🚲	mainly uphill day	🚲	bike trail/path
🚲	mainly downhill day	ⓘ	information center/board
🚲	climbs and descents day	-◊-	road pass
⛺	end has campsites	⊖	no entry/closed road
⛩	end has lodgings	🚏	rest stop/quiet spot
⛺/⛩	end has multiple options	🏪	local shop/convenience store
KM	distance of the route in km	🍜	restaurant/eatery
Hr	av. riding time for the route	🧋	cafe/tea shop
M	meters above sea level	💧	drinking water
to/for	off-map roads/locations	🍦	cold treats
Alternative Route	direction toward alt. routes	HOTEL	lodging

campsite

 free campsite

 train station

 ferry wharf

 national park

 national forest

 outdoor place of interest

 hot spring

 natural hot spring

 beach

 snorkel/swimming spot

 popular surfing spot

 water feature

 start/end point

 route

road

 bike path/trail

 tunnel

 bridge

 walking/hiking trail

 climbing region

 water (river/lake/ocean)

 turning direction on route

 compass

GPX maps

As well as our hand-drawn maps within *Roads above the Clouds* we also provide GPX files that digitally map our routes and match up with our daily itineraries. These files can be opened in most map or activity apps. The QR codes link to a secure download that requires a password. There are no limits to how many times you can download the .gpx files but access will expire after 2024, just visit addoilgo.com for updates. Please do not share, copy, post or distribute the maps, we worked tirelessly to produce them.

Password: RATC24

Complete map collection

All eighteen daily routes plus alternative routes in one download.

Huándǎo

One map of the main eighteen day route around Taiwan.

Taiwan Spine

DAY 1   Sanxia to Linsen
DAY 2   Linsen to Lishan
DAY 3   Lishan to Renai

Nantou

DAY 4   Renai to Sun Moon Lake
DAY 5   Sun Moon Lake to Heshe
DAY 6   Heshe to Tatajia Pass

South West

DAY 7   Tatajia Pass to Dapu
DAY 8   Dapu to Maolin
DAY 9   Maolin to Fangliao

292

Taiwan Tail

DAY 10 Fangliao to Kenting
DAY 11 Kenting to Dawu

South East

DAY 12 Dawu to Dulan
DAY 13 Dulan to Shitiping

Hualien & Taroko

DAY 14 Shitiping to Hualien
DAY 15 Hualien to Taroko
DAY 16 Taroko to Dongshan

North East

DAY 17 Dongshan to Jiufen
DAY 18 Jiufen to Dadaocheng Wharf
Taipei

Alternative
Route
Dapu
to Dapu

Alternative
Route
East Rift Valley

293

Notes

Notes

About the Author

Mark Tovell is the author behind *Bicycle Touring Taiwan, Roads above the Clouds*. A writer, artist, illustrator and designer Mark holds a post graduate from Chelsea college of Arts, London. But all of those self-aggrandising titles don't compare to the title Mark holds most dear, *cyclist*.

After years of travelling the world Mark gave up backpacking picked up his bicycle and started to cycle tour, he never looked back.

Years later, he came across a book, Wu, Ming-Yi's *The Stolen Bicycle*. Transported by this wonderful text Mark landed on the Island of Taiwan where the seeds of writing a new route to touring the heart of Asia grew.

*Bicycle Touring Taiwan, Roads above the Clouds i*s Mark's first book and is the culmination of years of exploring, writing and drawing on this wonderful island, as he still does today.

Mark currently lives in Tainan, south Taiwan with his bicycle, Jimmy. Mark happily helps any cyclist in need and is a host on warmshowers.org, so be sure to contact him if you happen to be riding through, the door is always open.

You can contact Mark at info@addoilgo.com or on instagram: addoil_go.